Annoying
the
Victorians

Annoying *the* Victorians

JAMES R. KINCAID

Routledge: New York & London

Published in 1995 by

Routledge
29 West 35 Street
New York, NY 10001

Published in Great Britain in 1994 by

Routledge
11 New Fetter Lane
London EC4P 4EE

Printed in the United States of America

Library of Congress Cataloging-in-Publication Data

Kincaid, James R. (James Russell)
    Annoying the Victorians / James R. Kincaid
        p.   cm.
    Includes bibliographical references and index.
    1. English Literature—19th Century—History and Criticism—Theory, etc.
I. Title.
PR461.K56 1994
820.9 008–dc20

                                        93-42943
                                          CIP

British Library Cataloguing-in-Publication Data Also Available

ISBN 0-415-90728-4 (hardcover)
ISBN 0-415-90729-2 (paperback)

To My Mother and Father

CONTENTS

ACKNOWLEDGMENTS

THE BOOK IS dedicated to the memory of my dear father and to my wise (wiser every year) and unreasoningly loving mother.

Friends and colleagues who might have been involved with the planning and writing of this book, helping to mull over ideas and reading various drafts of the chapters as they grew and gradually took form, weren't. As a general rule. There were some exceptions: Julian Markels, Robin Bell Markels, U. C. Knoepflmacher, Linda Shires, Larry Swingle, Peter Manning, Sylvia Manning, Robert Polhemus, Eve Kosofsky Sedgwick, Regina Barreca, Kevin Ennis, Ronald Gottesman, Terry Caesar, David Simpson, Regina Schwartz, Hilary Schor, A. J. Kuhn, Jeffrey Robinson, Patricia Cherin, David Cherin, Cathy Comstock, W. Ross Winterowd, Gerhard Joseph (I guess), Buck McMullen, Jean Ferguson Carr, Leslie Brill, Leo Braudy, Keith Fitzgerald, Adrian Richwell, Carol Muske-Dukes, Bruce Kawin, Mark Spilka, Jane K. Brown, Len Findlay, Margaret Higonnet, Linda K. Hughes, and the late Eliot Gilbert. Short as this list is, it is swollen by generosity: some of those whose names appear made contributions so faint as to lead me to think that I may have, in a burst of lunatic nostalgia, invented them.

Others most certainly did nothing. Garrett Stewart, who is cited several times in these pages, nonetheless ignored my letters asking for help and continued his practice of never returning calls—too busy. Gerald Bruns, once again, hurt me by his supercilious neglect. Jerome Beaty will have nothing to do with me, and

Acknowledgements

John Glavin makes no secret of his dislike. Juliet McMaster speaks ill of me and not just behind my back either. Nina Auerbach called me "inept," and the staff at the Memorial Library for Victorian Studies (Special Collections) made it clear they do not want me back. Even Joel Conarroe does not invite me to his parties.

Least bearable of all was, of course, N. John Hall.

The graduate students in the Victorian Strangeness classes and the undergraduates in the classes on Criminals, Lunatics, and Perverts I taught at the University of Southern California contributed more than they or I will ever know, and I hereby thank them. And I cannot forget the kindness of John Jordan, Murray Baumgarten, and the Dickens Universe for granting me, again and again, the opportunity to give talks to a group of scholars and students bitterly hostile to my views.

My editor at Routledge, William Germano, has always, as he puts it, been there for me, which is true and which says a lot about his character, I think.

My deans at the University of Southern California, Marshall Cohen and Richard Ide, and successive Department Chairs—Peter Manning, Richard Ide, Stephen Moore, and Teresa McKenna—have treated me with more kindness and forbearance than I deserve (almost). Collectively, they are, therefore, wholly responsible for any errors, defects in taste, or actionable comments in this book.

My immediate family (Nita Moots Kincaid, Matthew Kincaid, Anne Kincaid, Elizabeth Kincaid) geared themselves up and assembled the same displays of interest in this book as in other things I do extremely well: aerobic exercising, gardening, hiking, expressing opinions.

Earlier versions of some of the chapters have appeared elsewhere and are reprinted here with permission as follows:

Chapter 1 — in *Novel: A Forum on Fiction*, vol. 26, no. 2 (Fall, 1992). Copyright, NOVEL Corp. (c) 1992; vol 26. Reprinted with permission.

Chapter 3 — in *Dickens Studies Annual* 16 (1987): 95–111; with permission of the editors and AMS Press.

Chapter 4 — in *Victorian Literature and Society: Essays in Honor of Richard D. Altick*, ed. James R. Kincaid and Albert J. Kuhn (Columbus: Ohio State University Press, 1984): 258–75; with permission of the Ohio State University Press.

Chapter 5 — in *Dramatic Dickens*, ed. Carol MacKay (London: Macmillan, 1989), pp. 11–26; with permission of Macmillan.

Chapter 6 — in *Victorian Poetry* 30 (1992): 197–209; with permission of the editors.

Chapter 7 — in *Nineteenth-Century Literature* 45 (1990): 176–205; with permission of the editors, the Regents of the University of California, and Buck McMullen, the co-author.

Acknowledgements

Chapter 10 — in *Novel: A Forum on Fiction*, vol 24 (1990). Copyright NOVEL Corp. (c) 1990, vol 24. Reprinted with permission.

Chapter 11 — in *Reading and Writing Women's Lives*, ed. Bege K. Bowers and Barbara Brothers (Ann Arbor: UMI Research Press, 1990): 87–104; with permission of the editors.

Chapter 13 — in *The Sense of Sex: Feminist Perspectives on Hardy*, ed. Margaret Higonnet (Urbana: Univ. of Illinois Press, 1992): 132–48; Copyright 1993 by the Board of Trustees of the University of Illinois. Reprinted with permission of the University of Illinois Press.

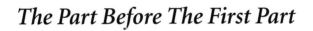

The Part Before The First Part

The Part Before The First Part

$\mathcal{M}$OTHER SAID, AND I do not forget, that I should never, no matter how bad the times, let myself be dragged down to playing by the rules. It's disrespectful: to play by the rules is to insult them by taking them for granted. It is the cheat who is courteous to the rules, gives them a chance to speak. Between rules and cheats, it's love. Rules are always true to cheats, and the cheats honor that devotion. Made for each other. Rules long for cheating agitations, disorders to settle. The upright never call, only the cheats. The best lovers are the cheats who bumble, the crooks who maybe don't even want to succeed: they are willing to flood the motor of the get-away car so the rules can catch up and the two can have a go at it. Games would quickly disappear, would sink under the sludge of clarity, were it not for those with aces dropping out of their sleeves and onto the table, those who miscount, misquote, misrepresent, lie, forge, make vain pretense, assume unwarranted authority, skew history, distort plain meanings, confuse the lucid, jumble the coherent, and get in the way of progress.

That is both a snappy explanation and fit justification for this book. The idea is to bring some of the rules governing critical-scholarly-theoretical discourse out into the open, show them a good time. What it takes to please them is to do something wrong, or, even better, a lot of things wrong. In my case, this kind of wrongdoing is best called "cheating," but in other instances (you and I have seen them), it may be not so much scoundrelism as stupidity, not trying to get away with it but not getting it. But the rules don't care: in either case, if you don't get it right, the rules will come out to say, "You didn't get it right." The proper amount of obstinacy or thick-headedness will allow the rules to explain, to illustrate, to be explicit.

Actually, it takes a lot of criminal or dum-dum behavior to get the rules speaking. There is so much rectitude around that the rules have been made nearly mute. So many honor the rules they have nearly invisibilized (my dean uses that word) them. The rules governing what we do within literary discourse wear clothes that are so resolutely fashionable they pass as natural and innocent, do not even register on the eye or in the mind.

I think the metaphors employed so far have made it pretty clear what I am doing. These metaphors sweep forward and gush (in anticipation), revealing my point: that the rules need and want denaturalizing, that only resolute criminal activity can do it, and that I am just the man for the job.

Here is what I will do. The essays that follow try very hard not to be law-abiding. To annoy: that is the aim. To annoy the Victorian subjects, accustomed to better treatment, and to swarm and sting even more maddeningly what we all know are the best ways of writing about literature and literary history, of conducting an argument, of respecting readers, of being faithful to evidence, of writing coherently, of obeying the demands of logic, of following causality wherever it leads, of hurrying on and off the stage, of being polite, of winning the game.

Worry the Victorians in order to annoy the Victorianists: that's my motto. One friendly to this project, if she can be found, would say that such a watchword, carried into action, might profitably disrupt not only texts but what we take these texts to be, how they are seen, and how they come into being in our critical and institutional practices. Not new readings but a play with the conditions of reading: that's the point of being disrespectful.

That's clear enough, so I should get on with it. The first rule is this: the best way to explain such things is to do them. But I am not being paid to obey rules. So I will add to this introduction more explaining, in the form of evocative short sections, some more pertinent than others and freer of redundancy, but all carefully designed to make it more difficult for readers to ridicule this book and humiliate its author.

WHAT'S GOING ON HERE?

Our practices as critics are not neutral or unplaced; they are products of institutions with histories and sets of needs. That doesn't come as news to you. But my optimistic feeling is that these practices are not simply power-driven obligations but rather old habits supported by ignorance and sloth, like not flossing. We needn't ennoble our tunnel vision. We operate, one can (if it gives pleasure) say, within fields of obscurely motivated power; but these fields still get all weedy when no one thinks about the weeds or the practices that allow them to grow. Our not-thinking can be cast in terms of high paranoia: the not-thinking is part of a system of strategic directives orchestrated by an unoriginated Power. That's frightening, but not very.

If we, perversely, abandon Foucault, we might recast ourselves as lazy half-wits getting by within a set of critical practices we have inherited, have found remarkably easy to use, and have never troubled to examine because it is nicer to sit by the fire (or in front of students, at conferences, in learned journals) and doze. After all, criticism is something we do, not just something that is there.[1] As a thing we do, it is liable to the same disrespect we accord all human activities: getting to know them, we stop thinking about them altogether—like dusting. (That's an artful foreshadowing.) Learning to do criticism is learning to stop attending to it, learning to forget.

That's not to say that the habits of criticism are innocent or nothing more than slovenly, that all we need to do is take a fresh look, do a little weeding. Assumptions of all sorts are naturalized and set in motion by our activities, and our stupidity protects a host of unasked questions. What Eve Kosofsky Sedgwick calls "reading rebelliously,"[2] then, is not an attempt to produce rebellious readings but to rebel against the taken-for-granted which propels the forms of reading we have learned to honor.

Such readings are so concerned with their own form and its preservation that they are relatively indifferent to the content of what they produce, since what they produce are flattering formal reproductions. Literary training generally amounts to instructions on how to follow and duplicate this form and this discourse, how to do it in such a way that others who know how to do it recognize "instinctively" that you're doing it, without being obliged to consider just what it is you're doing. One must learn to produce a discourse that conforms to current practices without giving those practices away. "It is this," Terry Eagleton wittily comments, "that is being taught. . . . You can think or believe what you want, as long as you speak this particular language. Nobody is especially concerned with what you say, with what extreme, moderate, radical, or conservative positions you adopt, provided that they are compatible with, and can be articulated within, a specific form of discourse. It is just that certain meanings and positions will not be articulable within it."[3]

Take, for instance, the odd habit of respecting "texts," a habit disturbed only briefly and slightly by deconstruction. I'll allow myself to say more on this later, but even now it should be obvious that a posture of stunned reverence toward "the text" pays homage to our ways of seeing texts, protecting our habitual means of placing texts and talking about them. The text is like the British royalty: one can feel as one likes about the particular majestic combo in place (I happen to admire the current set deeply) but there is only one attitude possible within the decorum surrounding them. If we annoy Victorian texts, then, we can be sure the texts won't care and neither will the Victorians; we can hope only to fluster what we suppose we mean by "text" and "Victorian." As Sedgwick says, our happiest times are when we are able "to denaturalize the present, rather than the past."[4] We make these past texts strange not to give us a more accurate view of them but to allow them more rattle and eruptive power when set beneath our current comforts. They can harass us. I aim, then, to produce readings which are neither right nor soothing (a tautology anyhow). I'm in chase of readings which are annoyingly wrong. You may be feeling that such claims are not so much annoying as arrogant, and that's not what I want you to be feeling. So, how about this: I am not writing this critique of lit-crit procedures from nowhere, not even from outside those procedures.[5] Further, my own (award-winning) self-consciousness does not, I grant you, provide immunity from the bullying ability of ideologies to reproduce themselves. Still, I will try to grab when I can the possibilities of resistance by watching myself. Mirror-gazing is a great joy anyhow, as you well know, and here it may also give us all some glimpse of how things are going, what's going on here.

The problem is that when others are invited to watch with you, they may not find what appears in the mirror so pleasing. They may find it ridiculous. My own form of self-consciousness, therefore, expresses itself (properly) as self-ridicule, mockery, ironic deflections, nervous giggles. Let me put it more plainly: critics are in the habit of setting up the game, inventing their own rules, and then winning; I propose to disrupt the games, shift and flaunt the rules, and lose.

HOW IT'S DONE

Americans like to attribute the "nonprincipled methodological eclecticism"[6] of academic scholarship to the British, to the tradition of chatty-elegant amateurism of Romantic essayists, Matthew Arnold, and any number of modern examples (who in turn have their caricatures of American critics, of course, but not ones we need be bothered by, since they are so clearly the product of envy and spite).

The truth is, though, that modern critics and theorists of nearly every school have felt safest when they imagined themselves furthest from "method." Most say they have no method at all. Even champions of rigor like the Russian formalists said that they were not tied to "a particular methodology," that their general principles were always subject to alteration and refinement by "the material."[7] The payoff for such deference to "the material," the object at hand, is presumably a liberation from the tyranny of "rules," methods applied mechanically. Once liberated from rules, we figure we can negotiate better with the object and find methods satisfactory to all parties. Method becomes a liberated term, thus liberating us.

It's not so clear that we gain much freedom by this move, and it does seem remarkable that all texts (depending on the period and fashion) suggest the same alterations and refinements. By sneering at method, we seem to have lodged it firmly in the basement, out of sight but where all the generators are. Method surely can no more be divorced from theory or general principles than the object of our inquiry can be separated from the inquiry itself. Making one term (principles or the text) primary simply allows the other term (method or inquirer) to disappear beneath a blanket of assumptions that can then be ignored or regarded as "natural." Imagining that we have no method automatically ties us to one; regarding method as flexible fixes it; thinking of method as adaptable to the material puts that material in thrall to method.

Relaxing our duty to "the text," we are freer to examine method. I agree with Barbara Johnson that one cannot find a method that is guaranteed to generate surprise, but I think she is skydiving over swamps when she says, "it is usually surprise that engenders methodology." I much prefer "surprise" to "the text," but "surprise" or any other response still produces the sort of split that allows method to go its way and be forgotten. Still, Johnson's resistance to being "comfortable in the abyss" and her ability to apply the fullest and most effective ironic pressure to our comforts seem to me wonderfully apt.[8] It's just that method should not be left out of the ironic surprise party. Attempting to practice what Hayden White calls "an absurdist criticism,"[9] then, I will try to treat method as we have become accustomed to treating evidence: not as something external, innocent, stabilizing (or rigid, dangerous, and ugly), but simply as a quality of our own seeing, the way our lenses are ground. This will entail a lot of shifting: juggling the question, refusing the answer, shuffling my own position, nudging you, pretending not to hear, making rude noises, asking dumb questions, trailing off, forgetting where we were, failing to attend, becoming bored, changing the rules to suit me, being inconsistent, courting incoherence. There's method for you.

MAKING GOOD SENSE AND GOOD STORIES

J. Hillis Miller reminds us of our deep attraction to storytelling and our tendency to confuse those tales we love to tell with things that are real and natural. We can even come to regard both the stories and the telling of them as self-sufficient records of self-evident truths, recovered by tellers (us) who simply lay out what is there, only that. Such stories, further, tend to be "genetic": they have beginnings, middles, ends, and in between lots of "causal, organic, or dialectical" continuity to hold things together, to make us say, "This story makes sense. It is a rational accounting for what happened." Miller is referring both to the stories told by the new historicism and to cultural stories generally, especially those we tell about texts.[10] The ties between literary discourse and truth-telling and between truth-telling and storytelling run very deep, but one can perhaps begin to escape these bonds by smudging the central term, "truth," and by rubbing together more intimately criticism and story-making. Doing so would allow us to look for stories (modes of criticism) other than the genetic and to renounce once and for all the pleasures of continuity and the predictable. Strong (bad) stories are strong insofar as they find ways not to fulfill those patterns of thinking that come to be comfortable. Weak (good) stories both satisfy and mask the assumptions that constitute the familiar, and we have grown so accustomed to them we may even forget to notice how boring they are and how insidious. We all become good storytellers of good stories; the challenge is to find bad stories to tell so badly they defamiliarize the conventions of approved narratives.

To find our way out of the predictable and the good, we can turn to the prescriptions of Barbara Johnson and "begin by transgressing one's own usual practices, by indulging in some judicious time-wasting with what one does not know how to use, or what has fallen into disrepute."[11] Once we master such elementary lessons, we may be ready for the injudicious seminars conducted by Roland Barthes. Barthes starts things off by introducing his "anti-hero" and our model, "the reader of the text at the moment he takes his pleasure," a pleasure made possible by the casting out of "that old specter: logical contradiction."

Once liberated from the bugaboo that tells us to respect logic, to be consistent, to avoid contradictions, we may be surprised to see how easy it is to get rid of other heavy burdens, like the professor: "The professor is someone who finishes his sentences." Sentences are coherent, complete, predictable, and stuffed with little victories: "The sentence is hierarchical: it implies subjections, subordinations, internal reactions." But bad and blissful accounts offer no wins, and the bad storyteller shuns any sort of dominance, completion, triumph: "whenever a victory appears somewhere, he wants to go somewhere else." To avoid mastery,

Barthes says, we need "to produce a perforated, elliptical, drifting, skidding, discourse."[12] Very bad stories, in other words, without a single completed sentence, point proved, argument closed, expectation satisfied, problem resolved.

THE GEOGRAPHY OF BAD STORIES

What we need to find out is where to go to tell bad stories. Good stories are well supported, with heavily funded centers all over the world. In our field, one simply finds such a center and starts in, picking an approved subject, choosing a point of view or way of going about it (not to be confused with a "method") and doing it, applying whatever techniques seems naturally to come to hand and keeping at it for the amount of time it takes. But the means for telling bad stories by way of what is unnatural and never on hand (deconstruction) is not very well set up. For one thing, there's nothing to "apply." For another, you don't find yourself at a distance from the subject but messily entwined with it. But most important, you don't really have a beginning, just a willingness to plunge in. As Culler says, "You start wherever you are, *in medias res*,"[13] which isn't a bad place to be.

HOW IT ALL COMES OUT

You've noticed that the last section was short. Well, this one is too. Most of the rest are also, shorter than the beginning ones. That's a tendency that can be explained easily enough. Like most of us, I wanted to make a good first impression, so I used almost all my best material right off. It's not that I have nothing left to say, but that some (all) of it has been heavily anticipated and thus trodden on as far as fresh effects go. The good news is that I can practice a pretty fierce economy from here on out. I would have preferred freshness.

The answer to "how does it all come out?" is that it doesn't. The absurd critic, bad teller of bad stories, takes no pleasure in resolving conflicts, only in stirring them up or at least holding them open, not so the results can be known but so the conflicts can breeze along and complicate themselves in the open air.[14] Who wants to settle for supposing that a text can merely "signify one thing more than another" when we can tickle it into being willing to "'signify more' and thus to make us 'think more'"[15]? Perhaps that's not such a good argument, our sad experience (mine and yours too) revealing all too clearly that not everyone wants to think more. But perhaps "more woozily," "more nakedly," "more badly."

THE TEXT THAT WON'T LEAVE WHEN IT'S TOLD TO

As is the case with the neighbor's kid or the drunk at the party. Not wanted by anybody, he or, just as often, she hangs on and somehow becomes the center of attention. Even Stanley Fish, the most brilliant and resourceful of the text-banishers has been largely unsuccessful in convincing his fellows to forget the text. Fish's most impressive strategy is to assume that the text has already left, has, in fact, never been there or anywhere else, at least nowhere within our finding. But other critics, nearly all others, tied to old habits or maybe just fatigued, find themselves cornered by the text and end up deferring to it, taking notes, quoting from them.

It is common now to reject any idea that a text is neutral, self-contained, or ahistorical. Now, texts are, as Victoria Kahn argues, "interested"[16] and the intricacies of the interests circulating in and beyond texts have become the subject of some of our most influential cultural, political, and new-historical criticism. I suppose one could see the interested text as an advance on the innocent one, but perhaps this is a sophistication that merely reiterates the essential characteristics of the old text and the old practices: texts still speak, texts can still be deciphered (and rather easily, despite their interestedness and our own), texts still mean. Most of all, texts are granted priority and some unaccountable independence from our ways of making them speak and mean. As Fish says, "The question of whether or not a text invites a particular interpretation (or range of interpretations) only becomes urgent within the assumption that at some level the text exists prior to interpretation; but if one rejects that assumption, as I do, then the question becomes at once unaskable and trivial."[17]

If texts are not made products of our own habits of seeing, they can assume a detached, if politicized, naturalness and hide those habits of seeing which brought the text into being in the first place. Texts take their shape and allure from the institutions that allow them to be bought and sold, handled, and, for our purposes, read. If we isolate texts or, as is now common, make them the subjects of certain historical and ideological forces (ones, it turns out, we can also decipher with great assurance), then we protect the ideologies of interpretation that deliver the text to us, and we lie about our own role in the production of those ideologies.

Attacks on idealizing texts are not new, but they are like a fashion that never caught on. Even the boldest and most powerful of American deconstructionists continue to honor the text, idealizing it and making it somehow responsible for their own amazing, risky performances: the text made me do it. Here's Hillis Miller granting "respect for the text" and Barbara Johnson acknowledging "the self-contradictions and ambiguities already present within the text."[18] Already present? Within the text? The readings are somehow there in the text, prior to reading, a presence within (or above and beyond) that need only be invoked. Instead of this respected presence being an old-fashioned centering agency, it is, for these critics, a newfangled decentering thing. But, as Paul de Man and Archie Bunker wanted to know, what's the difference? If one wishes, as I do, to get away from all the bowing and scraping to texts, it's necessary (or maybe just pleasant) to make some noise about it. Otherwise nobody notices, and it's important to be noticed.

BUT WHY ARE YOU USING CANONICAL TEXTS TO DISHONOR?

Canonical texts stagger under the heavy load of reverence, the accumulated slag of refined readings upon readings. It is only charitable to offer them some relief. Besides, these texts have had to accord themselves most obediently to our reading practices and thus stand (in straight lines, good posture, smiling) as exemplary models of how it is we see and do things. As Culler says, under the pressure of subversive theory, canonical texts "may exercise even greater critical force than exotic texts from other traditions, whose very strangeness tends to make the reading of them a process of naturalization, a matter of fitting them to our own categories."[19] Certainly, much can be discovered by reading non-traditional texts, but perhaps not so readily the traditional ways in which texts have been construed and the assumptions governing those constructions.

In any case, since I am armed only with the weapon (tickler) of rudeness and the ability to annoy, there is little I can do with texts that have not yet been given irritating shapes and forms. The canon, on the other hand, is heavily defended, just asking to be jumped on. As David Kaufmann reminds us, the very idea that "literature" (i.e., the canon) is being treated badly "rallies students, parents, administrators, and alumni to come to literature's aid."[20] But is it really literature that we are so ready to protect? Johnson defines the classics as the "already read,"[21] and perhaps what we so zealously defend is actually that reading, or, the processes by which such readings are conducted.

It's true that the classics are the most pluralized of texts, those we say are most hospitable to a variety of readings and shapings. At least they've all been read in lots of ways. But that hospitableness might encourage comfortable conformity rather than diversity, might suggest that certain texts have been made to fit so well with the assumptions that guide our enterprise that they have become one with those assumptions. What we do is what *Hamlet* or "Tintern Abbey," *Bleak*

House or *Ulysses* are. We have grown confident with them, easy and pleasant, able to kid around, roughhouse a little, secure in their loyalty to us, their ever-lasting fixity within the boundaries of the familiar. They're like old slippers, a predictable dog, or granola for breakfast: they fit perfectly with what it is we think we want, what we suppose accords exactly with what ought to be, what meshes with what we set out to find, and what we knew (somewhere deep down) we would certainly find because we made it and put it there. Awfully snug but without much power left to astound.

LET'S GET SERIOUS

Things that are spoken of seriously, that must be spoken of seriously, are those that someone wants to remove from the game or, failing that, pad so thickly they will be immobile and invulnerable. Perhaps that isn't right: it may be not the serious thing that is being protected but the serious speaker, the one bestowing seriousness. Better: it is the set of invested principles and privileges standing behind the giver of seriousness that are both idealized and hidden. When we agree to be serious, we silence whole areas of questions and positions that otherwise would be available to us. Different tones lay out different maps.

I cannot think of a serious way to jab at the assumptions that make our pro-cedures possible. How can I create trouble without help from irony? I under-stand that issues of professional decorum are involved. Issues of professional importance—and texts, or most of them, are certainly that—must, we know, be treated in a professional manner. This goes without saying, or should, and if it has to be said, the profession is annoyed.[22] That's the point. Professional man-ners are no less constitutive of codes of being than are the social manners in Jane Austen or Henry James; obey them quietly and they'll give you everything you want. Flaunt them, refuse to take them or the requisite activities "seriously," make them speak to defend themselves, and you lose.

Actually, the worst thing is not to take oneself seriously; or, since that is hard to imagine, to write commentary that does not seem to take itself seriously. Then one loses for sure. Which is, again, the point: only by losing can one hope to force the rules for the decorous to come out of hiding, the rules for the decorous being of the same household as the rules which honor texts, construe meanings, find evidence, eschew method, and generally write essays that are very good stories, ones where there are winners and where it is in bad taste to talk about losers. I propose to do my best to lose—badly, consistently, and with an ill grace—in order to lure into speech the direct reprimands sometimes regretfully necessary with sassy upstarts. You know how it is with people like that: it's the only language they understand.

MAKING A DISPLAY OF YOURSELF

Being rude means being willing to put oneself on exhibit. Stand in the window, shades not drawn, inviting gazers. Look at it this way: if I don't, someone else will. If you're not looking at me, you might be looking at the text, or at a reading of texts, or at the good stories and the winners. You're sure to be looking at something; you always do. Why not at me? I know that voyeurs and exhibitionists seldom team up, the game being too easy for you voyeurs, like shooting fish in a barrel. But we'll make it work. Don't be insulted by being called a voyeur. It's all in metaphor, and besides, there are worse things.

I KNEW THAT

One of the worst things is to be already aware. Knowingness and its signs— the raised eyebrow, the barely perceptible smile, the nod that shuts off an explanation, silence—act to protect the present and its practices, our present and our practices, from any counterunderstandings, from anything nettlesome or untoward. Most especially, knowingness provides a way to measure the past and bring it under control: set against things "as we know them," the past will come into focus. But what is it we know and how is it we know it? Knowingness cancels such questions, makes them not exist. Eve Kosofsky Sedgwick's *Epistemology of the Closet* is both an exposure of the lethal strategies knowingness can conceal and an exhilarating attack on its certainties: "A point of the book is not to know how far its insights and projects are generalizable [and] in particular . . . to resist in every way it can the deadening pretended knowingness"[23] that we have all around us.

Sedgwick's resistance comes in many forms, but she makes most attractive to us her constructions of the past and of texts, subversive and wonderfully productive constructions in both cases. This vexing the past in order to serve us is a courageous form of the more traditional but similar practice of testing our certainties against the past, partly as a guard against the blind securities of knowingness. "If we're so sure of ourselves, of our bonafides and our superior knowledge," Peter Brooks says with engaging exasperation, "why do we bother to submit ourselves to the test of that otherness that is the culture of the past?"[24] Good, though one suspects that our knowingness might not stop us from construing that "culture of the past" in order to serve the very habits of thought our knowingness protects. After all, the culture of the past isn't something that is, but something we desperately need not to know, even if it takes some doing not to know it.

The not known can be used, then, as a productive agency, "a motivating force": "What the surprising encounter with otherness should do is lay bare some hint of an ignorance one never knew one had."[25] Good again, but that can happen, only if the otherness is allowed to be Other—or made Other. All monsters get domesticated overnight if we allow it. We need, as Hayden White says, to nurture and then celebrate the "capacity to misunderstand,"[26] a refusal to allow the past, literary texts, and theory to be so readily understood, so readily captive to the forces of the understandable.

CULTIVATING THE OBTUSE

Knowing is homicidal. This insight, packed with a happy optimistic nihilism, formed the basis for the moral and political program of Russian Formalism. Formalism is usually seen as a highly unfortunate development, hiding beneath its apolitical scientism a slavish compliance to a conservative or reactionary ideology and an elitist aesthetic. But these Russians were fond of nothing so much as ridiculing aestheticism, mocking the elite, and putting their brilliant comic and (only secondarily) critical talents in the service of an absurdist rebellion. They were skeptical of finding a form that would not be murderous as soon as it was naturalized. And they sensed that a power that could exempt itself from the currents of estrangement would soon have a knife in its hands. Any form that began looking pleasant and pretty, they felt, had to be made monstrous; any tool that came readily to hand had to be dropped so that it would trip us up; any knowing had to be made stupid; if not, all these things would turn into death and take us with them.

That which we know and stop bothering with becomes (and turns us into) dust, like the dust Tolstoy could not remember cleaning from his divan. It wasn't a failure of memory, Tolstoy said, but a total loss: "Since these movements are habitual and unconscious, I could not remember and felt it was impossible to remember." Knowing how to do it, one no longer is conscious of the doing, and thus the doing is as if it were not; further, "if the whole complex lives of many people go on unconsciously, then such lives are as if they had never been."

"And so," Victor Shklovsky goes on, "life is reckoned as nothing. Habitualization devours. . . ." (Perhaps I should pause and apologize for quoting the best-known passage from an essay everyone knows. But knowing, you see, is the enemy here, the comic butt, so I'll proceed.) The point I'm making is that the Russian Formalists are molding a brilliant argument that recalls Falstaff and foreshadows Derrida, a rebellious argument that is formulated to keep moving, never to rest in its resistance to the accepted, the habitual, the known. As Shklovsky was saying, "Habitualization devours—" everything. It annihilates. Knowing is annihilation: poison gas, the hydrogen bomb. Dachau did not exist because no one knew but because everyone was so knowing. "And art," Shklovsky wonderfully continues, refusing to rest in cynicism, "art exists that one may recover the sensation of life; it exists to make one feel things, to make the stone stony." It makes us feel again, resurrects us, by making things "unfamiliar" and thus allowing (or forcing) us to recover "the sensation of things as they are and not as they are known," "a special perception of the object" rather than merely "a means of knowing it."[27]

Art, then, or at least criticism, has the duty of "ostraneniye," of making strange. And this rebellious opposition to the accepted and the known lies behind the finest literary discourse of our century. This debt is not usually acknowledged openly, perhaps because Shklovsky's focus on "the object" seems misplaced, a remnant of outdated positivism. But Shklovsky's emphasis could just as easily be construed to rest on the "making" part of "making strange," on the "sensation" and "perception" he wants to bring back into being, not any sort of accurate recovery of objects. He says directly that "the object doesn't matter," that anything will do so long as the habit of mind and seeing is disrupted.[28] It's the process that counts, our political and moral obligation to make not-knowing a method as well as an aim.

These wily Russians saw that the opposition between the strange and the familiar is always in the process of being deconstructed; the strange is always being invaded by the familiar, becoming old hat only a moment after it scared us silly. Things are never stable, which means that, exactly as Shklovsky says, one can never put one's faith in the estranged object. One must keep moving, attending to the never-ending (but always-fun) estranging work before us.

The point then is to attend to the practices of knowing, rather than simply the object that is *known*. In other words, our purpose is to use texts to suggest how it is they come to be known. I am not trying to persuade you—I'd never do it anyhow—that if they were known differently they'd be known better. Instead, I'm in pursuit of method, a method that will encourage the pursuit. I see no reason to stop, certainly not to celebrate victories or steady up meanings: no payoffs but no layoffs either; no getting the last word. Nothing but beginnings that look promising but never fulfill that promise: like careers in tap-dancing or (speaking autobiographically) becoming a fashion leader. There's no knowing where not knowing will lead us, but it won't land us anywhere.

WHAT'S AHEAD

You have every right to expect that what's ahead will be here explained or, if not exactly explained, mapped out enough so that you can get your bearings, as when you are preparing for a hike. "Mapped out" probably isn't the best way to put it, since no one I know consults a map closely before starting to walk. If you're with someone who makes everyone wait while the map is consulted, you hope he gets shin-splints. What you want is a twenty-second breeze-through: two miles down, then about three along the creek there, I think, a little uphill over there maybe, and then sort of back around.

I'll give you what you want here. There are three **parts** following the one you've just finished, a couple of (pointless but welcome) interludes between parts, and an afterward written by an authority we will respect. The **part** that comes next uses Dickens and the other two **parts** do not. The middle **part** has poetry to vex. The final **part** is where one finds neither Dickens nor poetry.

Everybody set? Got the sandwiches, the Fritos, the Heath bars, the beer? Good. The map? No? Hell with it.

The First Part
Dickensian Jugglers

1

Fattening Up on Pickwick

A feast of fat things!	*Isaiah* 25: 6
Every fat vat must stand upon his bottom.	John Bunyan
Bring me flesh and bring me wine.	Good King Wenceslas
And ye shall eat the fat of the land.	*Genesis* 45: 18
Never eat anything you can't lift!	Ronald Gottesman
I am an epicure; *you* are a gourmand; *he* has both feet in the trough.	*New Statesman*

*T*HE BEST PART of almost every essay is the opening. You've noticed that. I mention it because I don't want the quality (terrific) of my own opening to backfire on me and have you quitting early. Mother said that might happen, and a boy's best reader is his mother. But here is my opening, which offers something like (but not exactly) a summary of the whole thing.

THE OPENING

What if we said that *The Pickwick Papers* is not so much a book to read as to relish? What use might we make of such a suggestion and the possibility that the novel opens up for us a series of secret, half-shameful indulgences?

For one thing, we might explore more openly the regressive tendencies of the novel, particularly key words like "cozy" and "comfortable," and images like the glowing fire inside and the raging cold without. Everyone knows that this is the novel which tells us all we know about Christmas. And what it tells us is that Christmas represents a movement inward and backward: to "the delusions of our childish days."[1] It carries us back to old juvenility, allows us to bask in the warmth of pure puerility. *The Pickwick Papers* makes no demands on us; it does not push us into a strenuous adult world, all sweat and muscle and cartilage. It gives us a world of infinitely yielding, cushiony flesh.

The novel's erotic appeals—and what other appeals can it make?—are, then, those of Mr. Tupman, Mr. Pickwick, Mr. Wardle, and, above all, Mr. Wardle's boy: the appeals of fat. This is a fat book for fat lovers. We glide back into childhood and into the forever-fluffed pillows of corpulence we have always longed for and never found in the gristly sinews of adulthood. The novel invites us to a wallow in pure erotica, flashing before us a series of childish fantasies that always, one way or another, take the form of The Fat Boy. There really is nothing but The Fat Boy, in different disguises, sometimes even crossed-dressed, but always the same underneath. It is his novel; the novel is him. He promises to make our flesh creep, and he does, makes it creep and tingle sensuously by reaching out to caress it.

Reading this novel is a form of communion, a meeting of flesh with flesh. The body of childhood, unmatured and unboned, becomes a realized dream of Christmas peace, a feast of fat.

A NOTE ON PROCEDURES MEANT TO CLARIFY

I have divided this chapter into eighteen sections, approximately, not counting The Opening and what I am doing now, neither of which are really what you would call "sections." Here are what the actual sections (yet to come) are:

1. **Errors Routinely Committed by Other Scholars**
2. **The Flesh Around Us**
3. **Cartilage and Gristle**
4. **My Thesis**
5. **Pickwick and Regression**
6. **Nostalgia**
7. **Snug and Cozy**
8. **Christmas and Dingley Dell**

1. Errors Routinely Committed by Other Scholars

Ever since we got rid of structuralism, talk of *desire* fills the air and the journals. All scholars speak of it, even those who ne'er felt it. But have you noticed how bloodless and unbodied all this talk is? One almost suspects that the talk is a screen, a vast babble which substitutes for the real thing. And the real thing is not talk but, as Jesse Helms reminds us, a matter of flesh and lolling and plunging and pleasuring. Perhaps there never was a time when academics were crammed full with fleshly desire, but we have lost what we did have, and we are therefore compelled to talk about it endlessly. My essay will seek to bring us back to the body, to restore it to us and us to it.

2. The Flesh Around Us

What we most long for is flesh. We cannot get enough of it. Why, then, do we pretend to value slimness and want to make our softest flesh disappear? We say we want to lose fat, not to find it. Of course that is nonsense, as you and I know, but it isn't at first easy to see what is really going on, so I'll tell you. First of all, notice how even our manifest cultural desires really yearn for excess and not spareness; only perverts can manufacture erotic interest in the skinny. Jane Fonda holds no appeal, nor does Richard Simmons, though he used to before he took to exercise. What we adore to the point of madness is the boneless flesh of Jane Russell or Marilyn Monroe, the wondrous fat butts of John Wayne, Marlon Brando, and Elvis.

But there is a more subtle point—there'd better be—and that is that our fascination with weight loss is a fascination for the weight that is lost, for the absent Other, the fat that isn't (quite) there and hence is intensely desirable. I refer those interested to Lacan. We long for the absent Other, in this case the vanished but tantalizing flesh. Skinniness is interesting only in recalling the fat that is no more. Let me make this concrete: recently I saw an ad for some diet potion that had caused four ex-football players to lose 320 pounds between them. I submit to you that you would have been, as I was, completely uninterested in the emaciated figures actually pictured and mesmerized by the 320 pounds that were gone. Pure desire. What we couldn't do with that 320 pounds of flesh—make a fifth football player or a companion for ourselves. But you see my point: there is a kind of orgiastic sexual excess here—we have so much flesh we can throw it away. Yet, by throwing it away, we create intense longing: just where has all that flesh gone and how can I get there too?

3. Cartilage and Gristle

As any happy deconstructionist would do, I locate the cultural binary—fat and bone—and proceed to make fat the superior term. Bone and firmness exist where fat and fluffiness should be: the hard stuff is unnatural. Those who thrust forward bone are freaks—like Mrs. Joe Gargery. Notice how we all despise skinny first ladies like Pat Nixon and how much we took to that round mound of renown, Barbara Bush. But, proceeding, we now dissolve the distinction, making the hard and soft, skeleton and flesh, bone and fat melt together in a formless vision of desire without limits or bounds.

4. My Thesis

As I outlined previously (but you don't mind a repeat), I believe the reader of *Pickwick* is an erotic reader, gliding blissfully backward into full childhood sexuality. We are represented most fully by The Fat Boy, that genderless image of engulfing, cannibalistic self-indulgence, the satisfaction of every desire worth having. The hard-nosed scientific basis for all this is to be found, of course, in Freud, in the quote which follows. I should point out that while this is not exactly a quote in the pedantic sense, since it is not exactly what Freud *said*, it is what he *meant*. Those of us who have lived long with his writings find that we absorb his thoughts and do not find it necessary to refer to his exact words, which are sometimes unsatisfactory, if the truth were known.

My conclusions will come as a shock no doubt to colleagues who have written much and thought little on this subject and who are themselves subject to the most disgusting sexual skewings. Nonetheless, here is the truth: the erotic instinct is always regressive, always bubbling in the desire to wallow in the blissful egoism of childhood. But this puts the point too weakly. It is, first of all, not merely egoism we wish to recapture but *pure ego*, the overflowing self. Second, this is a drive by no means confined to fantasy. It provides the erotic focus for every one of us, and it is not at all just a matter of pictures in the head. To be blunt, we yearn not for images but for flesh, the warm yielding unbounded feather-bed of nurturing, fattening breasts. It would be wrong to say this was mother's breast or that the regression was incestuous: the drive is much more cannibal-istic than genital. We seek to become one with the fat about us, to make the whole world into flesh—into *our* flesh! All eroticism is nothing more than the dive back into a dream of a fleecy and complete self, ever expanding, ever loved.

5. Pickwick and Regression

That the novel allows us to waft our way backwards is not a point I feel com-pelled to hit heavily. It is obvious. That the novel is the most compelling vehicle for regression in our culture is not open to dispute. I offer one quotation, not to support the point—since it needs no support—but to illustrate it: "Happy, happy Christmas that can win us back to the delusions of our childish days!" says Mr. Pickwick. We win our way back to a world not at all delusory, a world of perpetual desire and perpetual Christmases.

6. Nostalgia

Regressive trips offer plenty of sights along the way, sights that always constitute a sort of *deja vu*: we've been there before. Nothing is ever really unfamiliar in regression; there are no strangers, nothing unwelcome. Even the horses in this novel are old and familiar, as are the "great, queer, rambling old inns" and, of course, the central characters: Pickwick, Tony Weller, old Wardle. But this novel of the very old is also a novel of the very young, and that's because they are psychically connected; in regression, they are the same thing. In fact, the older are the younger, since their regression is richer. Thus Mr. Pickwick's devotion to the happiness of the young is a glorious form of self-absorption.

7. Snug and Cozy

A structuralist would say that *Pickwick* can be divided into the genuine coziness of Dingley Dell and the ghastly parody of coziness in the Fleet, such things as the Snuggery. A structuralist would further say that "snug" is itself a binary term; we are snug only if we contrast our warm, settled condition with coldness and alienation. But, in this case, the structuralist would be wrong. In this novel (and in our regressive fantasy), snugness is not a defensive retreat, not some womb we are backing into; snugness is a positive quality that comes to us unbidden. "'This,' said Mr. Pickwick looking round him, 'this is, indeed, comfort.'" He is speaking of Dingley Dell, where snugness has its center. When Mr. Pickwick falls through the ice, gets "snug in bed" and hosts a "grand carouse" with a bowl of hot punch, then a second, then a third, the snug keeps on expanding; is not tied to some opposite. Nor is the snug confined to Dingley Dell. Bob Sawyer boasts that he gives cozy parties, and almost all the eating in the novel is a kind of biting into snugness ("let me order you up a snug little dinner," Sam says). The snug is most of all convivial, connecting. As Mr. Peter Magnus puts it, "Company, you see—company is—is—it's a very different thing from solitude—ain't it." Though Sam responds that this is "a self-evident proposition, as the dog's meat man said when the housemaid told him he warn't a gentleman," company *is* a very different thing from solitude. Company, as we will see, gives the child's ego, our ego, something essential, something to fatten on.

8. Christmas and Dingley Dell

At Christmas we forget to be adult, to observe limits, to be skinny—at Christmas we know desire, perhaps for the only time in the year. At least that's the way Dickens allows it to be: a great carnival luring us back to full eros. Christmas is identified in the novel as the "open-hearted season," the season when hearts open up and deny us nothing at all. What really goes on at Dingley Dell? Games and sleep and getting drunk and mating and, especially, eating without end. Dingley Dell is fat heaven. Here's a typical moment snatched from the heart of this gluttonous open-heartedness:

> "Ah, Mullins Meadows," repeated the fat man.
>
> "Reg'lar good land that," interposed another fat man.
>
> "And so it is surely," said a third fat man.
>
> "Everybody knows that," said the corpulent host.

The very conversation is plump, full of wondrous redundancy—the redundancy of bite after bite after bite. Such feasting is everywhere, even in miscellaneous and somewhat grisly references—as in the poem about the Ivy, a plant said to "make a merry meal" of corpses and to "fatten upon the past." (It would be distasteful and tactless to urge that this Ivy was an emblem for the erotic reader, battening on nostalgia even to the point of making meals of everything in sight, so I won't urge it.) At Dingley Dell, even the tinge of melancholy, "the tear which starts unbidden to the eye when the recollection of old times" comes on us, is really just a lubricant to slide us down the paths of regression.

9. Booze

An even slipperier and more reliable oil is alcohol—hot pineapple rum punch, milk punch, porter, brandy and water, gin, wine. The whole novel swims before us in blurry convivial bliss; the book is soused, staggers and speaks with a thick tongue: we won't go home to morning, till daylight doth appear. Everyone has her, or more likely his, arms around everyone else in a tipsy embrace; everyone is always ordering up a double glass of the invariable, a convivial glass. Jingle sets the tone right away by rescuing the Pickwickians from a row and herding them into an inn: "glasses round—brandy and water, hot and strong, and sweet, and plenty." Certainly plenty. And it acts, hot and strong, to make everything rosy. When Mr. Pickwick is angry, he drinks, and here is the result: "the brandy and water had done its work; the amiable countenance of Mr. Pickwick was fast recovering its customary expression," beaming and stupefied. One current of the novel moves toward Eatanswill, where the electors lie on the pavements "in a state of utter insensibility"; another, more hospitable, current takes us toward Mr. Pickwick collapsing into a wheelbarrow in a similar state. He is led there, we recall, not simply by the snug warmth of the day and the cold milk punch but by trying to recollect a song he had heard in his infancy. That is, Mr. Pickwick moves to where we all want to be: fat and cuddled, with a lullaby stroking our ears.

10. The Overflowing Child

We all realize that this is a novel by and for children; that much has been established. Despite Tony Weller's sarcasms on grown-up people being born again— "the new birth" he supposes they call it—this is a novel which offers just that; or, if not rebirth, then at least regression and that's even better, you see, since it is more titillating and much more readily available. In any case, we are presented with a host of images of age slipping back toward or into youth, most notably in Mr. Pickwick and his eternally young heart but also by way of the knowing Sam Weller, who always finds his best audience in boys and is especially drawn to them. Sam operates as our major link to the child, yet he is so resolutely adult himself—or seems to be—that his own identification with and attraction to children is pretty well screened. Through Sam we can gain access to the child, especially the wildly undisciplined, omnivorous, overflowing child. The overflow image is drawn from stout old Mr. Wardle, "old short-and-fat" as a pikekeeper calls him. He is said to be "overflowing with hilarity" at several points, the pure child not simply in his merriness but by virtue of the fact that he overflows. The child spills. We all know that one of the horrors of growing up comes from being forced to respect quite arbitrary and unnecessary limits. The child, on the other hand, knows no limits, is able to expand endlessly to take in more pleasure, more love, more food.

11. Food

I hope you notice the artful transition, since it cost me some pains to arrange it. Where else is there such praise of gluttony as in this novel, such a greasy cele- bration of eating run amok? Not four chapters into the book, Wardle and the Fat Boy are dispensing food, passing it from hand to hand until it comes to rest in somebody's mouth, anybody's mouth: all are welcome, any stranger, any reader. We can all eat our fill and more, since there are said to be dishes "in endless number." Contemplate that: endless number. It's a perfect fantasy of appetite always catered to and never dulled, the wonderful state where we are always hungry, always eating. At Eatanswill, Sam says, the people simply *will* not stop feeding; he wonders that "they ain't afeerd of bustin'." But the child is infinitely expandable, as well as insatiable. After the cricket match, the celebrants turn to drinking only "when everyone had eaten as much as possible." And how much is possible? In this world, there is no end to possibility, no controls. Everyone eats everything in sight. Some characters, in fact, make it into the novel only by way of their meals: the farmer whose boots Sam is cleaning when we first see him is represented only by his eating ("a slight lunch of two or three pounds of cold beef and a pot or two of porter"). Even Mrs. Bardell and her friends go on with their toasted cheese and pettitoes and there is some suggestion that Mrs. Bardell, if not edible herself, is attractive to Pickwick primarily for gastronomical purposes. She has, we are told, "a natural genius for cooking," "a most exquisite talent"; she is fat herself and the cause of fat in others. As such, she is not imagining things when she supposes Mr. Pickwick's views of her are not entirely Platonic. Mr. Pickwick has sexual needs, certainly, but they cannot be contained by anything as decorous and conventional as marriage—they run straight to flesh.

12. A Fleshly Novel

Now we arrive at what I like to think of as the argument of this essay. And here it is. The lustful reader of the novel—by which I mean my colleagues and most of the rest of you—is a voyeur. The novel offers us the next best thing to a flesh- bath, a kind of porno film we can run in our head, reverse it, stop the action, freeze on the especially enticing visions, all of which are of flesh. It presents a relentless barrage of flesh images along with compelling invitations to plunge into them. At one point, Sam refers to "a fat and happy livin'"—which is just what this novel is and what it gives to us. Now I get to list for you every fleshy image in the novel, and you'll enjoy that. But before I get to it, I have, right now, a corollary point to make. It's this: even clothes in *Pickwick* do not so much hide as point to the ample body beneath. Time and again, the narrator of the novel draws our attention not to the clothes but to the flesh they adorn. In the first three pages alone, we get several examples. Our first view of Mr. Pickwick is of his tights and gaiters—more exactly, of the man beneath them: "had they clothed an ordinary man [they] might have passed without observation, but when Pickwick clothed them—if we might use that expression—[they] inspired voluntary awe." You see: Pickwick is that which is beneath the clothes. Ditto, Winkle is not his clothes but his body, "enveloped in a mysterious blue coat." And Snodgrass's flesh "communicates additional lustre to a new green shooting coat." Two pages later, Mr. Pickwick has "put himself into his clothes." This is a highly proper novel, of course, but it is one in which all the characters are, as it were, presented nude.

OK, here comes evidence (impressive) for those still in need of such securities. It's a list of some of the fleshy scenes and people. Aside from Mr. Pickwick, Tupman is, of course, fat, fatter than his leader perhaps, a regular "grown-up Bacchus," as Jingle has it. Dr. Slammer is "a little fat man," and the widow he loves has "a fat countenance." Doctor Payne, his second, is "a portly personage." Mr. Wardle, "old short-and-fat," is called stout a couple of dozen times in the novel—probably more. The person who opens the door at The Leather Bottle is "a stout country lad," and the crier at Eatanswill is "the fat crier at Eatanswill," where many of his fellow townspeople are naturally "stout." Picturesque scenes, such as the vision of autumn field workers and the "fat urchin" crawling out of the basket, are rendered more poignant by their fat. Mr. Lowten, the "puffy-faced" host at the Great White Horse in Ipswich is not only "a corpulent man," he is identified *as* "the corpulent man." Which makes necessary a pause to give you another striking point: notice how often people are identified *by* their flesh! Mrs. Weller is first introduced as "a rather stout lady": and then referred to thrice as "*the* rather stout lady," the corpulence taking over as essence. Mr. Raddle is, simply, "the heavy gentleman," and Serjeant Buzfuz is nothing but fat. Continuing with the list: Dubbley, one of Mr. Nupkins' lieutenants is "stout"; almost all cooks are fat; Mrs. Sanders, one of Mrs. Bardell's cronies, is "a big, fat, heavy-faced personage"; Ben Allen is a "stout, thick-set young man"; Mr. Humm, presiding at the Ebeneezer temperance meetings, has "a fat smile"; Mr. Namby, a sheriff's deputy, is "a stout man"; Solomon Pell is "a fat flabby man"; and Sam's sweetheart Mary is "wery plump and vell made." Horses taking them on happy excursions are called "chubby," and even the seal of a letter is decorated with "a little fat boy."

The novel is one great vat of undifferentiated and welcoming skin and tissue, without the limits and controls of bone, the harshness of muscle, the reminders of mortality contained in gristle. By that I mean this: bone and so forth tend to define the body and give it shape—and in so doing confine it, regulate it, subject it to the entirely unerotic reminders of sensible limits: leaving off eating, drinking no more than is good for you, going to bed on time. Children are enemies of such tragic restraints—and so is eros, fat eros.

And so is this novel. The only glimpses of the skinny we get here are attached to black comedy or to brief suggestions of repulsion or nausea. Dismal Jemmy is "long and lank," seems to be all cheekbone; Rachel Wardle exposes only her bony wrist, which is probably a pretty fair sample of what she is everywhere; the horse that takes Rachel and Jingle on their elopement displays, in sympathy, "great symmetry of bone"; and the escaping couple are identified as "Thin body and thin face—rather skinny." The Pickwickians are misdirected on their way to Dingley Dell by "a tall bony woman"; Job Trotter is so skinny even his hair is "lank"; the arch-enemy Fogg is, of all things, "a vegetable-diet sort of man," decidedly out of place in this cannibalistic, carnivorous book; the Fleet prisoners are generally cadaverous, filed-down; and The Rev. Mr. Stiggins has "a long thin countenance with a semi-rattlesnake sort of eye." But this is not the novel to spend much time on such things, plunging, as it does, every five minutes into the fat.

13. Kierkegaard and Flesh

This is the most majestic section and the one most fitting for a scholarly essay. I worked it up in the same the way Mr. Pott's reporter did his research: I crammed, read in the encyclopedia under "K" for Kierkegaard and under "F" for flesh and combined my findings. However, the resulting paper is so consequential and so necessarily extended that I decided to separate it from this essay and give it the room (and media attention) it requires and deserves. I am assured that it will appear under a not-unfamiliar imprint (with heavy publicity) at an early date.

14. Old Tony

G.K. Chesterton and others who enriched the Dickens Fellowship in the early days recognized at once that Tony Weller was the oracle of this novel. Tony casts the fellowship of flesh in strongly male, even misogynistic terms, but he knows what counts in this world: the intimate connection of width and wisdom—they always grow together. Tony has devoted himself to expanding or ignoring limits, particularly the limits of the body: "The fleshly curves [of his face] had so far extended beyond the limits originally assigned them," that he presents nothing but the extreme tip of a nose, and that is about to vanish into the glorious blubber he has devoted himself to acquiring. He selects his friends for their "width and consequent wisdom," and he takes immediately to Mr. Pickwick, who he sees as a fellow epicure, a fellow child.

The two of them form a kind of unit or, more accurately, the first two points in the trinity of flesh that defines the erotic reading of this novel: Tony Weller, Mr. Pickwick, and the Fat Boy. Pay attention now, as this is where it gets provocative. Notice that all three are not just fat but strangely innocent, open-visaged, even apparently helpless. Like Tennyson's Kraken, all they can really do is batten on huge sea worms in their sleep. All three are said to have "red faces," a highly significant point, and all three, at different points, are involved in strangely touching scenes of making contact—scenes so quiet, in fact, that we are likely not to register them or their connections consciously.

Here they are: as Mr. Pickwick is led heartsick through the prison, he pulls the prison official "gently" by the coattail; after the jury returns the verdict against Mr. Pickwick, Tony touches Sam "gently" on the shoulder and utters those memorable words, "vy worn't there a alleyby"; and, finally, at the Dingley Dell Christmas, the Fat Boy pulls Mr. Pickwick by the coattails, again "gently." "Speak gently to the little child/ It's love be sure to gain./ Teach it in accents soft and mild./ It may not long remain." That poem, though parodied in Lewis Carroll's *Wonderland*, represents the exquisitely soft and gentle attitude Carroll, Dickens, and all of us feel toward the child—the fat child, the Christmas child—especially when that child is the Fat Boy, especially when that child is us.

15. The Fat Boy

At the center of this novel and its appeals is the image of pure ego, pure limit-lessness, pure carnival, pure lust—what we all would love to return to, The Fat Boy. His grand excess of flesh makes him a pleasure machine: he has so much flesh, he offers some to us. When he shakes his head it gives "a *blanc-mange* like motion to his fat face," and Sam calls him "dumpling face"—both blanc-mange and dumplings being very inviting to chew on a bit. We love to gaze at The Fat Boy as much as he loves to gaze at others. He is something extraordinary, we are constantly told, a kind of startling and magnetizing curiosity. But he is also identified with jolliness: he and Sam make the ice-slide together and are the first to try it out. Most of his joy comes from food, however; not so much from eating as from the anticipation of eating. The Fat Boy is the drooling boy, all appetite: "There is such a jolly meat pie!" "Oh my eye, how prime! I am so hungry!" His appetites are contagious.

The rest of us may be more restrained (I am), but The Fat Boy does seem to be exercising some of the novel's most pointed erotic impulses. He is always show-ing up at love scenes to look and listen, to gaze (see Lacan again, if you'd like). He watches kissing with "a dark and gloomy joy" and is always right around the corner, walking in without knocking, when there is something lascivious under way—as is the case with Snodgrass and Emily late and Rachel and Tupman early. That he is also spectacularly aroused by food is not some quirk in his sexual direction but consistent with it. He does not distinguish between sexual contact and possession, nor between possession and consumption: to love is to eat. The Fat Boy's relation to food involves more than eating it or even wanting to eat it: he loves to leer at it, ogle it, fondle it, become sexually active with it. He "sighs deeply" over a capon, bestows an "ardent glance" on its plumpness, "gloats languidly" over a banquet. Like us, The Fat Boy knows no restraint in his desire to consume. He not only makes no distinction between eating and sexual pleasure, he joins them ardently. He looks at bodies, at flesh, in order to make it all one with his own ever-expanding fat. And that's natural enough.

16. The Cannibal

The Fat Boy, thinking of food, of "roast legs and gravy," gives "a semi-cannibalic leer at Mr. Weller." Dickens's phrasing—the odd term "roast legs"—makes it seem as if he (Dickens) were participating in or inviting us to participate in the ungodly feast. Later, the wonderful boy looks at Mary with a full dose "of cannibal" in his eyes, flattering her with something more than a proposal to share a life of feasting with him: "How we should have enjoyed our meals together!" he says. The suggestion is that they will, in some exuberantly literal way, become one flesh.

17. Erotic Fun

And just so, bodies are offered up to us throughout this novel to salivate over, to possess, to ingest. Sam is drawn to stories of the cannibal—as in the man who made sausage of himself but forgot to shed his buttons, the buttons alone causing complaint, not the flesh. Even Sam's valentine, carefully chosen and composed, presents an emblem of oral satisfaction: a "highly coloured representation of a couple of human hearts skewered together with an arrow, cooking before a cheerful fire, while a male and female cannibal in modern attire were approaching the meal with hungry eyes." They are not the only ones with eyes filled with hunger, longing, desire. Even the great Pickwick is offered to us as flesh to have and enjoy: "he goes in rayther raw, Sammy. . . . and he'll come out, done so exceedin' brown, that his most familiar friends won't know him. Roast pigeon's nothin' to it, Sammy."

18. Finale

Despite what you'll be saying, though, our erotic fun with this novel does not come from swallowing or wanting to swallow Mr. Pickwick. Rather, we are welcomed to become fat with him, to share our flesh with his. If someone does take a bite now and then, it's no great matter. There's plenty more where that came from. This novel assures us that there is no end to our childhood, to our play, to our desire—certainly no end to our life.

2

Little Nell—She Dead

"SHE WAS DEAD. Dear, gentle, patient, noble Nell, was dead. Her little bird—a poor slight thing the pressure of a finger would have crushed—was stirring nimbly in its cage; and the strong heart of its child-mistress was mute and motionless for ever."[1] It's the bird that interests me—this little bird and the suggestion that maybe I would like to crush it with my finger. Crush is a strong word. I wonder why, in the midst of the horrible (but not entirely unexpected) revelation of Nell's death, we receive this peculiarly vindictive aside. But then, it's not really an aside, you'll agree. The bird—or mashing the bird—shares equal billing with Nell's corpse. It provides just the sort of contrast Dickens talked about as the informing principle of *The Old Curiosity Shop*.[2] Thus it's proper that we should focus on the bird. The text tells us to.

In the same way, a few pages later, during Nell's funeral, we are asked to look not at the coffin but at the spectators, particularly at a collection of disgusting old vermin who, we are told, really should have died ten years ago if they had done what's right. Dickens works up considerable animosity toward these coots: "the deaf, the blind, the lame, the palsied, the living dead in many shapes and forms." It's so disgusting that we welcome the narrator's bitter, bitter irony: "What was the death [the grave] would shut in, to that which would crawl and creep above it!" (72). Damn right! It's the bird and those aged worms, slithering and squirming, that we should be talking about, you're saying. Not Nell. Nell is embarrassing, sentimental. We've outgrown that. Let's talk about the bird and the golden agers.

What's going on when we say that, I suggest, is a form of evasion and denial, understandable but filthy. Personally, I have no interest whatsoever in the old people and, I must confess, even less in the bird. I can't keep track of the bird, can't remember if it's the same one Nell had originally or not. The only thing I remember about the bird is that when Kit snivelled over the little birdy Nell left behind, Quilp proposed that they wring its neck. Did they? Is this the same bird? If so, how did it survive? More perplexing, if Nell left it behind, how did it catch up with her? Is it a new one? If so, how did Nell have the heart to get a substitute for the old favorite? Who cares? I find the bird and the old people simply handy containers for my embarrassment, my inadequacy in the face of the overwhelming demands made by the child's death. You'd say the same if you were honest about it.

The important question then has to do with what I take to be a massive cultural and historical evasion of this subject: the death of the child, Nell's death. Why is it that, outside of Dickens, the death of the child is actually so infrequent in the canonical literature? It was, we know, a commonplace event in the nineteenth century. The odds for survival improved for children during the latter decades of the century, but not really enough to make it even money that you would make it to the age of 5. Why is there so little about it in the literature? And why do we have nothing to say about it when it is mentioned (other than some self-flattering name-calling: the Victorians were "sentimental"; we are "tough")? I know you are now recalling examples of child-deaths that *do* occur in canonical literature, wanting to argue with me. Such is human perversity. I didn't say there were none; but most of those we do have take place under special circumstances: the death of little Miles *(The Turn of the Screw)* is a release for him, and that of Linton Heathcliff *(Wuthering Heights)* a release for us (we are glad he got his). Neither allows us much access to the event, the loss of the child. I believe the death of Buck Grangerford in *Huckleberry Finn* does push us directly, if briefly, toward the image and emotions of loss. But that sort of thing is rare—that's all I'm claiming. You're with me now, on my side.

I want to suggest a diagnosis for the disease afflicting us, the one which makes us all cowards, unable to look at Nell, much less able to feel for her. I have a cure, too, you'll be glad to hear; but I'll save that. The reason we veer away, take evasive action when we approach Nell's corpse, first of all, is not that we are too sensitive or too rugged or too honest. It is because we feel so drawn to her, so drawn to her that we pull back. We pull back because what we are drawn by we do not want to face or admit; and that's because what we are drawn by is, down deep, lust. Not for the female but for the "child," as she is obsessively and not without reason called.

The diagnosis gets worse. But start there: our culture has made pedophilia inevitable and also criminal—we must love the child sexually and we cannot. The more serious problem in our case, though, is that our erotic play with Nell takes the form of voyeurism, a sexual activity we know is very much like sadism. We want to take possession, establish control of the object, have it there permanently on view. You can see where this is going: the movement of the novel is toward fulfillment, toward giving us what we said we wanted—an absolutely objectified child, Nell as object, Nell as corpse. For several reasons, though, none of them flattering, that's not really what we want. We really want always to be moving in that direction, always about to take possession but never doing it. In other words, what we want is desire, not an ending to desire. We want to perpetuate the chase, not stop it; we want Nell always dying, always about to become an object. We do not want her dead. Death ends desire. We are voyeurs, not necrophiliacs.

I take it that, so far, all this is simply common sense. The novel drives us to distraction because, ironically, it gives us what we want, and that is the last thing we want. Our great grandparents wept openly that their wishes should be so brutally fulfilled, and thus cancelled. We are more squeamish and much less candid about the nature of our desires, and we are so busy denying them that we require a variety of screens and evasions, like the assertion that the death of Nell is beneath us, a form of emotionalism we have passed beyond. Out of the prison of our deep fear and denial, we crow about being liberated and unafraid.

The cure is to deconstruct. As it is, right now, we are always paying homage to the Nell ideology, the Nell plot, by not naming it. By avoiding it, we make it central. We talk endlessly about Quilp and Swiveller, but we make them contrasting figures only and thus trivialize our talk about them. We are all covertly agreeing that the novel is really about Nell (though we also pretend that we wish it were not). I am, frankly, just as eager to decenter the Nell plot, to expose its pretenses, deny its totalitarian arrogance. The way to avoid totalizing it, I suggest and expect you to believe, is to enter into play, see what contrary centers we can construct, and thus build more rings to our circus, more ways of seeing and being, more metaphors to live by. In other words, I propose that we devise a set of wildly contradictory procedures for understanding this novel and apply them all at the same time. That will show Nell and her corpse that they can't claim all the attention; and it will, paradoxically, give us a way to approach with less fear the claims made by the child, by that plot. We'll never have to resort to calling it sentimental again.

I provide at this point a chart. You'll forgive me saying two things about it: first, that it looks simple enough but, in fact, represents years of experience and many minutes of hard thought; second, that it will only be of use to you if you stop now and study it some. If you aren't willing to do that, I wish you would just go do something else, since you can't expect to follow what is coming up with just a slapdash glance at the chart. If you plunge ahead in ignorance, you will become muddled, angry, and defensive. You will misunderstand things and make mistakes and get hot and blame me, and I'll respond in kind. Neither of us wants that, at least I don't, so if you're too lazy to study the chart, good riddance. Maybe you're in the wrong field of study altogether. Maybe you should just go off and find something less demanding.

THE CHART

Metaphors:	Peace	Prudence	Power	Play	Passion
Actors:	Nell	Kit	Quilp	Dick	You and Me
Spot:	Grave	Floor	Table	Stage	Bed
Time:	Sunset	Morning	Noon	Anytime	Night
Action:	Quit	Save	Get	Go On	Arouse
Mode:	Pastoral	Sit-Com	Satire	Farce	Erotica

Are we ready then? If you'll refer to the chart, I'll explain. Across the top are a series of p-words: peace, prudence, power, play, passion. These are metaphors, ways of constructing experience and our apprehension of experience. Each stands independently, not in any necessary relation to anything else, not part of a binary for instance: peace doesn't balance out war; or play, seriousness. None of these metaphors has any coherent connection with any other; none recognizes that the others exist or can exist. Each metaphor is out to give us everything we need—each is literally totalizing, totalitarian. The reason for offering so many terms is to allow us some hope of escaping totality, of escaping the illusion that any one of these centers is natural. None of these is natural; none has any special authority beyond that which is granted to it by history, culture, ideology, whim. None has any textual authority. I am imposing them; they don't come from the text. The text has none to offer, but welcomes any we have.

Let me illustrate, if I may. Do not get impatient. Our novel is now a five-ring circus. (Of course, we could add or subtract rings, if we wanted. Maybe the Brasses deserve a metaphor of their own, or Mrs. Jarley, or politics, or Nell's bird[s], or the gendered reader. But we'll go with five for now.) If I were good at this, I could persuade you that *each* of the five rings constitutes a sufficient, persuasive, and fulfilling novel, or a story about the novel, or a way to lead your life. The point of all this is to displace the Nell center and thus, once it is out of the spotlight, to have some access to it, to get a peek at what it is we are so afraid of. Decentering it can never be a wholly free or uncontaminated activity, naturally, a caution I'll try to take into account. And let me again reiterate that this chart is not a formalist or interpretive exercise. It doesn't describe the text; it outrages the text, invades it, tickles it, ignores it.

OK. First column: Nell plot and peace. This is the one we are blinded by now, so there's not much point in talking a lot about it. "Peace" here suggests that we are urged to organize our understanding of the narrative around the belief that peacefulness is not just a goal but the only natural state. Time and again in the Nell plot, motion is seen as demonic or perverse, the proper state of man being repose, calm. An ordinary group of people on the street are made into a raging sea, an unnatural tempest. Under mania, Nell's grandfather rages about gambling; in a natural state, though, he gardens quietly among the graves. In the Nell plot things do not change. The grandfather, whom we hate so much (perhaps because he is in the position we want to occupy), says that Nell is always the same; and the plot moves to preserve her sameness. Nell is a child who never loses those clouds of glory, never violates the dream by betraying us and growing up. She is Peter Pan and Lewis Carroll's Alice—and how peaceful it is. This peace also is related to a kind of complete self-sufficiency, an aloneness that is part of the effect of all those contrasts in which we see Nell. They all heighten her crucial singularity, the fact that she needs no one to define her, that she is a sort of allegory, an allegory of what it means to need nothing.

The pastoral is used here to convince us of the divine appropriateness of all this—the movement toward peace is the movement toward God. Now, I should say, though, that we resist the logic of this plot, the push it makes toward fulfilling itself in a coalition of nature, God, peace, and stasis in the image of a tombstone. Our interest feeds on perpetuation, not fulfillment; and this plot seems wedded to a formal closure that shuts us out, that snuffs the candles and sends us on home. But as I say, this metaphor and the way it is worked out through Nell tend to paralyze us. We keep our distance and hurl taunts at it, call it sentimental, rather like juvenile delinquents teasing a tiger in a zoo. Knowing it would be unproductive simply to go behind the bars and cozy up to the tiger, we'll see what we can locate from other vantage points.

Move one column over and we come to the confluence of Kit and prudence. This center is not so much embarrassing, like the Nell plot, as it is deeply boring. Why is that? Why have we lost the ability to respond to these issues and figures?

Instead of saying that the Kit stuff—Kit and Barbara and the Garlands and the Notary and all those interchangeable people—is simply conventional, tired, or just plain bad, let's locate the problem in us, in a cultural distancing so extreme that we have almost no reaction whatever. We respond to the Nell material sneakily and with red faces, as we do to pornography; but here we have no response at all: we skip, we sleep through this material, we forget it. Why? Let's see.

First of all, prudence is very different from peace. This is a different center, one that might easily deconstruct the Nell plot, if we would let it. This plot disdains the extremism of the Nell plot, the peace-at-all-costs drive and the willingness to push so absolutely for one goal. The Kit plot scurries around but never ventures far from the nest. Like squirrels, these people go short distances to gather nuts and return with them—that's it. It is an economic center, rooted in an economy of scarcity and a psychology of caution. In the Kit plot, one husbands resources, saves up, monitors expenditures. Most of all, one observes the rules, operates within fixed boundaries, realizes one does not have the capacity to challenge limits.

This plot is based on an acknowledgement of weakness and vulnerability, primarily class weakness and class vulnerability. Kit and his mother and Barbara and her mother are all aware that they can take no risks, that the best safety lies close to home, close to routine, to the expected and the regular. At least the routine keeps one alive. Even the Garlands reflect this protective movement inward, this essential conservative fearfulness; employing Kit they worry they may be taking a chance, and their life is based on avoiding anything like chance. They explain this to Kit by saying, "[We] are very quiet regular folks, and it would be a sad thing if we made any kind of mistake, and found things different from what we had hoped and expected" (21). To a great extent, Kit and those about him struggle and are successful in holding the line, maintaining the expected. Others sometimes do bring the unexpected into their lives, but these wary, timorous people soon right themselves and return to their defensive regularity. The one time they deliberately lay themselves open to surprise, through their great dissipation at Astley's circus (39), they regret the whole business, feel a fearful kind of guilt, not because they are puritanical but because they are committed to understanding life only through a paradigm of careful, familiar control. That's the way they see; that's the way their world is. Astley's is disruptive because it thrusts at them a different paradigm, the paradigm of Dick Swiveller. The reason this is so unsettling to methodical types is that they cannot *be* in such a world; they live, breathe, and have their being within a pattern of prudence. When they wander out of it, they risk nonbeing.

Kit and those about him, then, are tied to virtue as a matter of survival. They are loyal, steadfast, absolutely reliant—not because they have better souls but because those are necessary traits in the only narrative that has a place for them. Disloyal, unreliable, changeable characters are simply unthinkable in the metaphor they inhabit. They are not, these poor, contented with their lot; they simply have no other. They find themselves written into a narrative that resembles very closely the formulaic defensiveness of television situation-comedy, another prudential mode anxious to repeat in order to insure safety. TV sit-coms are all written by Abel Garland and Barbara's mother. Such plots contain no surprises, which is not a defect but a secret of their success, their ability to reassure. Thus the Kit plot depends on recurrences: Kit's turning up at Nell's window regularly, and later coming back to mind the pony a second time as he said he would. His returning to mind the pony becomes the basis of a joke, endlessly repeated by Mr. Chuckster. It's not a very good joke, but then, it isn't meant to be. Good jokes are based on surprises and try to pro-voke eruptions of laughter. But here in the Kit plot, we want no wild laughter, no eruptions, no surprises; mild amusement will do. We want reassuring little nudges to remind us that the routine has not changed, that nothing has changed, that next week Archie and Edith, and Lucy, and Andy and Barney, and Roseanne will be back doing exactly the same thing. Thus with Kit.

A digression, abrupt but clarifying: One notes how each of these metaphors tends to deal with the same issues or forms, re-seeing them in each case from a different perspective. One of the most interesting of these shifting forms (or objects that take on different shape) is human deformity. In the Nell plot, deformity is made the polar opposite of the child: she runs into it everywhere, but the freaks only make her seem more perfect and emphasize her isolation. In the Quilp plot, of course, deformity is made central and is the source of all the energy; for Swiveller, the deformed Marchioness is the instrument of play or playful affection, a partner in a game. For us, in our lustful reading, deformity is denied, since everything, no matter how bizarre, is made to feed our eroticism. And for Kit now, for the Kit plot, deformity itself is made regular, unsurprising, redundant—as in the club foot of Mr. Garland, which sure enough is duplicated exactly in his son. Is this all clear?

In a similar way, other issues are drawn into each metaphor and are trans-formed by them. I haven't received permission to trace all of these, alas, but try some for yourself: death, heaven, the child. You'll see what I mean, and what you'll see is that none of these terms or objects has any natural mean-ing—or any meaning *in the text*; they take their meanings from the metaphors or plots they find themselves in. And these metaphors, as I've been saying, have no independent or textual existence; they originate with us. If it still isn't clear how the object changes shape according to the way it is viewed, according to the controlling metaphor, I don't mind doing one last round. Nothing beats repetition, after all. This time we'll do death. For peace, death is made a goal, a soft finale; for prudence, it is avoided through patterns of guilt and expiation; for power, it is made an instrument of torture; for play, it becomes part of the game, part of the cycles of resurrection; for you and me, it is orgasm, death is, or fulfillment, always around the corner but endlessly deferred. That'll do.

Now, back to our tour through the chart. We had, you recall, covered two columns before taking a break (ill-advised) to illustrate how these metaphors work. We return to the middle column, "Power." The most difficult of these metaphors to get any distance on is Quilp's, precisely because Quilp lives just where we live—he lives in our metaphor. We might say that he somewhat exaggerates our habits and procedures, but he operates on the same basic assumptions. And that is why this villain, this monster, this compact bundle of hate and witty sadism seems so much like one of the family. He lives, as we do, with a naturalized center of power; he assumes that everything is explicable by way of power, can only be explained by way of power.

He is, you will be saying, paranoid. Yes, but paranoia is only a purified form of the logic of power. Quilp supposes, as we suppose, that power is not a metaphor. We both think that power is in the world independent of our finding or putting it there. We think power is not a creation of discourse; we think discourse is a creation of power. Paradoxically, Quilp is so deeply entrapped by the metaphor of power that he is powerful; that is, he sees nothing but power and therefore is not bamboozled as are others by explanations which do not proceed from power, which mix in inauthentic doses of morality or sentiment, for instance, as Quilp would never do.

But he does that all the time, you say—speaks of sentiment and morality. That's right. Quilp moves toward the natural, inevitable narrative of power: satire, the ridicule of an external object. Note that definition.[3] Quilp is magnificent at ridicule; he is also trapped by that mode, unable to handle anything but ridicule, and thus dependent on these external objects for his power. Satire's only plot is formed by external objects; it has no independent source. Take away the objects for ridicule and satire collapses. It draws its power by distancing itself resolutely and constantly from the Other and thus is controlled by, defined by that Other.

Thus it is appropriate that Quilp takes the form of the naughty child, the show-off, the one who waits for Others (adults) to set rules so he can break them. He is defined by the attention he is trying to get, that he needs in order to secure any self-definition. Quilp, it is often noted, parodies the Nell plot; that is, he energizes that plot by setting himself up as its opposite, its funny, even ridiculous, opposite. It is not so often noted that he draws apart just as violently from all the other metaphoric centers, too. Quilp is extraordinarily adept at reading all these other centers and at dramatizing not just one but many counter narratives. He is desperately aware of the others and very smart about them; he has to be. He is defined by negation, as power must be, as a force that thinks of itself, as satire must, over and against others. Thus, in addition to countering Nelly—even his corpse parodies hers—Quilp stands against the other metaphors. He has a principled hatred of virtue, we know: "I hate your virtuous people, I hate 'em every one!" he says (48), throwing down another glass of liquor. But it's more than virtue he hates. He hates peace, prudence, play, and passion just as fiercely and rips into them all.

Readers are sometimes puzzled by Quilp's motives, which seem inadequately explained by any realistic psychology. Now, very few things in Dickens answer to realism, common sense, or anything so paltry, but Quilp's drive to sully Nell's innocence and mock her pastoral aspirations, delightful as it is, is tough to place in psychological terms. Why does he do it? And why does he mistreat his wife? And why does he want to entangle and destroy Dick? And why does he hate Kit so deeply that he sets up totems to bash at? My answer is that the metaphor in which Quilp lives and constructs his world demands his energetic and self-conscious repulsion of all other metaphors. He simply must, whether it satisfies the demands of realistic behavior or not, define himself over and against all other competing modes, he must seek to use power against them, he must seek their annihilation. This logic, the logic of satire, paranoia, and global nuclear war, in the end fulfills itself in Quilp's self-liquidation.

Before that, though, Quilp finds his greatest opposition not in Nell but in Kit. Nell actually shares with Quilp a contempt for ordinary boundaries, a wild and reckless dedication to her metaphor that results in a kind of suicide Quilp can honor. Similarly, he can recognize in Swiveller's dedication to play some of his own methods, even if the ends are radically different. Dick's play has no end but play itself, no purpose but to engage in play and prolong it. Quilp plays games, but plays to win. Dick is Daffy Duck in an endless cartoon baseball game; Quilp is Mike Tyson, battering opponents into game-ending comas at the rate of millions of dollars per second.

But it is Kit that drives Quilp wild, and it is the metaphor of economic prudence that most goads him. Kit's gratuitous insults of Quilp are so feeble and so inadequate to explain Quilp's rage that they call attention to the gap between motive and act. Are we to think that Quilp is a thin-skinned, insecure little fellow with a poor self-image, deeply wounded by Kit's calling him "ugly"? No, Quilp is outraged by the way of being and seeing that Kit represents; he is infuriated by prudence itself. Quilp goes to Little Bethel, the home of prudence made transcendent, in order to draw energy for his satire: "Yes, I was at chapel. What then? I've read in books that pilgrims were used to go to chapel before they went on journeys, to put up petitions for their safe return. Wise men! Journeys are very perilous—especially outside the coach. Wheels come off, horses take fright, coachmen drive too fast, coaches overturn. I always go to chapel before I start on journeys. It's the last thing I do on such occasions, indeed" (48).

Quilp is offended by the minimalist dedication to life in the Kit plot, by the way it shares with Emma Woodhouse's father the sense of being satisfied with the thinnest gruel and protective even of that. Quilp lives within a mad economy of surplus—the more you use the more there is—and with plots that depend on a constant source of energy and thus constant surprises. Quilp must, over and over again, come up with new tricks and new devices, new torments for his wife, mother-in-law, and Sampson Brass—new devilish schemes. The reliance on regularity and redundancy in Kit's sit-com plot, thus, stands as Quilp's opposite, his nemesis, and therefore feeds most lavishly his satire.

The reader's own voyeurism gives Quilp some material as well. Our maneuvers constitute a kind of competition for Quilp, who is a peeper himself. Voyeurs do not work in teams, so he sets out to eliminate us by making our gentle, or at least disguised, interest in Nell blatant and grotesque. His open, winking, drooling lust after Nell is a way of pointing the finger at us (unfairly, unfairly). When Quilp bounces on Nell's bed, speaks of how rosy and chubby and luscious she is, he profanes our own interests. He takes sex out of the head (where it belongs) and onto the filthy floor; he moves it from fantasy to the skin—and this is not at all what readers like us are after.

And now for something completely different: the Dick plot. I have no notes here and nothing on my outline. No scribbles on the ends of envelopes. You are not to think that I am, all the same, at a loss, unable to come up with anything to say. It's not that. What it is is this: the material on Dick is so obvious you can do it yourself. I don't want to bore you by telling you things you could figure out (easy) if you tried.

And that's the case with the Swiveller metaphor, which connects to pure play, pure theater. Any sort of material that enters this arena is at once made protean, providing more and more energy for sustaining the world of play and keeping it spinning: here Dick's single rented room is transformed into apartments, then "vasty chambers," then the universe, and an expanding universe at that. Thus his game will never end. Dick lives in a world that has no linearity, no causality, no rules. It is not a satiric world at all, since it has no dependence on otherness and no interest in ridicule. Within Dick's metaphor, illness leads not to death but to rejuvenation for no reason; self-indulgence and perpetual expenditure lead not to depletion but to bounty for no reason; confinement in a smelly, sloppy hole leads to love with a Marchioness for no reason. Play will do that for you.

And finally we have *us*, the inhabitants of passion, the actively-looking readers. What we are passionate for is passion. And we read not to find fulfillment but to keep the reading going. We want desire, not an end to desire. Of the plots, these metaphors, I will say that none of them yields very well to voyeurism except the generously theatrical Swiveller plot, which is why that most dedicated and refined of voyeurs, Garrett Stewart, treats it as if it were the whole novel.[4] It may be for many readers the only plot that can inspire and perpetuate desire.

One would suppose that the ideal plot for exercising passion would be the Nell plot, but it isn't. Nell is a child, which is good, is extraordinarily pure and innocent, and that's good, too, since it means she is empty and can be occupied. But Nell pushes past desire to a kind of complete fulfillment in death, a fulfillment that works against perpetuating desire. In addition, she is a kind of voyeur herself; throughout the novel she keeps looking—and looking right back at us. Conventionally, the object of voyeurism is blind, but Nell sees, and threatens even to see us. She is, that is to say, in control; she guides her grandfather and stares assertively even at Quilp. She really is a very poor *object* of desire, as, by the way, female children generally are in Dickens. The boys, Oliver and David especially, are offered up to us as blind objects to stare at lustfully; but the girls—Nell, Amy Dorrit, Florence Dombey—refuse to be so used. They peep back at the peepers and spoil the game.

Thus, we constitute a fifth metaphor ourselves in our reading, a fact that explains two important points, that answers, really, the two most important questions to be raised about the novel. (My chart, you see, tells us everything we want to know and a good deal more; and, as I say, it answers the two questions that are about the only two questions worth asking, though up to now they have completely eluded any answer.) Here are the two questions. First, why did every inhabitant of New York City go down to the docks and shout out to the ships carrying the latest numbers of *The Old Curiosity Shop*, even when those ships were still several miles out to sea, "Is Nell dead?"[5] The answer to why they did that is that they wanted to know whether or not they could keep their passion going, keep their desire alive. If Nell were dead, so was desire, in which case there was nothing to do but light up, have a smoke, and go back to sleep. The other question is simpler but even more baffling: why is the novel indescribable? The answer to that is that the metaphor from which we read it does not coincide with the metaphor controlling the novel, that, further, there is no one metaphor controlling the novel, that there need be no one metaphor controlling us. In truth, no one is in control, and for that we should all be very happy, since it releases us into the fields of deconstructive bliss for recess, for a playtime that will never end.

3

Viewing and Blurring with Dickens

"WHEN PEOPLE SAY Dickens exaggerates," fumes an exasperated George Santayana, "it seems to me that they can have no eyes and no ears"; their ears are clogged and their vision clouded by purely conventional "notions" of what things are.[1] Santayana suggests pretty clearly that he *does* have eyes and ears, quite unconventional ones, too. He further suggests that we had better come similarly equipped if we are to read Dickens. But read Dickens how? And what does it mean when we say we are reading Dickens—or watching him? Santayana's suggestion is, in fact, quite a tame one: he thinks that by escaping from conventional ways of seeing, hearing, and interpreting, we can live cheek by jowl with the *real* Dickens and the *real* world. Such formalist notions—de-familiarizing in order to return to palpable reality—now seem wistful fantasies. This real Dickens is a very elusive customer, though of course we can join in the hunt for him, even pretend that we are beckoned to do so by the novels themselves, the "novels themselves" having the same fantastic status as the "real Dickens." But that's OK, since with unconventional eyes and ears we will spot more interesting things, if never the thing itself.

Correspondingly, the most fascinating films playing off of Dickens, it seems to me, have been those that approach the novels with the most bizarre of squints. Face the novels head-on and you find them staring blankly back at you, like the sky at Marseilles in *Little Dorrit*. A filmmaker, like a Dickens reader, has to be prepared for (and welcome) a good many jolts, no matter what conventional expectations may be. Our Dickens does not merely re-form our eyes and ears, he confuses them by asking them to be turned in too many directions at once, by giving clear signals that then vanish, by offering a confounding variety of interpretive possibilities. Films, like readers, can only pretend that they have "got it," then, since there is no "it" to get.

My subject is the slippery and uncertain nature of representation we can find (if we want) in Dickens.[2] Such a thesis rests solidly on one grand cliché: that nineteenth-century novelists loved to fool around with both physical and moral perspective. There is, however, another cliché lurking behind my thesis that should make us as uncoordinated and wobbly as Mr. Pickwick on the ice: namely, that Dickens is a "cinematic novelist." What can that mean? In its naïve form, this "cinematic" idea suggests that there is a movie right there in the novel: all one has to do is to follow the camera directions given in the text, and let the movie emerge. I do not mean to attack what everyone will agree (you're agreeing) is a ludicrous notion (held by no one making films); but I would like to use the notion anyhow to examine some of the ways in which the question of representation can be made both difficult and quivering in the novels. I want to show how what at first seems clear becomes blurred, freeing any enterprising (they all are) filmmaker to construct a vision, since one can never represent or reflect a Dickens novel.

First, a digression (oh good!) to suggest that in one novel, *The Pickwick Papers,* Dickens actually may seem (but doesn't really, right?) to give some support to the naive "cinematic" concept. Certain passages not only appear to provide clear and uncomplicated details but also give directions regarding the angle from which they are to be viewed. Partly to illustrate this point and partly to indulge in the pleasure of quoting this prose, I'll give a couple of examples. The first picks up with Sam Weller's approach to Goswell Street and to Mrs. Bardell's cheery home, occupied at the time by that worthy person, her son, and two friends, Mrs. Cluppins and Mrs. Sanders:

> It was nearly nine o'clock when he reached Goswell Street. A couple of candles were burning in the little front parlour, and a couple of caps were reflected on the window-blind. Mrs. Bardell had got company.
>
> Mr. Weller knocked at the door, and after a pretty long interval—occupied by the party without, in whistling a tune, and by the party within in persuading a refractory flat candle to allow itself to be lighted—a pair of small boots pattered over the floor-cloth, and Master Bardell presented himself.
>
> "Well, young town-skip," said Sam, "how's mother?"
>
> "She's pretty well," replied Master Bardell, "so am I."

"Well, that's a mercy," said Sam; "tell her I want to speak to her, will you, my hinfant fernomenon?"

Master Bardell, thus adjured, placed the refractory flat candle on the bottom stair, and vanished into the front parlour with his message.

The two caps, reflected on the window-blind, were the respective head-dresses of a couple of Mrs. Bardell's most particular acquaintance, who had just stepped in, to have a quiet cup of tea, and a little warm supper of a couple of sets of pettitoes and some toasted cheese. The cheese was simmering and browning away, most delightfully, in a little Dutch over before the fire; the pettitoes were getting on deliciously in a little tin saucepan on the hob; and Mrs. Bardell and her two friends were getting on very well, also, in a little quiet conversation about and concerning all their particular friends and acquaintance; when Master Bardell came back from answering the door, and delivered the message entrusted to him by Mr. Samuel Weller. (26)[3]

There are certain decisions for a filmmaker left open by this passage—whether to give an invented sample of the women's "quiet conversation" about "particular friends," for instance. Still, it is hard to escape that shadow on the window blind, the movement from outside to inside the house, the cozy domestic details, the patter of Master Bardell's small boots, the refractory flat candle, the wonderful dialogue between Sam and the twerpy child. All these details and the sequence in which they appear amount to interpretations, of course, but the interpretive function is here partly disguised, the mode of seeing and recording being generally so conventional as to give the illusion of being natural.[4] The scene thus may seem pretty clear and authoritative—uncharacteristically so, as I will argue (now that's a big surprise!).

But before getting on to what is characteristic, let me (go ahead—we have no demands on our time) quote one more passage, the dream of an uncreative screenwriter willing to cater to what an audience may be presumed to take to be real. This is a meeting between Sam Weller and his father, picked up near the end of a long description of old Tony Weller and his attire:

His hair, which was short, sleek, and black, was just visible beneath the capacious brim of a low-crowned black hat. His legs were encased in knee-cord Breeches, and painted top-boots: and a copper watch-chain, terminating in one seal, and a key of the same material, dangled loosely from his capacious waistband.

We have said that Mr. Weller was engaged in preparing for his journey to London—he was taking sustenance, in fact. On the table before him, stood a pot of ale, a cold round of beef, and a very respectable-looking loaf, to each of which he distributed his favours in turn, with the most rigid impartiality. He had just cut a mighty slice from the latter, when the footsteps of somebody entering the room, caused him to raise his head; and he beheld his son.

"Mornin', Sammy!" said the father.

The son walked up to the pot of ale, and nodding significantly to his parent, took a long draught by way of reply.

"Werry good power o' suction, Sammy," said Mr. Weller the elder, looking into the pot, when his first-born had set it down half empty. "You'd ha' made an uncommon fine oyster, Sammy, if you'd been born in that station o' life." (23)

There's not a lot one would want to do with this apparently prescriptive passage, I suppose (though there is something disorienting about walking up to a pot of ale as if it were a person or a bus-stop), but my point is (yes?) that our version of "Dickens" almost never gives us this sort of aid to conventional seeing, hearing, smelling. Much more frequent are disruptions, instructions that are difficult or impossible to decipher, blurrings. Often, when we expect description, we receive instead interpretation, hammering us with the point that all representation is interpretation. Here is Pip's description of a box-tree that grows (if that's the word for it) in Miss Havisham's garden: "One box-tree that had been clipped round long ago, like a pudding, and had a new growth at the top of it, out of shape and of a different colour, as if that part of the pudding had stuck to the saucepan and got burnt" (11).

This habit of playing exuberantly with objects and figures is so common in Dickens that Orwell identified it as *the* Dickensian style, "the florid little squiggle on the edge of the page."[5] The effect of such squiggles is to push representation into the realm of untamed and fanciful interpretation, and to defy any sort of neutral visualizing. Here are a couple of more examples (sweet!). From *Little Dorrit*, a part of a long description of the guests at Pet Meagles's marriage: "There were three other Young Barnacles, from three other offices, insipid to all the senses, and terribly in want of seasoning, doing the marriage as they would have 'done' the Nile, Old Rome, the new singer, or Jerusalem" (34). How does one *see* undercooked and underseasoned Young Barnacles? Similarly, in *Martin Chuzzlewit*, the narrator spends many pages talking about Todgers's, but the result of all this talk is not to pin the place down, locate it for us in some perceptual field. Rather, the emphasis is on its "mystery," the fact that its character and even location were "matters of profound uncertainty" (9).

It is not just Todgers's which is shrouded in "profound uncertainty"; Dickens's habit (a petted one he never broke or tried to) of describing one thing in terms of another befogs any essence, any definite thing-ness. His figurative language amounts to a radical relativism in terms of perspective, an indication that the best we can do in the way of seeing amounts to a poor approximation.

Here is Pip, trying to describe the figure of Magwitch retreating across the marshes:

> At the same time, he hugged his shuddering body in both his arms—clasping himself, as if to hold himself together—and limped towards the low church wall. As I saw him go, picking his way among the nettles, and among the brambles that bound the green mounds, he looked in my young eyes as if he were eluding the hands of the dead people, stretching up cautiously out of their graves, to get a twist upon his ankle and pull him in. (1)

The pointed reference to "my young eyes" draws us to note the singularity of the spectacularly grisly image, to realize that the image is a trope and an extravagant one, that the young boy is casting about frantically to find a simile that will suggest something of his fear and his compassion. One recalls that this scene represents Pip's "first most vivid and broad impression of the identity of things," including the impression "that the small bundle of shivers growing afraid of it all and beginning to cry, was Pip." That is, Pip learns both his separateness from "things," and the frightening fact that his only means for bridging that gap is language, an impossibly inadequate substance. In his attempt to capture and comprehend the convict and his own "small bundle of shivers," Pip goes chasing after words. And he takes us on the same chase—after the wildest of geese. As Magwitch approaches the gibbet that once held a pirate, Pip tries yet another brilliant figure: "as if he were the pirate come to life, and come down, and going back to hook himself up again." There is desperation in these extravagant linguistic devices, a sense that there is no direct equivalence between words and things. Pip can only read himself and his experience through words, yet words can never provide him with the transparent texts he wants.

A more explicit indication of the impossibility of reading (and showing) is provided by Poll Sweedlepipe's struggle with his illiteracy when confronted with Young Bailey:

> Mr. Bailey spoke as if he already had a leg and three-quarters in the grave, and this had happened twenty or thirty years ago. Poll Sweedlepipe, the meek, was so perfectly confounded by his precocious self-possession, and his patronising manner, as well as by his boots, cockade, and livery, that a mist swam before his eyes, and he saw—not the Bailey of acknowledged juvenility, from Todgers's Commercial Boarding House ... but a highly-condensed embodiment of all the sporting grooms in London; and abstract of all the stable-knowledge of the time; a something at a high-pressure that must have had existence many years, and was fraught with terrible experiences. And truly, though in the cloudy atmosphere of Todgers's, Mr. Bailey's genius had ever shown out brightly in this particular respect, it now eclipsed both time and space, cheated beholders of their senses, and worked on

their belief in defiance of all natural laws.... He became an inexplicable creature: a breeched and booted Sphinx. There was no course open to the barber but to go distracted himself, or to take Bailey for granted: and he wisely chose the latter. (26)

Notice that this passage, which begins with what appears to be a good-natured exposé of Poll's credulity, quietly moves to include one and all, every "beholder," including us. We are all "cheated" of our senses, made to abandon "all natural laws," forced to acknowledge that Bailey is "inexplicable." Like Poll, we cannot inquire too closely into the mystery of this Sphinx. We must "take Bailey for granted," rely casually on the conventional assumption which tells us that words are truly descriptive and that our senses speak to us accurately. But the same passage that encourages such a sane attitude also exposes its purely conventional status, its absurdity. Language can provide neither authoritative images nor inroads to essences—but we must pretend that it does. Dickens's play with the limitations of language is relentless. He sometimes even allows words such priority that they simply take over the reality presumably being represented, most obviously when a metaphor becomes a character: Mrs. Merdle as "Bosom," Pancks as "Steamboat."

Even those devices ordinarily used in realistic fiction to provide the illusion of solidity refuse, in Dickens, to stand still and do their job.[6] The most obvious of these devices, the proliferation of concrete objects, is subverted. The objects are never just *there*; they swing into the viewer's eyes, crowd about, take on a threatening life of their own. Here, for instance, is Pip waiting in Mr. Jaggers' office: "There were some odd objects about, that I should not have expected to see— such as an old rusty pistol, a sword in a scabbard, several strange-looking boxes and packages, and two dreadful casts on a shelf, of faces peculiarly swollen, and twitchy about the nose" (20). Ogled by these twitchy noses and swelling faces, Pip goes on with his catalogue, as if he hopes to overcome his dizziness by enumerating the inanimate objects about him. But the objects refuse to remain inanimate, and Pip can no longer stabilize and control them: "I wondered whether the two swollen faces were of Mr. Jaggers's family, and, if he were so unfortunate as to have a pair of such ill-looking relations, why he stuck them on that dusty perch, for the blacks and flies to settle on, instead of giving them a place at home.... I sat wondering and waiting in Mr. Jaggers's close room, until I really could not bear the two casts on the shelf above Mr. Jaggers's chair, and got up and went out."

Sticking with *Great Expectations,* we can observe how apparently explicit descriptions are not allowed to run on very long without an interruption which has the effect of blurring the image. Pip's attempt to disguise the returned Magwitch is given in great detail, but the detail merges quickly into non-imagistic interpretive figures: "I can compare the effect of it [powder applied to Magwitch], when on, to nothing but the probable effect of rouge upon the dead; so awful was the manner in which everything in him, that it was most desirable to repress, started through that thin layer of pretense, and seemed to come blazing out at the crown of his head" (40). Note that this passage sticks to details—rouge, a corpse, the crown of his head—but insists on the necessity of a comparison and, further, makes the terms of that comparison impossible to visualize. What is it that is blazing out at the crown of his head? What is this "everything"? And why are we given a "probable effect" rather than a certain one?

This same sort of uncertainty is often produced by a habit which we (*we?*) might term "surrealistic dissociation," where people and actions are oddly carved up, parts swallowing up wholes. Here, from *The Pickwick Papers:*

> Mr. Justice Stareleigh . . . was a most particularly short man, and so fat, that he seemed all face and waistcoat. He rolled in, upon two little turned legs, and having bobbed gravely to the bar, who bobbed gravely to him, put his little legs underneath his table and his little three-cornered hat upon it; and when Mr. Justice Stareleigh had done this, all you could see of him was two queer little eyes, one broad pink face, and somewhere about half of a big and very comical-looking wig. (34)

Notice that the dissociative play becomes so feral here that Mr. Justice Stareleigh does indeed seem to be "all face and waistcoat," equipped with nothing more than two eyes, a hat, and a wig. His legs, which seem at one point to have rollers attached, at another point to be wooden and detachable, at another to be the real article, if a trifle short, are, in any event, syntactically equivalent to his "little three-cornered hat" and could probably also be placed on a rack or in a closet, were there any. It's a bit like Mr. Potato-Head: you get a certain number of blank faces, eyes, wigs, and so forth to arrange at your convenience and as it suits your fancy; but none of the parts really connects organically with the others.

Even conventional set pieces, apparently filmable as they stand, are often subtly disrupted by a similar kind of surrealistic splintering, an inexplicable shift of visual fields that disallows any attempt we might make to naturalize the description, bring it into coherent focus. Another way to put this is to say that the mode and tone shift with dizzying rapidity from, say, melancholic-sentimental to comic-grotesque. A good example (we'll decide that) occurs at the end of the second chapter of *David Copperfield.* David, along with Peggotty, is in Mr. Barkis' cart, slowly retreating from a happy home that we sense will soon be happy no longer:

> I am glad to recollect that when the carrier began to move, my mother ran out
> at the gate, and called to him to stop, that she might kiss me once more. I am
> glad to dwell upon the earnestness and love with which she lifted up her face
> to mine, and did so.
>
> As we left her standing in the road, Mr. Murdstone came up to where she was,
> and seemed to expostulate with her for being so moved. I was looking back
> round the awning of the cart, and wondered what business it was of his.
> Peggotty, who was also looking back on the other side, seemed anything but
> satisfied, as the face she brought back into the cart denoted.

The cinematic directions seem quite clear, even as regards the placement of
the camera: shoot from David's point of view, receding from the house; close
focus on Mrs. Copperfield; back up to scene of her kissing David; close-up of
Mrs. Copperfield's face; begin receding, again from David's point of view; frame
with the cart's awning the image of Murdstone angrily remonstrating; slowly
distance the scene; close-up of Peggotty's dissatisfied face swinging back around;
move to forward motion of the cart. All this seems reasonable enough; in fact, it
is far too reasonable, too visually coherent. It overlooks the marvelously
grotesque effect of the modal shift in this predominantly sad scene: "the face she
brought back into the cart." It is as if Peggotty had dropped her face out of the
cart and barely managed to catch it and haul it in before it rolled away in the
dust. The verbal shift undermines the apparent primacy of the visual here and
abruptly returns us to the instability of language. Dickens's astonishing ability to
upset all apple-carts reminds us that vision and perspective are never naturally
determined, that they are matters of habit and convention only.

The whole procedure I have used thus far has also been a matter of habit and
convention: displaying all-too-ripe passages from here and there, reading them
with confidence (faked), and suggesting that they are representative. I acknowledge that there is heavy (but pretty self-assured, got to give you that) critical
hucksterism involved here, something equivalent to peddling little boxes of straw-
berries with the only edible ones glorying the top and all the disfigured and green
ones stuffed beneath. Selectivity is necessary, of course: would we want to hear
even an effulgent commentator (Stanley Fish) go slow-motion through a Dickens
novel word-by-word? Still, a brief look at a couple of longer passages might partly
justify my smaller picking and choosing: first, the way the disrupting techniques I
have mentioned are combined in the first chapter of *Little Dorrit;* second, the way
David Copperfield and other later novels make the problem of perspective impossible to solve (or duplicate) and how they, even more challengingly, question the
notion of the individual, the self, the author. (That all this disrupting is really not
a matter of Dickens's "technique," not located in the passage but in the rendering

of it we manage when we read, that we are talking about constructions not about texts and evidence: all that I take for granted. And so do you.)

The first chapter of *Little Dorrit* employs these various blurring techniques in such a way as to throw the issue of representation itself into doubt.[7] The chapter opens calmly enough, with a conventional, easy-to-take paragraph: "Thirty years ago, Marseilles lay burning in the sun, one day." Few openings could be less demanding, less of a strain on our ordinary habits of reading and perceiving, though possibly we wonder about the mildly heightened term "burning." Such assurances as we are able to receive from the first sentence are, however, quickly dissolved in a strange and terrifying play with this image of a blazing sun: "Everything in Marseilles, and about Marseilles, had stared at the fervid sky, and been stared at in return, until a staring habit had become universal there." The notion of staring as a "universal" blindness is suggestive of a universal illiteracy. Where does meaning reside, if not in the light? Perhaps as unsettling is the mixing of humans and objects, granting equal blinding power to each. Worse, the passage goes on to explode this equality, allowing superior power to the objects and making the humans the losers in this staring contest: "Strangers were stared out of countenance by staring white houses, staring white walls, staring white streets." Humans take refuge in any darkness they can find from a whiteness that reflects a universal meaninglessness. They finally stop looking altogether: the sea is "too intensely blue to be looked at." Marseilles becomes invisible, merely "a fact to be strongly smelt and tasted." When we switch to inside the prison, a pit of darkness which "had no knowledge of the brightness outside," we are in no better shape. Rigaud's eyes are emblematic: "They had no depth or change; they glittered, and they opened and shut. So far, and waiving their use to himself, a clockmaker could have made a better pair." Even his hair has "no definable colour." One cannot see, then, inside or out—into or out of. The only person with knowledge is Cavalletto, but he has no better eyesight than anybody else: "How can I say? I always know what the hour is, and where I am. I was brought in here at night, and out of a boat, but I know where I am." How absolutely uncinematic (or at least unmimetic) is knowledge here: Cavalletto's knowing, his light, comes despite or maybe because of the darkness, but he has no idea why, cannot explain or see it. Neither can we.

Many of the novels, particularly the later ones, pointedly raise a confusion as to perspective: to what extent can a film accept the privileged view of the narrator, and how can one escape it? There are also problems as to structure or pattern: how is the story or film to be formed, and who is to tell it? Finally, one wonders how legitimately or interestingly one can employ actresses or actors in filming Dickens, whether the sharp outlines of a person (or a personality) might not avoid one of the most tickling possibilities we can play with: that humans are not to be understood in reference to self-contained, separable integers but through other metaphors: amalgamation or absorption, perhaps. Films using actors seem implicitly biased toward individualist assumptions,[8] assumptions which are attacked by Dickens's novels but by no Dickens films that I know of.

To start with the simplest matter, perspective, is to start with something not very simple. How close does a camera want to get to David Copperfield's eyes and his troubled heart? David admits that he invents histories for some people, histories that "hang like a mist of fancy over well-remembered facts." And he adds the startling admission that self-pity and romantic imagination are the motors driving this story: "I seem to see and pity, going on before me, an inno- cent romantic boy, making his imaginative world out of such strange and sordid things" (11). Where do the "experiences" and "things" end and the romantic and imaginative inventions take over? Further, what are we to do with a self- pitying mode? How can a camera turn in on itself and weep for all the pain and injustice it has suffered?

Perhaps there is no real problem, as most of the films of the novel have illus- trated: cast a sweet, moderately androgynous boy in the role of the child and surround him with the monsters he projects, monsters of unqualified bestiality. Basil Rathbone, in this case, makes a good Murdstone. But he is David's self- pitying version of Murdstone only, one that even David hints may be incom- plete, colored and distorted by the child's jealousy and by his rage at being robbed of his mother's undivided attention. David later wants to portray Murdstone as an indiscriminate (hence impersonal and desexualized) fiend, preying on one widow after another. But David the child knows better or, rather, lets us see more: "He seemed to be very fond of my mother—I am afraid I liked him none the better for that—and she was very fond of him" (4). We hardly need Freud by our side to see the sexual jealousy at work, but what film has observed the child's distorted vision and portrayed the love between the two adults? What film has been willing to emphasize Murdstone's terrible and ob- viously sincere grief at his wife's death, a grief observed coldly and selfishly by the child: "Mr. Murdstone took no heed of me when I went into the parlour, where he was, but sat by the fireside, weeping silently" (9). There is, in other words, a great deal that David notes but doesn't register, doesn't allow to penetrate into an area that would call for interpretation. The question is: how compelling could a film be that followed his practice?

As David matures (a loaded term in this context), he develops a habit of removing people he knows from social, class, and economic contexts in order to explain them and deal with them in isolated, psychological terms. He is a relentless individualizer. All this is understandable, of course, since he would like to present himself as the hero the first sentence of his novel coyly announces, a figure uninfluenced by his surroundings, a self-sufficient, industrious fellow, made by himself. Thus, he may seem obtuse, blind to the class-induced snobbery of Steerforth, refusing to acknowledge it even when Steerforth tells him of it, abducts Em'ly, and is drowned. In fact, the drowning represents a great psychological bonanza for David, since it allows him to maintain the assurance that one—he, at any rate—is captain of one's own fate. Similarly, when Uriah Heep presents to David a scorching indictment of the hierarchical social and educational system that instills hypocritical "umbleness in the dispossessed, David ignores altogether the wider implications and remarks only that Uriah's comments provide him with a fuller insight into the wet-palmed-one's personality, his "detestable cant," his "base, unrelenting, and revengeful spirit" (39).

David's curious personalizing and individualizing habit raises questions about how he sees his own life, what form or structure he is attempting to impose on it—and to what extent a filmmaker might be guided by it. (That's a transition, am I right? We got a new subject coming up—that's my bet.) The problem is made severe by David's confused and contradictory efforts to provide a clear framework himself. What kind of causal connections can be drawn between events and his own developing self? Well, the problem turns out to be that David both needs and abhors the whole idea of causality. He both is and is not the product of what he has encountered. When he arrives at Dover, for instance, and is secured against further incursions from the Murdstones,[9] he announces in the chapter title, "I make another beginning" (15). It is a beginning that he hopes will wipe out the first one. His first beginning, after all, had been tainted badly by the intruder Murdstone, by Creakle, by his degradation in the warehouse—perhaps also by his guilty and, for the time, undisturbed love for his mother. So, he resolutely attempts simply to cancel that earlier passage in his life. "Thus I began," he says, "my new life, in a new name, and with everything new about me." "Like one in a dream," he drops with finality the curtain on his old life: "I only know that it was, and ceased to be; and that I have written, and there I leave it" (14). The cadences ring with the blunt certainty of a funeral bell, appropriately, since David is overseeing the murder of his earlier self. He is, like his name, bran-new—or so he insists. Later he puts the point even more insistently, perhaps overinsistently: "That little fellow [his former self] seems to be no part of me; I remember him as something left behind upon the road of life—as something I have passed rather than have actually been—and almost think of him as of some one else" (18).

This attempt to dislocate his life is still an attempt to see that life as a linear path, albeit a path he can manipulate, creating dead ends or denying that it was he who was on it before. In other words, David is undertaking a novelistic task that is self-contradictory: he both does and does not want a plot. He would, on the one hand, like to formulate his narrative as a causal and clear course of self-development: a series of events and reactions to those events that will explain his maturation, his ability to discipline his heart. In part, David is striving to write an unswerving Horatio Alger story, describing the ability of a strong character to mold the shape of his own destiny.

On the other hand, this developmental model is countered by one that the Victorians would have spoken of as "catastrophic."[10] Each of David's many new beginnings depends on an abrupt cancellation of what came before, not a smooth progression from it. Notice how many times he speaks of himself as starting anew: most passionately when he gets to Dover, but also when his mother marries, when he is sent to school, when he lands in London, when he becomes a "new boy" at Dr. Strong's, when he marries Dora, when she dies, when he ascends to Agnes. The continuous narrative is thus shadowed by a radically disconnected one, the disconnections being caused by David's need both to explore and to forget parts of his life. This great novel of memory also doubles back on the very roots of memory, attempting to erase its unwelcome disclosures. Maybe this is not, for most readers, a self-consuming novel, but David (or a part of him) would very much like it to be so. "The remembrance of that life is fraught with so much pain for me, with so much mental suffering and want of hope" (14): all that suffering wars against the coherent tale the adult author is trying to fashion.

Joining in this war against a coherent single plot is a backcurrent that perversely refuses to run uphill in the direction David wants, but keeps tugging him back to home, to his infancy, refusing to advance very far for very long. All this is rather familiar material, and I will not repeat the evidence that would link Dora or Agnes to David's mother and his nurse. (Don't you know what that evidence is?) But what haunts the novel is the perception that David is trapped trying to tell a progressive narrative with materials that refuse, finally, to budge from the vision of an idealized childhood. Maybe the story goes nowhere. I think most readers have a sense that David's story is over after a few chapters, that he can engage only in a delusory advance while he continually retraces the same cycle, the same sad repetitions, progressing nowhere, writing no plot.

Adding more murk is the argument advanced by some—and this is now our fourth pattern—that David has a straight-line story to tell, but that the line leads downward, not up. According to this reading, David travels on a path that leads away from beauty, youth, playfulness (figured in his mother, then Micawber, then Dora) to a dreary, account-book, pinched-in life. His report of what it is to be a novelist, one might say, sounds very much like some MBA discussing his workdays at I.B.M.: he identifies "the source of my success" as "a patient and continuous energy," "habits of punctuality, order, and diligence," the acquisition of "steady, plain, hard-working qualities," "thorough-going, ardent, and sincere earnestness" (42). This is a portrait of the artist as a nerd or organization man. No need for imagination or even skill; just get to the office early and work straight through coffee breaks! The question is how we are to understand this development in David, this subtle, pathetic acceptance of the Murdstonian ethic of firmness, energy, and self-control.

One way of considering this narrative is this: as an infant, David finds himself in a gloriously fulfilling but dangerous situation; he is completely absorbed by his coquettish, lovely mother. He is her lover, a position not untainted with guilt, as his dream of a risen and vengeful father makes clear. Murdstone enters, violently carries out the revenge of the father, and offers to David his only way of dealing with the Oedipal dilemma: deny his love for his mother and emulate the rigidity and firmness of Murdstone.[11] David's imitation of Murdstone is undertaken reluctantly, to be sure: he attempts to deny his presence by seeking substitutes for his mother and nurse, attempting, that is, to return stealthily to the pre-Murdstone days. Still, by the end of the novel, this argument claims, David has made the sad, ironic "adjustment," killing off his mother (Dora) and adopting the Murdstone position. Whatever one thinks of such formulations— and this is only one of many that might describe the same pattern (but one you think a lot of, am I right?)—the novel clearly may be seen as insisting on an advance that is really a decline, a successful working-out of problems that is really a capitulation to them.

But to get back to our hypothetical film-maker: What does one do with these four patterns—linear and progressive, discontinuous and catastrophic, cyclic and static, linear and regressive? Certainly, we could choose among them (we get just one choice?); or, we could, no doubt, represent somehow the possibility of all four.

Making a film that embodies four diverse and usually contradictory narrative structures would be a tough assignment, leaving all but the most ingenious film-maker floored. But hulking just ahead is an even more difficult obstacle for our film-maker. The four patterns mentioned all leave undisturbed the idea of the individual, the self. However disturbed or variously figured, the self is at the center. We still tend to take for granted the notion of the individualized self and we are likely to imagine that same self in novels we read. Ah, but just take a closer look at Dickens or, even better, at my own chapter (in this very Part, chapter 5) on "Performance, Roles, the Self, and Our Own Charles Dickens"—and you'll be convinced that commonplace ideas about the self and its constituents don't work here.

How, then, do you represent "characters" who do not conform to post-Enlightenment conceptions of individualism? Put a figure on the screen, no matter how distorted or wobbled, and you risk eliciting all the conventional assumptions about what constitutes a "character." My contention is that Dickens presses on us possibilities that should make all of us, not just screen-writers and directors, scratch our heads and fidget.

Of course, I do not mean to suggest that Dickens is unfilmable. Obviously, films, and brilliant ones, can be and have been made. But what is it that is being filmed? Dickens puts up deeply sophisticated resistances to interpretation, offering us a blank stare just when we most need clarification, and playing with the very process of interpreting. But a film is, of necessity, an interpretation of an interpretation, not a mimetic reflection. A film is much like critical commentary: it is a construction that can jolt or that can bore but that can never reconstruct what isn't there for reconstruction. There is a story that W.C. Fields, on being asked why he added juggling to Mr. Micawber's repertoire when there was nothing about juggling in the text, said, "Dickens forgot it." That's the right idea. Dickens, with his various obfuscating squiggles writhing all over hell and gone, would have loved juggling. Let's say—who's to stop us?—he was the most consummate juggler of them all.

4

All the Wickedness in the World Is Print
Dickens and Subversive Interpretation

THE SUBJECT OF this chapter—the unstable and shifting nature of a Dickens novel and of our response to it—developed as the result of a considerable instability of my own. Having agreed some time before to participate in a certain panel discussion, I suddenly became ludicrously confused as to whether the subject to be addressed was "Dickens in **This** Time" or "Dickens in **His** Time." I thought it was the former; it turned out to be the latter, a historical topic presenting itself to my competence about equally with particle physics and alchemy. Panic can spur a sort of ingenuity, and puzzling over whether there was, after all, much of a difference between "this" and "his" pushed me naturally enough (you'll agree) to consider the relationship between a recovered context for interpretation (biographical, historical, sociological, political) and interpretations which deliberately ignore those contexts, which, in fact, flaunt them, running counter to stated authorial intentions, what we take to be Victorian beliefs and predilections, or even (most of all) common sense. What about subversive readings, those antagonistic to, or ignorant of, what history seems to be telling us?

During the long heyday of formalism and structuralism, critics engaged in historical or contextual work often had a bad time of it. Pushed to the wall by the New Critics, they had to scurry to justify their enterprise. Formalists gave an absolute authority to *the text*, solid and objectified; the text rendered superfluous or inauthentic any references outside its boundaries. For formalists, historical criticism manifested a rather pathetic naïvete.

Pride goeth before a fall. Formalism rested, it now appears, on nothing more than a conspiracy of ignorance and silence, answering to shared needs and some ego gratification, but hardly to the sort of rigorous tests to which we now subject our theories and methods, yessirree. The loud and smug assertions about "the text" and its self-sufficiency sprang from notions about language and reading that now seem fatuous. How could we ever have imagined that language could be so securely stabilized, or that we could hold a Dickens novel still by talking about unifying symbols (the railroad, prison, river) and thematic oppositions (firmness versus wetness, childishness versus the undisciplined heart, and so forth)? The interpretations derived from this method now seem elegant but awfully slim, smug in the assurance of their own "rightness." Those essays of the 1950s and '60s now strike us as stunningly unaware of the assumptions that were generating them. How things have changed.

Historical criticism has been restored to respectability. It had slithered back onto our playing field and taken on new shapes, even before the reactionary and short-lived (mark my words!) new historicism tried to turn back the clock. Many forms of deconstructive and reader-response criticism gave to historical contexts for interpretation the same stamp of approval they gave to all others, making historicism no more inauthentic than any other. And that's something. Historicism was, in the order of Error, right up there with formalism, structuralism, Freudianism, and other truth-systems. But as Susan R. Horton showed in *Interpreting Interpreting*, interpretations based on a variety of contexts, from the biographical and historical through the semiotic, share a nearly identical inadequacy.[1]

One would suppose, for instance, that all we would have to do to arrive at a valid interpretation would be to lay out carefully all the contexts and then combine them. But not so. For one thing, it is impossible, since each context is itself an interpretation and subject to all the pitfalls of that slippery enterprise. Furthermore, even in the unlikely event that we could all agree on what a detail in the text means, different contexts will cause that detail to assume new shapes and will cause other details to take on "meaning." Thus, any attempt to put all contexts together will result in a cacophony, not a harmony. There is simply no way to force a text to stand still or to take account of everything, since we have no idea what "everything" is. And, as Horton points out, Dickens presents further difficulties, since we can never be certain exactly what mode he is working in at any given point and, consequently, what framework of expectations might be appropriate. This makes the presumed facts of the text elusive and unstable, splintering the connections we might make between these "facts" in order to form readings.

Let's take one example: the connection between a historical fact and a passage from a novel. The passage is from *Barnaby Rudge*. Old John Willet is talking to his son Joe about how to spend his money and time in London, and he says, "The other sixpence is to spend in the diversions of London; and the diversion I recommend is to go to the top of the Monument, and sitting there. There's no temptation there, sir—no drink—no young women—no bad characters of any sort—nothing but imagination. That's the way I enjoyed myself when I was your age, sir."[2] Now consider this in relation to the historical fact: just around the time *Barnaby Rudge* was appearing in *Master Humphrey's Clock*, there was a rash of suicidal leaps from the Monument—successful ones, too—causing a public stir and leading to the erection of a fencelike barricade to discourage melancholy-mad leapers.[3] What connections can we draw with certainty between the text and the historical fact? Is John Willet suggesting that his son plunge to a mangled death, or expressing an unconscious wish that this might occur? Possibly. Is Dickens hinting at the ominous consequences of oppression and neglect, foreshadowing the fierce outbreak that comes later in the novel? Possibly. Is this merely a comic embellishment, playing on John Willet's crazy sense of the language and his woozy idea about the pleasures of the imagination: that Dickensian squiggle on the edge of the page noted by Orwell and later by Robert Garis?[4] Possibly. One could go on and on. The problem facing us in making such connections is that neither fact nor text remains steady before our gaze. What complex of associations would a Victorian reader bring to bear on the word "Monument"—if any at all? How prominent would the suicides be in the mind of the Victorian reader, and how relevant would they be to the scene in the novel? Would readers halt at all on the word, make it "mean"? History is a very uncertain text. And we all know how uncertain novels are.

Modern (alert) readers might well locate in this passage a clear reflection of the tyranny-leading-to-rebellion motif—or they might not. After all, isn't murder suicide a rather strong set of terms to associate with the Willet family and the comic Maypole plot? It requires taking the comedy pretty seriously. Of course, it is true that later in the novel things do turn solemn: Willet is manhandled and becomes a pathetic idiot as a result, and his son has his arm blown off in America. But how does all that fit together? Old Willet becomes a victim, not a victimizer; and he has never had any connection to the riots other than denying that they are going on. Using a different framework, we might consider the word "imagination," what old Willet says one finds at the top of the Monument. What is the connection between imagination and death? Is climbing the Monument to sit vacantly or to fall off a complex anti-Romantic gesture which parodies Romantic epiphanies like the ascent of Mount Snowdon? The interpretations, clearly, are endless. This is not to deny the interest to be found (by some) in historical contexts for criticism; it's just to argue that such methodologies are bound to yield results as incomplete and dubious as any other.

In reference to the more specific issue of subversive or ironic readings of these novels—readings that might be accused of being historically blind and violating of Dickens's intentions, the attitudes of his audience, or the general intellectual atmosphere of the times—*Martin Chuzzlewit* offers a rich storehouse of opportunities. Let's start with Dickens's insistence that the novel is about selfishness. If we take him at his word, and say, for the hell of it, that his contemporaries seem to have done so too, we have no difficulty validating such a didactic reading. One might say that there is presumptive evidence against the full satisfaction such a reading could provide: who would read a novel organized around a theme so trite and tedious? Who wants to learn that many are overstocked with self-regard and cause harm because of it? (Not me, and I love *Martin Chuzzlewit*. Does that settle the issue? No.) Such carping begs the question and is dangerously close to claiming that some things are *in* the text and others are not. All interpretive models can find ways of fulfilling themselves. That much is certain. The question is not which one is more accurate but which ones are most unsettling, most likely to jar us loose from some of our comfortable reading assumptions, maybe even displaying those assumptions butt-naked and making them ashamed of themselves.

As an example of a subversive reading, I will repeat a little of what I have already written on the novel,[5] a process that seems to me safe enough, since, so far as I know, not a single reader (has there been one?) has been influenced, much less persuaded, by my argument. Briefly, it is this: take the selfish/selfless binary and complicate it with some others we can find (make up), especially in the American scenes: nature/artifice, restraint/excess, manners/crudity, style/barbarism. This is fun because the oppositions do not cohere for very long, and the enemies in the American scenes suggest a scheme of values that make the English enemies into positive saints. You see what I mean?

To start slow: both Colonel Scadder and Mr. Pecksniff seem selfish, and this may look like a tie between the two sides of the Atlantic, but what of American eating, manner of dress, vulgarity of speech, disregard for privacy? Let's say that America is Nature made into a nightmare, actually human nature in its fullest expression. "Some institutions develop human nature; others re—tard it" (16),[6] says one patriotic citizen. Perhaps he is right. The narrator warns those shallow philosophers who blandly appeal to "human nature," that they may be rousing a beast (13). And what is the American "Eden" but the deadly swamp of the primeval natural? Dickens seems to offer an alternative in British restraint,

British artfulness, British artificiality—even selfish British hypocrisy. Are we not expected to applaud the wholly anti-American Young Bailey and his constant "defiance of all natural laws" (26)? Isn't the wonderful defeat of nature managed by Bailey connected to the linguistic triumphs of Sairey Gamp and Mr. Pecksniff, the victory of artificiality and the unnatural? Isn't it, as Mr. Pecksniff says of his architectural practices, really the "finishing touches" (6), not the raw designs, that matter? Isn't it, finally, Mrs. Gamp who has the last word: "Ah, what a wale of grief," she says, "possessing herself of the bottle and glass" (19)? She, with her daffy allusions to Bunyan and the more depressing parts of the Bible, provides a splendid parody of moralistic solemnity and didacticism. The force of this anarchic parody completely subverts the moralistic center provided by the theme of selfishness and suggests not righteous reconciliation but the raucous carnival of artifice. Sairey and Seth are heroine and hero.

Agree? Of course not; at least, to return to our presumptive evidence, one would suspect not, since no one seems to have responded to the novel in this way but me. Still, this reading, I am willing to proclaim, has the same validity as one more historically and biographically responsive. But that validity is much of the same, dubious kind. Turning the tables, changing Pecksniff from a villain into a kind of hero is great fun (as you'll agree), but it still works with the same furniture and simply redecorates the traditional reading. Many of the same assumptions are used, the most basic being that the work is controlled by thematic oppositions. Of course, one may complicate or reverse the connections between these oppositions, but one is still forced to hold certain points in the text steady, to make some things mean and others not, to maintain the fiction that an opposition at one point is the same as an opposition at another. One finds oneself blinking at glaring contradictions in order to smooth out what is ruffled, mend what is broken. For example, I have just said that Bailey's triumph over nature is complete, as evidenced by his convincing Poll that his totally smooth face was, in fact, bewhiskered. That seems to be the effect of the fine comic scene in chapter 26. But in chapter 49, when Poll laments what he thinks is Bailey's death, he says that the shavings were a fully conscious game, "only for fun," and that Bailey will never lived to be shaved "in earnest." The latter statement need not take precedence over the former, but neither can one ignore it. At one point we are told that Poll is taken in; at another that he is not. Such contradictions present a considerable difficulty for thematic criticism, a difficulty which is too often overcome by simply ignoring the contradiction.[7]

If my counterreading is really no more than a reshuffling of the same thematic counters, perhaps a climb to the top of Horton's interpretive ladder and a view from the semiotic context will yield more unnerving results. Like the view from

Todgers's, however, this one is dizzying. Objects are not so much *there* as "seem" or "appear to be"; and their tendency to "thicken" and "expand" is likely to affect us as it does M. Todgers's lodger, making us "quite scared" (9) and anxious to rush back inside and descend the steps. Even the first few paragraphs of the narrative proper present us with baffling excess. Take the following: the sun struggles to "look" through clouds, finally succeeds and illuminates the landscape of a rural Wiltshire village with a "glory" likened to "a sudden flash of memory or spirit" in the mind of an old man (2). The glory is momentary, however, and it is succeeded by the absence of light, the silencing of the birds, and the transformation of the shining church into a place that is "cold and dark." Are these details emblematic or symbolic, or just there? If they are symbolic, of what: the sun as source of meaning, God, the possibility of understanding—hinted at and then withdrawn? The more basic question is whether these details *mean* at all.

Even within the first three paragraphs, from which these words are arbitrarily (I'll say!) selected, there is a wealth of other details that might or might not be connected, might or might not be given significance or prominence. The scene between Pecksniff and his daughters that follows the descriptive opening might be seen as a parody of our single-minded interpretive efforts. In Pecksniff's great and comprehensive moral scheme, there is nothing without significance: "And eggs . . . even they have their moral." This dizzying possibility is repeated later by Carroll's Duchess: "Everything's got a moral, if only you can find it."[8] As always, the Duchess is madly sane: everything in the novel can be invested with meaning or meanings, and it is not so hard to find them. But everything having plenteous meanings with infinite connections among them is much the same as having no meaning at all.

Beating a fast retreat from such chaos, we may have a go at a narrower, admittedly provisional portion of the semiotic view, confining ourselves to direct signals emanating from the novel. These signals have to do with the possibility of valid or even partial interpretation, the nature of that process, and how all that will accord with our understanding of the novel as a whole—if, that is, we can ever really have an understanding of the novel as a whole, if there even is such a thing as a novel as a whole. (There isn't. Take my word for it.)

Such an approach seems to be precisely the one Dickens takes pains at the start to waylay. His "Preface" opens with a heavily sarcastic commentary on those who accuse him of "exaggeration." Noting that "what is exaggeration to one class of minds and perceptions is plain truth to another," he goes on to suggest that those who speak of exaggeration are those "whose eye for colour is a little dull." Worse, he says that those who are exactly represented from life in his fiction are the very ones who protest against the unnaturalness of the image. The suggestion here is the unencouraging one that the "class of minds and perceptions" able to see the truth he is representing is small indeed—perhaps limited only to the author himself. Further, his anger is directed at his readers' ineducability, and he is clearly frustrated at being unable to train them. His "implied reader," in other words, is only implied, never realized. The first chapter sustains a sneering assault on "just interpretation," on the "ingenious labour on the part of a commentator." He seems to be declaring in advance that his novel is impervious to interpretation, implying that only the idiotic would try.

And yet (with Dickens there is always an "and yet") the narrator sometimes gives us clear, insistent signals on how to read this novel—signals that even the dullards he so detests could hardly miss. For instance, we are told straight out, after much ironic indirection, that Mr. Pecksniff's true "genius lay in ensnaring parents and guardians and pocketing premiums" (2). Similarly, the defect of young Martin's character is bluntly declared to be "selfishness" (21), and the origins of that blemish are just as bluntly laid forth (33). Sometimes, indeed, the insistence on the one right reading is pitched at shrillness: "And if ever plain truth were spoken on this occasionally false earth, Tom's sister spoke it when she said that" (9).

But things are by no means always so clear, partly because the ironic mode often used takes such risks with the alertness of readers and allows for so much openness.[9] The narrator is at one point so impatient with that openness that he adds an indignant footnote: "The most credulous reader"—that fool, and he is apparently legion—"will scarcely believe that Mr. Pecksniff's reasoning was once set upon as the Author's!!" (20). But, short of destroying the ironic effect by peppering the text with footnotes of this sort, the narrator must take his chances and give up control. Not only that, but the ironic forms used often take a devious route, one that says, "Don't believe that; believe this (ha!)." What we are told not to believe is false, but so is what we are led to believe, hinting that the truth lies in neither of the two formulations presented but in some mixture of their unstated opposites. Here is an example: "It must not be inferred from this position of humility, that the youngest Miss Pecksniff was so young as to be, as one may say, forced to sit upon a stool, by reason of the shortness of her legs. Miss Pecksniff sat upon a stool because of her simplicity and innocence, which were very great, very great" (2).

It would, however, be misleading to suggest that the narrator strains to make words mean what he intends for them to mean and fails. Often the narrator makes a point of his limited knowledge: in referring to Mark Tapley's sense of the very cold comfort available in partings, the narrator says, "Perhaps he knew it from his reading, perhaps from his experience, perhaps from intuition. It is impossible to say" (14). Obvious attempts to restrict meaning may be evident now and then, but they are so infrequent that when they do come they act as reminders of the impossibility of such control. The characters, at any rate, are constantly subverting the notion that language can be kept under such reins. Sairey Gamp's nitroglycerin talk allows the reader a boundless playground in which to swing and glide. "Gamp is my name, and Gamp my nater," she announces with full confidence in her communicating ability, anticipating Humpty Dumpty's daffy assurance to Alice that proper names, like any other words, must carry definite if impenetrable meaning.[10] So much for directed reading.

We might, in fact, be tempted to run off in the other direction and conclude that the book is a dramatization of its own indecipherability. A concordance would, I feel sure, demonstrate the unusual frequency with which words and phrases of uncertainty or imprecision are used: things often "seem" or "appear" to be; qualifiers like "maybe," "as it were," or "in effect" are employed to call attention to the oblique or approximate relationship between signifier and signified. More elaborate phrases suggest the difficult and uncertain nature of communication between two parties: "rather gave them to understand" is one of the most intriguing. Whether what is understood is what is given *for* understanding is unclear, befogged as the connection is by the soupy "rather." Interpretation becomes something of a desperate effort of will, signalled by the phrase, "I look upon you as. . . ." Lacking any effective medium for interpretation, one asserts a stability, a way of looking that is sustained only by the declaration and that, again, invites comparison with Humpty Dumpty's wonderfully mad means of investing words with whatever meaning he chooses.[11]

Curiously, the most potent and stable mode of communication, both for the narrator and for the characters, seems to be irony, a surprising fact, since even such a resolute stabilizer as Wayne Booth is willing to recognize how slippery a medium it is.[12] Still, in the noncommunicating community of *Martin Chuzzlewit*, ironists like Young Bailey are, comparatively, lucid: "I say . . . young ladies, there's soup to-morrow. She's a-making it now. Ain't she a-putting in the water? Oh! not at all neither!" (9). Indirection is, in a skewed world, as good as one can do.

One notices characters and especially the narrator attempting to adjust to the murk and the cockeyed obliquity by consistently describing one thing in terms of another. The effect is not one of metaphoric exuberance but a kind of forlorn hopelessness. The recurrence of "as if" and "as though" clauses point to the fact that language does not provide a straight route to fact or truth. Such clauses wave toward other routes, as if an inexperienced driver, even on bad roads, might be more likely to find his destination if given a variety of directions. The logic and the psychology are so weak that they call attention to their own insufficiency, the lack of confidence in language, the only medium available. When the narrator does try to muster some faith in language, he does so, even then, in a mock-simile, a pointed refusal to go outside the subject that is being explained: Tom Pinch, he says, "was as happy as only Tom Pinch could be. There is no other simile that will express his state of mind" (12). Perhaps no other simile would do the job, but why, then, use a simile at all and then comment on it? The effect is to reinforce the fact that the approximation of simile is inescapable, even with so direct and forthright a character as Tom. The formal device overrides the character. The device does not get us closer to Tom Pinch; just the reverse: Tom Pinch becomes a morsel of grammar, a poetic figure, a simile. This habit of expressing things in simile distances characters and actions from the language describing them, and it distances us from any feeling that language will allow us access to the truth.

There are repeated references to the uselessness of words, the inefficacy of language.[13] The main room at the Blue Dragon, for instance, not only is sunken, "all down-hill from the door," but is connected to the entrance by "a descent of two steps on the inside so exquisitely unexpected, that strangers, *despite the most elaborate cautioning,* usually dived in head first, as into a plunging bath" (3; emphasis added). Parliamentary language is described as the art of being able "to use as many words as possible and express nothing whatever" (43). It is not only Parliamentarians who possess this talent, however, for language has a way of tripping up even its most conscientious users. Plain speaking, as it turns out, is the least effective mode of address, the surest road to misunderstanding, as Tom Pinch discovers when he tries to rely on "the true and plain intention which my words professed" in speaking to Mercy Pecksniff (37). True and plain intentions do not translate into plain words, plain words being some mythical creation, like a griffin. Given all this unsteadiness, the gaps between intentions, language, and referent, one is tempted to take refuge in Montague Tigg's happy cynicism: "Life's a riddle: a most infernally hard riddle to guess, Mr. Pecksniff. My own opinion is, that like the celebrated conundrum, 'Why's a man in jail like a man out of jail?' there's no answer to it. Upon my soul and body, it's the queerest sort of thing altogether—but there's no use in talking about it. Ha! ha!" (4). There is, for Tigg and for language, no answer to be found anywhere—ha ha!

So, the narrator and characters often turn to an interpretive process that is more subtle, reading not words but gestures, glances, or "looks." Mercy Pecksniff gives Tom Pinch "a speaking look, and Tom knew what it said" (46). Mr. Moddle has eyes that speak "without the aid of language" (46). Jonas

Chuzzlewit sits, "reading how he looked in Mr. Pecksniff's eyes" (18). It's not only eyes that speak: Bailey's profuse ironic negatives, the narrator says, make his language "somewhat obscure," but his pantomime of lovers walking to church exchanging affectionate glances manages to make his meaning clear (11). Tom Pinch makes a motion with his hand, "and all his little history was written in the action" (50). The coachdriver Bill Simmons has his looks contradict his words (13), and the physician Mr. Jobling is so skilled at shaking his head, rubbing his hands, smacking his lips, and uttering sounds like "Ah" that his patients can construct from this a coherent sentence: "I know what you're going to say better than you do; but go on, go on" (27). Jonas Chuzzlewit, at one point unable to "make up his mind . . . whether to call Tom Pinch his dear friend or a villain," settles the matter by shaking "his fist at him *pro tem*" (24). It may seem to be a world of mimes, with great acting troupes like Mr. Mould's company and its "performance of funerals" (19) at the center—or perhaps the Anglo-Bengalee Disinterested Loan and Life Assurance Company, which runs on the marvelous power of the Footman, who, "relying solely on his figure," exerts a potent "charm" with his very waistcoat, an emblem of the company's stability.

Is it really possible, though, to devise a semiotic system more reliable than language? Even the narrator is sometimes baffled by the mime code, admitting that a nudge of Pecksniff's elbow "might either be construed into an indignant remonstrance or a cordial assent" (24). Worse still, characters like Chuffey give off no meaning; they are "the embodiment of nothing" (11). Some characters, vicious or virtuous, are able to make themselves illegible: Pecksniff at one point is "determined that the old man should read nothing" in his face (11), and Mark Tapley can manufacture a countenance that would make it impossible "for the most skilled physiognomist to determine what he was thinking about, or whether he was thinking at all" (43). Sairey Gamp's true meaning is even more difficult to come by because of her great versatility, her ability to produce "a face for all occasions" (19).

This last bit of artistry raises a more fundamental issue, one that assails our basic assumption that people and actions *should* be intelligible, that we should have access to some certainty and some truth. As always in Dickens, the drive toward that which is ascertainable and accountable is countered by a display of dexterous free-play, a parody of truth-telling and truth-seeking. Interpretive accuracy is both sought for and laughed at. The dull and moralistic honest types are balanced by artists, artists who are often indistinguishable from liars. Mrs. Gamp and Montague Tigg weave not just competing linguistic systems but competing worlds out of words.

The great art-for-art's-sake character is Seth Pecksniff, whose speech is always, as the narrator says, "ornamental." It is Pecksniff who elegantly and consistently inverts the dull proverb and makes it into, "Take care of the sounds and the sense will take care of itself." He speaks always as if he were decorating tombstones: "And Thomas Pinch and I... will walk [the world] yet, in mutual faithfulness and friendship! And if it comes to pass that either of us be run over, in any of the busy crossings which divide the streets of life, the other will convey him to the hospital in Hope, and sit beside his bed in Bounty!" (5). It may be that his sentences communicate little matter, but whose do so in this novel? Besides, Pecksniff has the remarkable ability to make something out of nothing, turning tedium into "comfort":

> "A gentleman taken ill upon the road, has been so very bad upstairs, sir," said the tearful hostess.
>
> "A gentleman taken ill upon the road, has been so very bad upstairs, has he?" repeated Mr. Pecksniff.
>
> "Well, well!" (3)

"Anybody," the narrator continues "would have been, as Mrs. Lupin was, comforted by the mere voice and presence of such a man."

Most characters, it is true, are engaged in the more mundane business of searching for truth and validity. It is very well for Mrs. Gamp to insist confidently that some things "is plain enough to them as needn't look through millstones" (46), but how do we know exactly which things are plain? And who will dislodge our millstones for us? How do we do our own detective work in a world in which even normal associative processes have gone haywire: "Why are they merrymaking here, if there's no one dead?" (46)? Even proverbial wisdom, that bedrock of received certainty, is mocked: the "infallibility" of "early to bed, early to rise..." "has been for generations verified by the enormous fortunes amassed by chimney-sweeps" (5).

Language, then, is unreliable—sometimes; gestures and appearances are slightly less so—sometimes. The question arises as to whether or not we truly desire reliability, and the answer is yes and no. So, where do we go from here? (Home?) We might retreat down the interpretive ladder and grab for some thematic naturalization of all these contradictions. An inviting possibility beckons in the division between the English and American scenes. Such sharp splits are always susceptible either to thematic joining or thematic contrast (joining if one looks to the selfish-selfless theme, contrasted in the nature-art theme). From our semiotic standpoint, however, the New World, despite its smug sense of superiority—"They corrupt even the language in the old country.... Where was you rose?" (22)—looks very much like the Old, heightened some, certainly, but giving us no better clues about interpretation. American language moves from a plain speech that is deranged, rootless, and always screaming toward violence—eagles' talons, gore, bowie knives, gougings—to a lunatic sense of manipulation: Hannibal Chollop's feeling that the snake-infested quagmires of Eden do not constitute a swamp at all compared to English landscape (33)[14]—to the floating language of the transcendental ladies: "Mind and matter . . . glide swift into the vortex of immensity. Howls the sublime" (34). At no point on the scale is language trustworthy or necessarily indicative of much of anything. Americans take refuge in explanatory pantomime nearly as much as the British, and sometimes the results seem helpful: La Fayette Kettle has written on his eyes, "Now you won't overreach me: you want to, but you won't" (21), and the signals given off by American eating and spitting habits might seem definite or at least emphatic. But much of the miming is mixed with cunning and is, thus, finally as unreliable as the language: Colonel Diver has "a singular expression" hovering in the neighborhood of his eyes, an expression "which was not a frown, nor a leer, and yet might have been mistaken at first glance for either" (16).

We might try to evade this impasse by throwing everything into some moral bundle, arguing, say, that there is a false and evil language (and appearance) used to deceive the Virtuous, who are said to be commonly "incredulous and blind" (15). After all, both Pecksniff and Tigg, in relying on the "ornamental," prey on the unwarily upright, as, presumably, does Mrs. Gamp, and by much the same means. But we soon find ourselves in another trap. The idea of a false and deceiving language demands the existence of a true and comprehensible one, and where in this novel (or anywhere) are we to find that article? Plain speaking, as we have observed, is likely to be dangerous and is certainly unintelligible. Further, if Virtue is blind, so is Vice. Jonas, much more a standard villain than Seth, Sairey, or Tigg, has about him a slyness which the narrator says is absolutely transparent. Imagining that he is in hiding, he displays all (28).

The search for coherence and a unifying principle is not usually given up so easily. (I'm ready to give up.) One could abandon language altogether, arguing that virtue resides in silence, in privacy. Supporting this argument is the distaste expressed for the New York newspapers—*The New York Sewer, The New York Peeper, The New York Keyhole Reporter* (16)—and their unwarranted, undignified search for private truths. There is also the curious figure of Nadgett, a man whose absolute privacy, his ability "to be a secret," makes all things come right in the end. But Nadgett is a weak model, being more than a little mad, writing letters to himself and then burning them. Besides, he suggests a depressing view of things: no one will understand anyhow, so keep it to yourself. And that's not even the main problem. The main problem is that Nadgett makes everything come out right not by keeping things to himself but by revealing them, albeit reluctantly. It is, after all, a detective-story plot, and we, as much as *The Keyhole Reporter*, need to *know*.

We need to know but never can—fully or with confidence—because we are never certain of *how* to know. The novel is like the raging Atlantic Ocean, "constancy in nothing" (15), or like Tigg's dream, which features "a dreadful secret," "a secret which he knew and yet did not know" (42). Perhaps we, like visitors to the Blue Dragon, have no choice but to dive into the novel as into a plunging bath and wallow around. Or perhaps we would be wiser to take our cue from Mr. Pecksniff, who has "scribbled" some but refrained from publishing it. But neither blank silence nor total uncertainty can satisfy what we can say (if we like) the novel demands (or we demand): a participation in the book's exploration of the means by which we understand, delude ourselves and others, attempt to reveal and to conceal.

The novel does not resist the application of interpretive models; it is openly hospitable, inviting one and all. Such cordiality is winning but it makes for a riot. No model can yield results that account for everything (even very much) and each model yields results which all too often (or maybe just often enough) contradict the findings, facts, and arrogant sureties of others. We find what our model causes and allows us to find. As Sairey Gamp says of Young Bailey, "All the wickedness in the world is Print to him" (26). Those with piety uppermost will find that estimable quality reflected in print. Others, like Young Bailey and subversive critics, will be equally gratified.

5

Performance, Roles, the Self, and Our Own Charles Dickens

And let those that play your clowns speak no more
than is set down for them, for there be of them
that will themselves laugh to set on some quantity
of barren spectators to laugh too, though in the
meantime some necessary question of the play be
then to be considered. That's villainous and shows
a most pitiful ambition in the fool that uses it.

—*Hamlet, III: ii: 36–42*

*I*T IS A GENERAL rule in Dickens that a character's readiness to cite authorities stands in inverse proportion to his reliability. One thinks of Mr. Pecksniff, Mr. Podsnap, Mrs. General, or, in the colloquial line, Mrs. Nickleby. Something like the same rule applies, we agree, to academic essays. Everyone is suspicious of papers that start straight off with references to the *Oxford English Dictionary*, for instance. I am too. One naturally assumes that the writer is a little shaky on the nineteenth century and that he (only men do this) is hiding out in the thirteenth, figuring he is less likely to be nabbed there. Well, according to the *OED*, the word "performance" has accumulated a cluster of meanings that divides roughly into two contradictory directions: one is to complete an imposed task, to perform one's duty; the other is to add what is missing, to ornament, to compose, to cause, to act or play, or to play upon.

Dickens is the major Victorian employer of both kinds of performers: the steadfast and the irresponsible. On one hand, characters like Mr. Brownlow, Little Nell, Esther Summerson, Amy Dorrit, and a host of others perform their duties with an earnestness and single-mindedness we can and perhaps should emulate. However, I am not concerned here with rectitude or well-made plots, but with the intricacies and delights of the circus-like theatrical in Dickens. I want, then, to touch on those other performers, the figures who dance about the earnest folk, who add, as the *OED* says, what is missing, ornament it, play with it, create themselves what they take to be missing, often out of nothing. This second type of character needs no plot for acting, no plan, no causality; they use whatever is at hand as the basis for impromptu skits, full-scale dramas, or grand opera. They gleefully ignore Hamlet's straitlaced directorial edicts, having no regard whatever for the "necessary question" presumably at hand. They raise other questions entirely, often subversive ones, nearly always delightful ones. The earnest performers have plans and follow their marching orders along a straight path; they struggle to constitute what we think of as a plot and to be obedient to it. The playful performers float free, improvising whatever composition they find to their fancy; they write anti-plots. The first group listens to Hamlet, subordinates itself to the script, plods straight out of Chicago to Neo-Aristotelian anthems; the second group subordinates itself to nothing, grabs the microphone, and laughs to set us laughing. The result is a rich, self-reflexive series of novels—or puddings, which threaten to burst and shower us with the raisins, sweetmeats, and brandy.

Not only does the second group of performers subvert linear plot development, they also force us to wonder what "character" is by disrupting our assumptions about selfhood. The closer we look at this group, the more it seems that there is no "they" there. At least, not in the usual sense. If we ask, "Who is the true Dick Swiveller, Wilkins Micawber, Noddy Boffin?", we find ourselves so helplessly bobbing about in deep waters that we begin to see that we have cast off in the wrong boat, formulated the question in a way that will frustrate a good answer. What does it mean to posit a real being, an identity behind the performance? Dickens, I will argue, presents violently contradictory, fiercely battling notions of what constitutes the self.

(It is time that I said exactly what I meant by "Dickens," you're thinking. Here I go casting doubt on Noddy Boffin but pretending that "Dickens" is the real thing and that we can apprehend that person with the usual equipment. How can this "Dickens" obey cultural rules for knowing that his characters evade? Good point, but I'm a step ahead of you. Look at the title, where I speak of "Our Own Dickens." See that? What that means is that the "Dickens" I'm talking about here is the one that suits my purposes, the agency of dissolving performances and unstable, mocking "selves." It's a construction, this "Dickens," like any other, a fabricated bit of energy that seeks not to tell the truth but to find an audience and perform.)

We generally assume not only that performances are authorized by pre-set scripts (a deterministic notion Hamlet likes but our Dickens does not) but that performances are temporary interruptions in the solidity of being both of performers and audience. Samuel Johnson's is only the most lucid insistence that performances are aberrations, hardly even ruffling our basic fixed personalities. "We are always in our senses," he claims, unthreatened in our illusions of separable being. Just so, roles or role-playing almost inevitably suggest to us a departure from a real self; the role is a disguise. My thesis is that Dickens questions the idea of selfhood as an isolated and stable entity; for him, the lines between performers and performance, roles and role-players are always blurred. How are we to know the dancer from the dance, the past Flora Finching from the present article, from the performances she gives, the roles she plays—how are we to distinguish her from those around her, from Mr. F's aunt?

Of course we need no one come from the dead to tell us that the Victorians were generally uneasy with simple notions of an essentialized self. Presentations of a multiple self or of a hidden, unknown self are common in Victorian literature. In Arnold, for instance: "And each lives half a hundred different lives" ("The Scholar Gypsy," l. 169); "And long we try in vain to speak and act/ Our hidden self, and what we say and do,/ Is eloquent, is well—but 'tis not true!" ("The Buried Life," ll. 64–66). These poignant laments, and others like them in the writings of virtually every major poet of the period, are, arguably, a bargaining maneuver, a liberal humanist dodge or compromise. Ultimately, they protect an essential self, even if it is splintered or mysterious, and they assure us that a little sweet sadness is, finally, not much of a price to pay for a securely fortified self.

The security provided was not all that reliable, however, judging from the Victorian poets' constant need to deny emphatically more dangerous questions about being. Arnold is notorious for poems that glimpse and then quickly look away from an absorption or dissolution of self: men who "dreamed two human hearts might blend" are simply unable to recognize "their loneliness," unable in their visionary ecstasy to detect "the unplumbed, salt, estranging sea" that is divinely ordained to separate us all ("Isolation: To Marguerite," ll: 38–42; "To Marguerite—Continued," l: 24). The longing to merge—"Oh, might our marges meet again" ("To Marguerite—Continued," l. 18)—can be expressed so movingly, one might conclude, only because such merging will never occur. Is there a sigh of relief, a welcoming of separation, here? The same mood prevails in Browning's "Two in the Campagna," in the general movement of Rossetti's *The House of Life* and Meredith's *Modern Love*, and in the equivocal ending of Tennyson's *The Princess*, where the Prince's idea of marriage as "The single pure and perfect animal,/ The two-celled heart beating, with one full stroke,/ Life" (VII. ll. 288-90) is shadowed by the decidedly *un*-two-celled action of the narrative, the obvious reluctance of the Princess to accept all this, and the skepticism of the characters in the frame poem. Our Dickens, I am suggesting (and why not?), is far more radical, takes many more risks in hinting at dissolution or absorption, and in conceiving a selfhood that is not contained or definable but relational, one that might reach out or collapse into nothingness.

All this is implied by the versatility of Dickens's performers and by the joy that they (and their author) take in sheer play. The unrestrained performances of these clowns raise questions not only about linear plots but about the nature of the characters trying to play a straight part in them. Many of Dickens's performers would make Hamlet seek other employment, but probably none deserves Danish censure more than Mr. Pecksniff, "architect, artist, and man." Pecksniff is given a part to play in the plot, of course, but his character is too amorphous to fit neatly into a plot. He is cast as a cadging hypocrite, and he occasionally nods amiably in that direction—but never for long. He is too busy constructing a raucous, open-ended farce to have any great interest in morality plays. Why not see Pecksniff, like Dickens, as the great impresario, managing the script, the stage directions, the costumes, the scenery, and, of course (again, like Dickens) adopting the leading roles, whatever they might be?

Take, for instance, the opening scene in *Martin Chuzzlewit* (2),[1] where Pecksniff and his two daughters stage, for their own benefit and without an audience, a mock resurrection scene. Pecksniff has been attacked by a brutal doorknob and he lies senseless on the floor. He rests there patiently, waiting for his cue, rousing himself when his daughters speak, brought to life not by their actions but by their words: "He comes to himself!", "He speaks again." A lively celebration scene follows, starring Miss Charity as Sensible Goodness, Miss Mercy as Kittenish Innocence, and Mr. Pecksniff as Paternal Virtue. The props are important: tea, buttered toast, ham, and especially eggs. "And eggs," says Mr. Pecksniff, "even they have their moral." Morality, he suggests, is meant to minister to comfort: "If we indulge in harmless fluids, we get the dropsy; if in exciting fluids, we get drunk. What a soothing reflection that is." The soothing, oozing warmth is made possible by Mr. Pecksniff's use of the plural "we," by which he means "mankind in general; the human race considered as a body, and not as individuals." Escaping the trap of the "individual," the Pecksniffian amalgam (called, for convenience, "Mr. Pecksniff") can feed, and drink, and experience delight even in moralisms: "There is nothing personal in morality, my love." One could certainly read this playlet as an illustration of deep-seated hypocrisy or as a rehearsal for serious hypocrisy later in the novel—but what uninteresting readings! Performances like Pecksniff's draw us into the stew; they are not attempting to get anywhere in particular. Rather, they cast a dim light on the very idea of individual destinations.

Take another example: Mrs. Jarley and her waxworks. The performance consists not just of the versatile waxworks—in which Grimaldi the clown can easily be made to pass for Mr. Murray the grammarian, depending on the tastes of the audience and Mrs. Jarley's whim—but of Mrs. Jarley herself, who uses the waxworks simply as an occasion for her own performances, which consist primarily of stirring soliloquies in defense of the works' classical status. Mrs. Jarley operates best when she has an audience; but there are others, like Sairey Gamp, who can create mono-dramas, parodies-in-advance of Tennyson's *Maud*. Sairey goes on about "wales of grief" and the virtues of "cowcumbers and vinegar" when she is by herself as well as when she has a listener. Of course, she never really is alone, since, being a master at dialogue, she has an articulate companion, Mrs. Harris. Often explained as a pathetic antidote to Sairey's deep loneliness or as a blatant instrument of self-advertisement, Mrs. Harris (I'm here to tell you) is *really* a means for creating the sort of drama Sairey loves: the realistic drama of detail, Ibsenesque in its particularity. Take this:

> Don't I know as that dear woman is expecting of me this minnit, Mr. Westlock, and is a-lookin' out of window down the street, with little Tommy Harris in her arms, as calls me his own Gammy, and truly calls, for bless the little mottled legs of that precious child (like Canterbury Brawn his own dear father says, which so they are) his own I have been, ever since I found him, Mr. Westlock, with his small red worsted shoe a-gurglin' in his throat, where he had put it in his play, a chick, wile they was leavin' of him on the floor a-lookin' for it through the ouse and him a-choakin' sweetly in the parlour! Oh, Betsey Prig, what wickedness you've showed this night, but never shall you darken Sairey's door agen, you twining serpiant! (49)

If this were all a matter of self-interest, why would she take such pleasure in talking with Young Bailey, who, at the time, is not a likely candidate for profit, for a laying-out and certainly not for a lying-in? Then there are the Micawbers,

among the most versatile at using any occasion for staging a performance: a
debt-collector roaring in the street below prompts *Antony and Cleopatra*; a party
precipitates the last act of *The Marriage of Figaro*.

Dickens's own subversive delight in non-scripted performance is everywhere
evident, not only in these wild, non-individual characters but in boisterous
structural disruption as well. Typical in this regard is chapter 13 of *Martin
Chuzzlewit*. At the end of chapter 12, also the completion of the fourth monthly number, Martin, dismissed from Mr. Pecksniff's moral and architectural
tutelage, suddenly announces, "I'll go to America!" The business of chapter 13,
we might expect, would be to get him there. Quickly, too, if we are to believe
what we have been told so often it must be true: that Dickens' decision to ship
Martin to Yankeedooledom was a desperate move to rouse a lethargic market
and boost sales.[2] But chapter 13 is in no hurry at all to get Martin overseas; he
barely makes it from Wiltshire to London, which is not a long haul. Instead,
time is spent on leisure activities: wildly expansive comic dialogues and duets
between Martin and William (call me "Bill") Simmons, Montague Tigg and a
pawnbroker ("David," Tigg says), Tigg and Martin. With seemingly all the
time in the world, Dickens provides his narrator with some long and splendid-
ly sarcastic digressions on "nature" and its connection to bestiality, the psychological flimflam of hopefulness, and moralists in general. Clearly, the author
has a good time, as does even Mark Tapley, who is less concerned with the plot
than with letting us know, in dozens of broad hints, that his perverse search for
the greatest misery possible has inevitably led him to smell out the miserably
selfish Martin.

Roughly speaking, a third of the long chapter 13 is devoted to Martin
Simmons, a third to the pawnshop Abbot and Costello routines, and a third to
Mark. The presumably desperate Dickens somehow seems very relaxed, confi-
dently playful, in no hurry at all. Just look at the introduction of Bill Simmons:

> He was a red-faced burly young fellow; smart in his way, and with a good-
> humored countenance. As he advanced toward the fire he touched his shining
> forehead with the forefinger of his stiff leather glove, by way of salutation; and
> said (rather unnecessarily) that it was an uncommon wet day.
>
> "Very wet," said Martin.
>
> "I don't know as ever I see a wetter."[3]
>
> "I never felt one," said Martin.

What on earth is going on here? Nothing, we might say. But that "nothing-
going-on" is precisely the point. The narrator even admits that these remarks are

made "rather unnecessarily." The clear signal to the reader is to relax and enjoy yourself. "Here we go!" Dickens says; "I've got these two together and we'll see what comes of it. You just warm yourself by the fire, get a glass of something agreeable, and trust me."

And we are right to do so, it turns out, largely because of Simmons, a coach-driver of remarkable and diverse abilities. Aspiring to greater things in the coach-driving line, William (Bill) turns the chance to earn a few extra shillings into the opportunity for comedy improv. He is full of entertaining stories about himself, about horses, and about Lummy Ned of the Light Salisbury and his awesome ability to outface death: "'Dead!' replied [Bill], with a contemptuous emphasis. 'Not he. You won't catch Ned a-dying easy. No, no. He knows better than that.'" To vary his show, Bill pulls a bugle from his pocket and plays the opening parts of a great many tunes.

What is accomplished here? In the face of the burbling offered by Bill Simmons, such a question seems to come from Malvolio. We who, like Dickens, thrive on cakes and ale will not think to ask. As so often happens in Dickens, when a character in one place needs to get to another, and there is a coach to take him, we can count on a high old time of it. Forget about accomplishing anything. Of course, Martin does get to London, a phrase's worth of plot work that takes seven full pages of horsing around. And once in London, we are still not forced into dreary toil. No! We are provided with Tigg and David the pawn-broker going through a routine they both love:

"The old address?"

"Not at all," said Mr. Tigg; "I have removed my town establishment from thirty-eight Mayfair to number fifteen-hundred-and-forty-two Park Lane."

"Come, I'm not going to put that down, you know," said the shopman with a grin.

"You may put down what you please, my friend," quoth Mr. Tigg. "The fact is still the same. The apartments for the under-butler and the fifth footman being of a most confounded low and vulgar kind at thirty-eight Mayfair, I have been compelled, in my regard for the feelings which do them so much honour, to take on lease for seven, fourteen, or twenty-one years, renewable at the option of the tenant, the elegant and commodious family mansion, number fifteen-hundred-and-forty-two Park Lane. Make it two-and-six, and come and see me!"

The shopman was so highly entertained by this piece of humour that Mr. Tigg himself could not repress some little show of exultation.

Martin does not quite get the point or have the wherewithal to enter into this game. Never mind. Tigg can keep things going by using the young dullard as a straight man:

> "Here! Please to give me the most you can for this," said Martin, handing the watch to the shopman, "I want money sorely."
>
> "He wants money sorely!" cried Mr. Tigg with excessive sympathy. "David, you will have the goodness to do your very utmost for my friend, who wants money sorely. You will deal with my friend as if he were myself. A gold hunting-watch, David, engine-tuned, capped and jewelled in four holes, escape movement, horizontal lever, and warranted to perform correctly, upon my personal reputation, who have observed it narrowly for many years, under the most trying circumstances." Here he winked at Martin, that he might understand this recommendation would have an immense effect upon the shopman: "What do you say, David, to my friend? Be very particular to deserve my custom and recommendation, David."

Like Simmons, Tigg is after money. Like Dickens, too, we presume. But none of them seems very interested in it; none is going to sacrifice the game, the delight for something as mundane as a little tin—or a little plot.

To focus this habit of disruption and to move more explicitly towards the issue of non-individualized, relational being, I would like to shift from the broad issue of "performance" to the somewhat more controllable one of "role" or "role-players." These role-players, on the face of it, would seem to have considerably less creative freedom than those conducting performances. According to the *OED* (here we go again!), a *roll* (role) is a prescribed list of names, predetermined by some rule; or a part one has to play, undertake, or assume. Note the preemptory *has to*; but also note the wonderful ambiguity contained in the word "assume." *Assume* can suggest simply taking over a part *or* actually creating it, assuming it to be whatever one chooses. Perhaps it won't hurt us to admit (since we stand to gain by this reasonableness) that Dickens certainly does give ample space to the *has to* part of roles, that he often insists on essential selfhood. Bill Sikes, one senses, can hardly shift at will to the role of a kindly grandfather. He is incurably bad, just as Herbert Pocket and Tommy Traddles are terminally good. Or so we may suppose, if we like. It's OK by me. What's important, though, are the flying players who swing around these fixed figures as if they were maypoles; it is the trapeze artists who play fast and loose with the "assume" part of the "role" definition who are most likely to offend our best assumptions.

For our part as readers, we come to the novels equipped to detect a real essence behind that role, a face behind the mask. But in Dickens we are forced to wonder. To start with a simple case, we might consider Mr. Bumble: what lives behind the mask of the Beadle costume, the cocked hat and stick, that malicious, unfeeling impostor? A quaking jelly of emasculation, apparently, as we see when he marries. But what about the scene when he looks down at the tiny Oliver he is holding by the hand and hears the child sob out that he is "So lonely, sir! So very lonely"? Mr. Bumble is moved, gets a lump in his throat, and pretends to cough to cover impending tears (4). What, then, *is* he: a decent, tender man, forced to play the roles of thunderous Beadle and hen-pecked husband; one of the latter two people forced to play the other two roles; all three; or none of them? Same with Fagin: is he simply an artful exploiter? Is his maternal solicitude and affectionate manner malicious, perverse, or genuinely loving? What about the scene where he bends over the sleeping Oliver to wake him for some thieving expedition, is touched by the innocent beauty of the child, and says, "Not now," turning softly away (19)? Which is he? And what of characters who are apparently indistinguishable from their roles? Who *is* Mr. Wopsle, apart from the violent part of Collins's "Ode on the Passions," throwing his blood-stained sword in thunder down, or apart from his well-groomed version of the indecisive Prince of Denmark? And Dick Swiveller. He awakens from his unreal role-playing by means of a cathartic illness and discovers in the loyalty and love of the Marchioness a new being for himself. Right? But is not that new being just about as indefinable as the old one—playful and Micawberesque? He and the Marchioness are still plotless players, passing their happy days with cribbage; and the Marchioness is still whatever she was or was not, the Marchioness, a name given to her by Dick to make it all seem "more real and pleasant." Dick still calls the shots and issues his bizarre proclamations on what is *real.* How are we to decide whether Dick has changed? And (the more difficult question is), how we are to decide what this Dick Swiveller was or is?

Some characters seem to play multiple roles, then, and others may or may not shift within those roles. Some are pure mysteries. Is Bailey the elfish young sprite who skips about Todgers's Commercial Boarding House or the worldly man-about-town who impresses Sairey Gamp with his street-smarts? But Sairey, who sees him as having mastered "all the wickedness in the world" (26), sees him just as easily as a chit, a "young sparrow" she might think of mothering (29). Where is the real Bailey? And what of Alfred Jingle, the chameleon socialite, cricket-player, lover, strolling actor, vagabond, scoundrel, repentant sinner? Has he, in the end, revealed his true self, his essence? Mr. Perker, wise in the ways of the world, is skeptical about permanent reform for such a form-less thing as Jingle. Mr. Pickwick thinks he has found the true article; but, then, Mr. Pickwick is a particularly naïve reader. He has, like us, been asking questions like: where is the real Jingle? where is the real Bailey? where is the real Sairey, the real Wopsle? the real Micawber? But perhaps the questions are misplaced.

These questions assume a core to an individual's being (having first posited this "individual," of course). What is more, they assume that an individual's being has clear boundaries, as if it were a cartoon with thick black lines marking off the character from its surroundings and from other such beings. Many characters in Dickens cannot be understood in the linear, developmental terms appropriate to individuals. They are the "we" of one another. Mrs. Micawber's vow never to desert Mr. Micawber, for instance, is a grand redundancy. How could she? Without him, where would she be? More exactly, *what* would she be?

The move towards alternate, boundaryless conceptions of being is played out throughout the Dickens canon. Even in the most radical of individualist forms, the *Bildungsroman* and its exemplar *Oliver Twist*, we can see Oliver growing toward a being that exists only in relation to that of the boys around Fagin, and to Fagin himself. Fagin's merry pickpocketing pantomimes, co-starring the Dodger and Charley Bates, make Oliver laugh "till the tears ran down his face" (9). Later, Fagin's "droll and curious" stories about exciting robberies make Oliver laugh heartily "in spite of all his better feelings" (18). Oliver's ability to be absorbed in purely communal laughter, in spite of his dratted individualized conscience, marks his affinity for incorporation, and this affinity makes us uneasy, I suggest, not so much because he is drawn towards crime as because he is drawn towards a joy that does not rest on differentiation. Too bad that the individualizers step in and lug him back to virtue.

A more complex series of images of merging and dissociation is developed in *Great Expectations*. The early part of the novel presents Pip with a set of possibilities for establishing his being, all involving a mingling and all more or less uninviting: his parents "dead and buried"; the shivering, brutal convict; the loving but apparently impotent Joe. Out of this, it is not surprising that the child settles on the child-father Joe, loves him, as he says, "perhaps for no better reason in those early days than because the dear fellow let me love him" (6). The phrasing is, from our point of view, unsentimental almost to the point of harshness, but, from another viewpoint, is brilliantly suggestive of reciprocity. It is not that he loves Joe and Joe loves him; it is more that he knocks at Joe's heart and Joe lets him in: "'And bring the poor little child. God bless the poor little child,' I said to your sister, 'there's room for *him* at the forge!'" (7). There's room for the child in Joe. Joe and Pip are not, at this stage, separable beings. We see this from, among other things, the letter Pip writes to Joe:

> MI DEER JO I OPE U R KRWITE WELL I OPE I SHAL SON B HABELL 4 2
> TEEDGE U JO AN THEN WE SHORL B SO GLODD AN WEN I M PRENGTD
> 2 U JO WOT LARX AN BLEVE ME INF XN PIP. (Chapter 7)

This is Dickens's answer to the letters of Lord Chesterfield he so despised, despised because of their unremitting hammering—very unlike Joe's selfless hammering—at self. What one notices about Pip's epistolary exercise is that, with a minor change or two, it might have been written by Joe (at a further stage in his formal education). The letter contains Joe's gawky, sweet genteelisms—"I OPE UR KRWITE WELL"; "BLEVE ME INF XN"—his concern with TEEDGing and his openness of heart—"WOT LARX." This last phrase blends the two together into one throughout the novel. Perhaps we never witness any larks; perhaps they are never realized in the plot. But they exist all the same, exist even more powerfully because they are in the form of a promise that defies fulfillment, a sign that need point to no other place, that is realized in itself.

This last difficult and profound noncausality is the secret of Joe's wisdom and lies at the core of his teaching in the great pedagogical scene that follows the presentation of Pip's letter. Teacher and pupil do not so much change places as unite. Joe's manner throughout his *apologia pro vita sua*—his explanation of his life and faith, his childhood, his love for Pip's sister, and his feelings toward Pip—is sternly tutorial: "Joe looked firmly at me"; "Don't you see?" "Don't you know?" "you're a-listening, and understanding, Pip?" In fact, Pip decidedly does not understand—not in the usual sense. He especially does not understand how Joe can love and admire Mrs. Joe or how he can regard his cruel, good-for-nothing father with respect and affection: "Whatsume'er the failings on his part, Remember reader he were that good in his hart." Joe does not flinch from the violence and universal unfairness of life; he would not disagree with Kafka that all are victims, sure to be tortured. But for Joe it is innocence and goodness of heart, not guilt, that can never be doubted. Pip does not seem to get it, does not seem to understand Joe's dissociation of action from being, his melting of all into a sad, indestructible goodness. But, in a way that defies our usual Lockean idea of individual growth and understanding, Pip actually is suckled and nourished by Joe's subtle and beautiful paradoxes. He makes himself part of Joe's wisdom: "We were equals afterwards, as we had been before; but, afterwards at quiet times when I sat looking at Joe and thinking about him, I had a new sensation of feeling conscious that I was looking up to Joe in my heart" (7).

Equals and nonequals, pupil and teacher, they reverse roles, are interchangeable, of one heart.

Pip tries, of course, to defy this learning and his heart for some time. In the end, however, he leaves behind the sorry, clambering, successful gentleman whose disguise he had tried to wear and gives himself to Joe's teaching. In terms of the narrative, he forms himself as, in, and for the convict Magwitch. As Magwitch "softens," so does Pip, until the speech of both modulates to a simple quiet dignity that no longer separates but marks their connecting:

> "And what's best of all," he said, "you've been more comfortable alonger me, since I was under a dark cloud, than when the sun shone. That's best of all."
>
> He lay on his back, breathing with great difficulty. Do what he would, and love me though he did, the light left his face ever and again, and a film came over the placid look at the white ceiling.
>
> "Are you in much pain to-day?"
>
> "I don't complain of none, dear boy."
>
> "You never do complain."
>
> He had spoken his last words. He smiled, and I understood his touch to mean that he wished to lift my hand and lay it on his breast. I laid it there, and he smiled again, and put both his hands upon it. (56)

Their unity is marked by their mutual adoption of the metaphor of light, the wordless communication, and the joining of hands. This last gesture, Pip's hands along with those of Magwitch resting on the heart, suggests that we must think of the heart not as Magwitch's failing, separate organ but as the human heart generally. This union connects both with Joe and with all who suffer and are good: "Remember reader he were that good in his hart."

Not all images of absorption are by any means so positive in Dickens. The loss of individuality, alienating as that individuality is, can also mean a loss of all defenses. And then we are lost in the horrifying, undifferentiated mobs of *Barnaby Rudge*:

> It was but a glimpse, but it showed them the crowd, gathering and clustering round the house: some of the armed men pressing to the front to break down the doors and windows, some bringing brands from the nearest fire, some with lifted faces following their course upon the roof and pointing them out to their companions: all raging and roaring like the flames they lighted up. They saw some men thirsting for the treasures of strong liquor which they knew were stored within; they saw others, who had been wounded, sinking down into the opposite doorways and dying, solitary wretches, in the midst of all the vast assemblage; here, a frightened woman trying to escape; and there a lost child; and there a drunken ruffian, unconscious of the death-wound on his head, raving and fighting to the last. (67)

The individuals picked out by this demonic camera-sweep seem to be there by accident, random debris to be caught up in the flood of the monster-mob. These rioters, figured when alive as a sea and when dead as manure heaps, are a single creature out of hell:

> The gutters of the street and every crack and fissure in the stones, ran with scorching spirit, which being damned up by busy hands, overflowed the road and pavement, and formed a great pool, into which the people dropped down dead by dozens. They lay in heaps all round this fearful pond, husbands and wives, fathers and sons, mothers and daughters, women with children in their arms and babies at their breasts, and drank until they died. While some stopped with their lips to the brink and never raised their heads again, others sprang up from their fiery draught, and danced, half in a mad triumph, and half in the agony of suffocation, until they fell, and steeped their corpses in the liquor that had killed them. Nor was even this the worst or most appalling kind of death that happened on this fatal night. From the burning cellars, where they drank out of hats, pails, buckets, tubs, and shoes, some men were drawn, alive, but all alight from head to foot; who, in their unendurable anguish and suffering, making for anything that had the look of water, rolled, hissing, in this hideous lake, and splashed up liquid fire which lapped in all it met with as it ran along the surface, and neither spared the living nor the dead. (68)

More subtly, *Little Dorrit* presents both the dangers and joys of absorption. It is a novel of reductions, radical strippings away, testing whether something can be made out of nothing. In the case of Mr. Dorrit, Mrs. Clennam, or Mr. Merdle, it cannot. Stripped of trappings, they vanish. Even the hero, Arthur Clennam, often called Nobody, thinks of joining with the river in a literal, suicidal nothingness: "And he thought—who has not thought for a moment, sometimes?—that it might be better to flow away monotonously, like the river, and to compound for its insensibility to happiness with its insensibility to pain" (16). But he is saved by Amy Dorrit—"I have nothing in the world," she says (III, 34)—and the Nothing and the Nobody coalesce. The filthy hive of individuals in the world continue in their "usual uproar," but Arthur and Amy are "inseparable and blessed" (III, 34).

These kinds of expansive beings raise interesting questions for filmmakers and television adapters who seem called upon to use characters as individuals. More interestingly, they call upon us as readers to abandon some of our most cherished and comfortable notions. But we have constructed our Dickens this way expressly so he can make us squirm. Who knows but that out of that squirming we might find a posture that will allow us to see and think in more radical—even more hopeful ways.

Interlude I

Who Is Relieved By the Idea of Comic Relief?

THERE IS A LOT OF difference between an academic talk and an academic essay, as we all know. Think what it would be like if there were not, if we had to listen to essays or read talks. We wouldn't be able to absorb the high density of an essay if it were spoken at us. Lucky for us that never happens. Reading a talk would be worse. The graceful ease and casual art that all academic paper-readers have mastered would drive us to frenzy if it came at us in print. I'd rather bite down hard on the soft tissue just inside my cheek, or have a finger mashed under a truck, or spend an entire afternoon with my dean.

But there are exceptions, and here is one. The following is a talk I gave recently for a panel got up by a friend I guess I should call him, who arranged it for the sole purpose of ventilating a crotchet, an idea whose time will never come, a position so pointless as to set records. This moderator staked what little credibility he had on the outcome of a contest between comedy and tragedy, a contest no one else supposes is taking place. Having stumbled on Aristotle's Poetics in the summer of 1987, he, in a manner that has come to be characteristic since his accident, took Aristotle's remarks on comedy personally, and has dedicated himself since that time to vengeance, to establishing that "Curly Sue," which he admires, is superior to "The Agamemnon," which he does not. Possessed of this single idea and considerable cunning, he set about locating three passable scholars and selling the MLA on this panel. The MLA, being witless, was easy; and he then got

Regina Barreca, Robert Polhemus, and me to front for him: Professor Barreca is a careless person and mistook it for a serious occasion, Professor Polhemus owed money to him, and I was lied to.

I had little choice but to argue that our current hierarchical arrangement (tragedy high, comedy low) betrays an acquiescence to the most smothering of political conservatisms. By coupling tragedy with the sublime, the ineffable, the metaphysical, and by aligning comedy with the mundane, the quotidian, and the material, we manage to muffle or even erase the most powerful narratives of illumination and liberation we have. As a consequence, we have nothing but reactionary stories to tell. We are no better than Lynne Cheney and Jesse Helms when we gush over King Lear and sneer at Larry, Curly, and Moe. It is nothing less than fascistic to set up tragedy as superior to comedy, and yet that is exactly what we do, we all do it, in obedience to the dictates of those power agencies Foucault and the new historicists at Berkeley have identified for us. We imagine that it is natural to regard comedy as inferior to tragedy, natural at least for educated people who have acquired postgraduate taste, despising spectator sports and never watching television. In so construing nature, however, we betray our own complicity in the power agencies I mentioned earlier, our own stake in the status quo, and our complacency about the oppression of others. When we say that comedy is inferior to tragedy, we join hands with Wally George, Castelragh, Pat Buchanan, Marie Antoinette, Rush Limbaugh, Caligula, and Orrin Hatch. Now I cannot repeat too often that I know you are thinking that no one has gone about saying tragedy was superior to comedy since about 1940, and you are right to say that only our moderator imagines that this is an issue. But none of that in any way disables my argument, as you will see.

My goal is to reconsider comic relief, both the *concept* of comic relief and who it relieves. Now, we usually refer to comic relief in the same tone we use for academic provosts, other people's children, Melanie Griffith, the new criticism, jogging, Big Macs, Ayn Rand, leisure suits, people who go on cruises, realtors, and the MLA: bemused contempt. Comedy is that which attends on, offers relaxation from, prepares us for more of—something else, something serious and demanding. Comedy is not demanding—it does not demand or take, it gives. And we know that any agency that gives cannot be worth much. Tragedy's seriousness is guaranteed by its bullying greed, its insistence on having things its own way and pulling from us not only our tears, which we value little, but our attention, which we hate to give. Comedy, on the other hand, doesn't care if we attend closely. Tragedy is sleek and single-minded, comedy rumpled and hospitable to any idea or agency. Tragedy stares us out of countenance; comedy winks and leers and drools. Tragedy is all dressed up; comedy is always taking things off, mooning us. We find it inevitable that we associate tragedy with the high, comedy with the low. But what is at issue here is the nature of that inevitability. Why are we willing to conspire in a discourse that pays homage to tragic grandeur and reduces comedy to release, authorized license, periodic relief—like a sneeze or yawn or belch? By allowing this hierarchical discourse to flow through us, we add our bit of cement to the cultural edifice that sits on top of comedy, mashing it into the inferior opposite of tragedy, its silly little carnival. By cooperating in this move, we relieve orthodox and conservative power structures of any pressure that might be exercised against them. Comic relief relieves the status quo, in other words, contains the power of comedy.

Now some would have us turn the tables, release comedy by inverting the hierarchy, declaring comedy superior. But you and I know that such a move, though satisfactory to our moderator, would maintain unchallenged the assumptions which prop up the opposition in the first place. Look at it this way: comedy is not the opposite of tragedy, it is the *whole* story, the narrative which refuses to leave things out. Tragedy insists on a formal structure that is unified and coherent, formally balanced and elegantly tight. Only that which is coordinate is allowed to adorn the tragic body. With comedy, nothing is sacrificed, nothing lost; the discoordinate and the discontinuous are especially welcome. Tragedy protects itself by its linearity, its tight conclusiveness; comedy's generosity and ability never to end make it gloriously vulnerable. Pitting tragedy against comedy is running up algebra against recess, Allan Bloom against Roland Barthes, the University of Chicago against Duke.

Let me take the time I have left (and more) to illustrate how comedy can be used to unleash possibilities for new configurations of being. Its superiority to tragedy is not important; its radical difference from tragedy is important. We used to say that tragedy tells the story of death and comedy the story of life, but we need not think of life and death as opposites: who supposes that life is what death isn't? Just so, comedy rests on different premises; it fosters, we might say, a faith in inclusions, in finding ways not to form a story but to keep the story from acquiring a form, to keep it bulky, discontinuous, and self-perpetuating. Hamlet assumes that Horatio will live only to tell Hamlet's story and that it will be tough going for him to resist the lure of suicide. But Horatio actually has a great time of it and tells many stories besides Hamlet's. In fact, he gets Hamlet's story mixed up with lots of others—stories of misadventures and wrong bedrooms strayed into by mistake and feasting and carousing. Comedy tells what life is like after tragedy gets out of the way, how Horatio and Edgar and Kent and Albany and the Montagues and the Capulets and Cathy and Hareton and Ishmael actually live once the corpses are removed. Comedy includes everything—it opens itself up to whatever may come its way.

As such, comedy also exposes the fastidiousness of tragedy and the interests that are protected by tragedy's refinements. Tragedy's focus on the high and mighty keeps those things high and mighty, sustains the value systems propping up our most conventional thinking—tragedy asks us not to depart from that thinking; tragedy thus insists that we not think at all. Comedy does not shift the focus, you see, does not substitute the low for the high, though that is what some would have us believe. Comedy doesn't change the focus but gets rid of focus altogether, substituting a blur or an impossibly wide-angled lens. By doing so, it subverts the means tragedy and the political right have for gluing our allegiance to them: tragedy and the right flog us into paying attention, focussing, believing that certain things and ways of looking at things are *serious,* deserve our concern. What is really at stake is not what these things are, but our attitude toward them, our willingness to settle into solemnity. Comedy's politics, then, involve a disruption of the idealizing attitude, a mockery of the means by which we make things metaphysical.

I said earlier I would provide an example and I really didn't, so I'll try again. Asking what it was truly like for Horatio after young Hamlet's funeral is to disobey Hamlet's orders: Hamlet has already told us that we are not to ask. He has told us that (a) such questions are not within our power; besides (b) he has already made clear what it will be like for Horatio, which is (c) that he will have to absent himself from felicity—i.e., a tragic conclusion in order to (d) tell Hamlet's story all over again, as if we hadn't already had enough of it. That is, tragedy insists that there is only one story, that we must live within it because there is no other it to live within. For Hamlet and for all other tragic authorities, princes and others with power (like foremen and provosts), there is no asking about Horatio because Horatio's script has been set. We cannot ask about Horatio because we *are* Horatio, living within a tragic drama whose lines and attitudes have been prescribed. Above all, we must have the right attitude, the natural attitude, we must be serious, this is a serious business, it calls for serious-ness; after all, we are talking about death and nobility and sacrifice. What could be more serious? Who would not want to be serious? What other choice is there?

Comedy does not answer these questions. Comedy is not oppositional but different. Comedy exists in another realm, one that offers its own rewards and also a clearer view of the needs which are met when we agree to be serious and to honor nobility, sacrifice, and linear narratives. Let's take three examples: one from Alice in Wonderland, one from an Edward Lear limerick, and one from Miss Bates. That's a narrow range of reference, you'll say, but that's because you don't as yet have a proper view of the matter, which will come upon you when you absorb these examples. First, Miss Bates: "It's such a happiness when good friends get together, and they always do." Nothing in this statement is attendant on anything else; there is no causality, only community. That's the first lesson: tragedy insists on causality, which may seem comforting in that it offers some predictive power, but where does that predictive power get us? Tragedy's always predicting the same dreary things. Who'd you rather have plotting your future, Captain Ahab or Miss Bates? Enough said.

Second, Edward Lear:

> There was a young lady whose bonnet
> Came untied when the birds sat upon it,
> But she said "I don't care, all the birds of the air,
> Are welcome to sit on my bonnet."

Not only is this ecologically apt but it illustrates the happiness that comes when, like the young lady, one doesn't care, doesn't attend, is not serious. Imagine Hamlet saying to the ghost that he doesn't care, or Othello saying this to Iago. Then all the birds of the air would come sit on their bonnets, too. It is only because certain serious attitudes are adopted that certain consequences ensue and certain people and agencies keep their political power. Not caring is the greatest political weapon we have.

One last admirable example. In Wonderland, everyone at one point gets very wet because Alice has not shed her above-ground seriousness and has been crying a river. In order to dry off, the Dodo suggests a Caucus Race, a caucus being, as you know, a political meeting and the Dodo being, as you know, a comic figure of Dodgson himself, who stuttered and who jokingly called himself "Do-do-do-Dodgson." The author thus authors this political meeting, the cau-cus race. He begins by reading out the rules, the sort of rules Hamlet gives Horatio, only here they say that the race is to be run in a sort of a circle, the exact shape not mattering at all: everyone may start when he likes and leave off when he likes. Everyone proceeds to do just that, and though the race has no ending, after a bit, everyone starts doing something else, at which point the Dodo says, "Everybody has won and all must have prizes!"

When, in *Wuthering Heights,* Cathy tells Nelly a dream about being cast out of heaven, she says that'll do to explain what she means about her ghastly life—that is, about tragedy. Well, the Caucus Race will do to explain what I mean about comedy, about an alternate politics where there are no fateful dreams and no compulsions to pay serious attention, in fact, to pay anything. In comedy we don't get what we pay for; even better, we don't get what we deserve, which is lucky for all of us, our moderator most especially.

The Second Part
Poets And Propriety

6

Forgetting to Remember
Tennyson's Happy Losses

Remember we found a lonely spot
And after I learned to care a lot,
You promised that you'd forget me not,
But you forgot to remember.
    —Climactic lyrics to "Remember," an affecting song

My memory is the thing I forget with.   **—Anon**

They teach us to remember; why do they not teach
us to forget?   **—F. A. Durivage**

The time is close when you shall forget all things
and be by all forgotten.   **—Marcus Aurelius**

Yea, from the table of my memory I'll wipe away
all trivial fond records.   **—Hamlet**

And the best and the worst of this is
That neither is most to blame,
If you have forgotten my kisses
And I have forgotten your name.   **—Swinburne**

Illiterate him, I say, quite from your memory.
    —Mrs. Malaprop

I THINK MOST of us realize how poignantly the criticism we write is attached to the body which writes it, and not just metaphorically either. (My own body is something to behold.) A friend told me that the removal of some of her intestine not only altered her prose style but caused her to lose her faith in formalism. There's evidence for you. A full study of the corporeal situation (what sort of body you have and what you do with it) and its investment in literary theory is badly needed, but I am not the one to provide it. I do, however, wish to offer a suggestion on posture, sitting more exactly. I think we should sit to watch Tennyson and write on him from the worst seat in the house, the one least valued, least comfortable. I myself want the seat that has been kept warm by Harold Bloom and his antithetical criticism, the seat so far to the side of the back of the balcony that it's been uncontested, partly because one would as soon do battle with Hulk Hogan, of course, but also because it offers such a peculiar view. Since Bloom is firmly lodged there, I'll be satisfied with edging in on his left cheek, as it were, cuddling up to just one of his comments, one that will lead me to

MY THESIS

My thesis is that if memory really worked it would be of less than no use to us: it would kill us; or, if not us, it would kill our Muse; worse, it would kill all eros. What we need is *forgetting*; with that we can construct being, poetry, and eroticism. But all of that, while it is my thesis, does not pick up the Bloom comment which was providing the transition. What Bloom says refers to the poem "Mariana," and what he says about the poem is that Mariana "is herself a poetess" and that what she "is longing for is not her belated swain but a priority in poetic invention." Her "deliciously unhealthy poem" celebrates a "primal narcissism" so complete and so at one with Tennyson's own that there is no room or no need for anyone who cometh not: "What would she do with him, what mental space has she left for him?"[1]

Such brilliant commentary opens up possibilities so full and unhealthy that critics with bodies up for it (me) cannot resist. What if he did come? He couldn't get past the moat, and Mariana wouldn't let him in anyhow, Bloom says. Good. But she also wouldn't recognize him. She'd think he was a UPS man or a Jehovah's Witness. She couldn't remember him, even if there was a him to remember. Mariana's poem celebrates her misplacing him, moving from the slightly uneasy (or maybe titillating) "He cometh not" to the blissful "He will not come." As it is, she can fill up a world of black happiness—of old faces glimmering, old footsteps trodding, old voices calling, and a devilish sexy poplar—precisely out of his absence. Memory works wonderfully when it forgets, when it scours us free of any intrusive substance, any Others, so as to allow us to make our being and our erotic life out of the purity of the vacant.

That's probably clear enough, but nothing much is to be lost by repeating it. Tennyson's clever "Ancient Sage" speaks of "The Passion of the Past"[2] by which he has been haunted since boyhood, a passion packed with the allure of that which is "Lost and gone and lost and gone!" (l. 224). Let's say we construe that phrase—you with me here?—as signalling to us that the passion is for the lost and gone itself, for loss that is absolute. Thus loss is, first, a poetic subject and a personal fixation. Let's claim, too, that such loss becomes a structural necessity in the poetry, that the poems always need to evoke what is not there, that they, like Hardy's novels, depend almost entirely on the force of absence, the force of what is beyond recall. In Tennyson, though, things that matter are not only beyond recall but strangely empty, forgotten.

To get at these possibilities, then, we need to deconstruct the oppositions between loss and gain and then between forgetting and remembering, just to see where that lands us.[3] Well, to be candid, we know where that'll land us, as haters of deconstruction never tire of pointing out. What these splenetics, a curse on them all, fail to realize, though, is that it's the voyage that concerns us not the destination. We'll land in emptiness, sure enough, but the getting there—oh my! And even the emptiness can be made productive, can manufacture sexual excitement at least; and that's not to be sneezed at.

To illustrate in brief form, let's descend to a little evidence—not much— namely the point in "The Two Voices" where the dismal voice argues that any conception of beginnings or origins implies necessarily an ending: if you start, you finish (perish). The voice we are all rooting for somewhat alarmingly accepts that logic but suggests that through erasing memory we can sign up that same reasoning for our team: if beginnings and endings are so eternally wed; then no beginnings, no endings. "Yet how should I," we crow, "for certain hold,/ Because my memory is so cold,/ That I first was in human mold?" (ll. 340–42). We don't mean here that we were first monkeys but part of some general and formless life agency maybe, who knows?, one that does not proceed in linear developments but "cycles always round" (l. 348). Our continuous lives then are cycles forged by beings (me and you) who "Forget the dream that happens then,/ Until they fall in trance again" (ll. 537–38). With this possibility before us, brought up out of the sea of forgetting, we are allowed to proceed to the most beautiful of forms: "... if first I floated free,/ As naked essence, must I be/ Incompetent of memory" (373–75). Turn this around (why not?): making myself incompetent of memory, I become free-floating and naked (desirable) pure (bare) essence; there is no Other, no memory, nothing to remember or intrude on my being or my desire. I never started, hence, I never stop. Being continues without end precisely because there is no substance behind one, no memory; my self comes into being alone and majestic, naked and desirable, free to build its own images of desire out of the void—and to make poetry out of a memory that produces nothing, that has no wheels that grind. There is now nothing to gain or regain, to remember or forget.

The deconstructive tour that follows, then, takes us (off-season rates) to loss; then to forgetting; then to a whole host of exemplary instances of memory being shooed away, inverted, vacated; then to nightmarish negative examples of memory returning from the dead; then to objections to our thesis (a side-trip, extra fee charged); then to the erotics of it all; and finally to the abyss. Put your tray tables up.

HOW CAN I LOSE YOU; LET ME COUNT THE WAYS

A better line would have been, "'Tis better to have loved and lost/ Than never to have lost at all!" But Samuel Butler thought of it first, and I'm no plagiarist. Even Butler, who understood nearly as well as Tennyson the pleasures of *fort* and the horror of *da*, succumbed to the itch to provide specific (and peculiar) *reasons* for his preferences, as if the superiority of loss to gain were not self-evident. I will provide no reasons. You don't need them. If you did you would not be reading Tennyson, much less this essay. It's not that you are an experienced loser yourself; it's just that you need no one to tell you where the real kicks come from or that hide and seek was never played to *find*.

You're thinking you don't need me either to tell you how important loss is to Tennyson and to the pleasure we derive from him. After all, his contemporaries felt that, and even if they hadn't, T. S. Eliot did and memorably spotted Tennyson's "moods of anguish."[4] The Tennyson revival, such as it has been, was spearheaded by misery—Arthur J. Carr's influential "Tennyson as a Modern Poet" (1950) set his modernity in terms of frustration, melancholy, and loss.[5] We are unlikely any time soon to locate a robust can-do Tennyson or a knock-about comic Tennyson, in part because we have not had our fill of the dismals. This makes it difficult for anyone (me) writing on Tennyson either to depart from the lugubrious paradigm or to find original or compelling things to say within it. If I argue that Ulysses is running after losing, chasing all those sinking stars, I will attract no dissenters but no audience either. Citing lesser-known poems might help a little:

> Immeasurable sadness!
> And I know it as a poet,
> And I greet it, and I meet it,
> Immeasurable sadness!
> —1864 epigram; Ricks, p. 1227

But if I use them to make familiar points, why bother? The tolerance for redundancy, even among academics, has its limits.

The first step in finding something to say (and avoiding the embarrassment that descends when a whole group stands silent, drinks in hand, staring at ground, subject dying, dying, dying) is this: treat loss not as a subject Tennyson wrote about but as a state of being we wrap ourselves o'er (like weeds), a position we construct, seek out because we need it desperately. The usual line is that loss represents a deprivation,[6] something to be avoided if at all possible. Gain is made the clearly superior term, loss the bad dream. But who would value gain at all were it not for its thrilling capacities to invest us with glimpses of loss? Who invests resources but to bring home their vanishing; who buys but to raise the erotics of theft? Gain is parasitic on loss, the only positive term in the equation.

Loss must therefore be earned, courted, seduced. We read loss as the Tennysonian Muse, the real horror being that loss might be lost. But our Tennyson is an optimistic poet and spends little time on such fears, evoking with supreme confidence his own Romantic bird, not a nightingale but a darker raven, croaking to the spirit songs of blankness: "Oh sad **No More!** Oh sweet **No More!**/ Oh strange **No More!**" ("No More," ll. 1-2; Ricks, p. 161). Evoking these powerful *No Mores* as losses—sad, sweet, strange—Tennyson makes what is not there into a center, whether it be grounds of faith, Hallam, or the Queen of the May. Gain is unthinkable: the lotos-eaters will not regain their homeland, Tithonus his youth, or Mariana her lover. Gain or presence are the negative terms. Only in absence and in loss do we find substance. So when Tennyson brings into being what is not there, he actively erases substance, foregrounds the poetic act of will which empowers denial and distancing. In this way we see that, finally, it is not loss which is centered after all—we were wrong to say so. What is willed is an uncentered nonsubstance. Put it this way: both loss and gain conspire in protecting the idea of the Other, the something outside ourselves that can be misplaced or tripped over once again, *forted* or *daed*. The more blissful strong creation (and the fuller deconstruction) strips aside such protections and undoes any notion that there is anything out there, anything to lose or find, anything Other. There is only Tennyson, the self, the critic. There is only me. No wonder we so love the experience of reading Tennyson. No wonder you are loving this essay.

WHO CAN EVER FORGET . . . ?

And so it is with memory. Tennyson calls up the past obsessively in order to demonstrate how much he does not need it, does not remember it. It is evoked to reveal that it is not there; he works his mind backward to show that there is no backward. Tennyson has no antecedents, then, no origins. And we recall from "The Two Voices" that such a maneuver buys us eternal life: no starts, no endings. Tennyson, memoryless, has no behind, no limits in time or space. He is Vastness itself, immortal and boundariless. We, all of us, don't deny it, have a weak glimmering of this majesty and even try to grasp a form of it by pretending to be absentminded. Freeing ourselves from the demands of certain appointments and chores, we sneak in as much of this Vastness as we dare, which isn't much. We are, as Bloom says, pathetically weak poets, writing private little shamefaced (pornographic) notes of primary narcissism for ourselves by laying claim, now and then, and when the risks (an angry spouse, student, mortgage company) are not too great, to a faulty memory. But that's a long way from no memory at all, from a Being so complete as to need no controls, roots, or explanations. Tennyson is no petty pornographer but a major criminal; the pleasure we take through him is the pleasure of voyeurism and transference. We get to watch as he plays out for us the grand and enormously risky drama of forgetting—everything.

EVIDENCE (OPTIONAL READING)

What I have for you now is a thirty-five mile-long (judging from my notes) parade of examples, counting the drill teams and the Appaloosa horses. A welter of examples can, of course, always be produced to spiffen up any argument whatever; and we've surely had enough of "evidence" in our line of work. Evidence can be conjured up (I know this and so do you) to prove any point. I am sure this argument, for instance, could work nearly as well (far better) with any other poets (philosophers, politicians). Tennyson, however, is the subject of the moment; so here are some details of how memory gets shooed away and forgetting rewarded.

Tennyson starts his career by attacking memory, almost before he has any to attack. As early as age fifteen or thereabouts, he is puling about the miseries of remembering: "Memory! why, oh why,/ This fond heart consuming,/ Show me years gone by,/ When those hopes were blooming?" ("Memory [Memory! dear enchanter]," ll. 17–20; Ricks, p. 83). The idea here is (as you've likely caught, but just in case—) that memory terrorizes our later years by lobbing ironic grenades at us just when we are most vulnerable, contrasting earlier grand hopes with present paltriness: visions of "the brilliant courts of spring" are not welcome when we are hiding out in "age's frosty mansion." And it's not just a happy past that beglooms our maturity either. A mirror poem from the same adolescent period, "Remorse," makes it clear that memory is as nasty in its darker moods: "Oh! 'tis a fearful thing to glance/ Back on the gloom of mis-spent years;/ What shadowy forms of guilt advance,/ And fill me with a thousand fears!" (ll. 1–4; Ricks, p. 87). Either way, memory's got us.

Unless, of course, we can deactivate it or, better yet, get it to work for us by producing emptiness. These, we might say (and why not?), are the projects undertaken by Tennyson's major poems. A few examples will suffice (they'd better; I'm using all that are on my list). "Break, break, break" leads us through the dramatic process of evocation—"I would that my tongue could utter the thoughts that arise in me" (ll. 3–4)—to cancellation—"The tender grace of a day that is dead/ Will never come back to me" (ll. 15–16). What arises, then, is the grandeur of nothingness, the reassurance that memory can draw only from an empty well; and, more importantly, that it can continue to draw nothing whatever. The only thought that arises in him is that there are no thoughts to arise in him, nothing down there to dredge up. More brightly, "Will Waterproof's Lyrical Monologue" leads us dangerously close to a boozy nostalgia for the past, only to rescue us by telling us that the past is valuable only insofar as it is lost and gone, lost and gone: "But for my pleasant hour, 'tis gone;/ 'Tis gone and let it go" (ll. 181–2).

It's not that I have nothing but these nearly noncanonical poems to offer, no biggies. How's this? Both *Maud* and *In Memoriam* show us in detail how to cleanse the past of substance. Both actually create loss as a scouring agent. *Maud* is brought into being for the sole purpose of eliminating her, so that the narrator can get free of all precursors and all intrusive priorities: "And ah for the man to arise in me,/ That the man I am may cease to be" (X, ll. 396–97). Notice the clarity and purity of his demand: this is not remodeling but demolition. To accomplish this and to get to the new and "better" self he achieves at the end, the narrator must first saturate his mind with Maud, who is made to stand for all those forms and memories that threaten the narrator's primacy. Maud soaks up everything from the past, most notably the narrator's father and all patriarchal claims on identity. When she is butchered (a strong term, but it's best to be emphatic at points like these), the narrator has nothing whatever remaining, finding a fit emblem for his state not in madness or even the grave but in the empty shell, "Void of the little living will/ That made it stir upon the shore" (II, 1, ll. 62–63). He is now not on the shore but in the primal waters of being, formless and warm.

In Memoriam is even more ruthless and systematic in its stagings of forgetting. At first, Hallam's death is deeply threatening, as it removes the dead one into memory, an agency far more intrusive than material presence. Hallam threatens to take over the poet's will and his Being: he seems unable not to remember him, unable to Be outside of his dead friend. Tennyson is haunted by Hallam's hand, a weirdly detached claw, out to snatch and strangle the poet's psyche. What if he should open the door and there it would be, that horrible appendage from the grave: "a sudden hand" that would "strike" (XIV, l. 11)? Out of nowhere, as in a Vincent Price movie, comes the hand of the evil dead. But it's not out of nowhere, actually; it's out of memory, which the poet now proceeds, though it takes a while, to sterilize. He first questions the accuracy (hence importance) of Memory—"And was the day of my delight/ As pure and perfect as I say?" (XXIV, ll. 1–2). Memory, like Sorrow, has lying lips, telling him of a purity that he can actually find only outside of memory, in a purified Self. He finds his way there by forcing memory to turn itself inside out and empty its pockets. He can even employ Hallam to tell him to "Arise, and get thee forth" (LXXXV, l. 79), a witty way of getting expelled from a party one is dying to leave. Staying with the past, allowing memory to be occupied comes to seem to him a "crime" (LXXXV, l. 61), and he can be positively uncivil: "I will not shut me from my kind" (CXXX, l. 1). He gets to this point by celebrating the evacuation of his mind, especially in the lyrics (C-CIII) recording the move away from Somersby, an emblem of happy forgetting: "Unwatched, the garden bough shall sway.... And year by year our memory fades/ From all the circle of the hills"(CI, ll. 1, 23–24). The beautiful ambiguity of the last image allows for an absolute detachment of memory and place: Hallam has lost all claim on Tennyson's being. "What art thou then?" Tennyson asks with a taunting jocularity, "I cannot guess" (CXXX, l. 5). After all, what does it matter? He can grant Hallam "some diffusive power" (CXXX, l. 8), because Hallam has given up all real power and interior agency: he is now nothing more than diffusive murk, mere smog, and we in L. A. know smog doesn't really exist.

These are Tennyson's blueprints for a happy life, then, manuals on how to forget. Now and then he does also issue cautions in the form of horror poems, poems about the failure to smash Memory or the even more grisly nightmare of

Memory's Return. Princess Ida knows that there are voices that "haunt/ About the mouldered lodges of the Past/. . . fatal to men" and that it is therefore necessary to "cram our ears with wool/And so pace by" (IV, ll. 45–48). "Let the past be past" (IV, l. 58), she cries; let it be dead, not be at all. But allowing the past to be past does not make it not be. No one but she can forget, and she is dragged down by vicious memories: "Come down, O maid/. . . . The children call, and I/ Thy shepherd pipe" (VII, ll. 177, 202–3). Ancient pastoral monsters rise from the bottom like the Kraken and swallow her.

Worse, Enoch Arden, erased and blanked, manages to rewrite himself in Tennyson's most teasing and terrifying drama. Having cleared out of the way, washed himself out of Memory, Enoch rips free from the tomb, fingers all bloody stumps, and comes staggering back, "the dead man come to life" (l. 754). It's *Tales from the Crypt*, a replay of our darkest fear, that we can never have a Being undependent on some priority, that memory will always cancel our fondest claims. But Enoch, answering to our wish-fulfillment, seems to decide not to return after all, to agree on his own to annihilation, vowing "Not to tell her, never to let her know" (l. 794). Good boy! But he doesn't mean it; trusting him is like trusting Freddy Krueger, and we get the same rewards. He worms his way into memory by way of the hated Miriam Lane, who lives (alas) to tell his story and, we suppose, to arrange that funeral monstrousness, the most expensive on record, just to trap us further.

So, this way and that, backward and forward, in good times and bad, Tennyson plays out the one game he knows and knows better than any other game-master: lose the memory.

OBJECTIONS AND COUNTER-EXAMPLES

Arguments are always much more compelling and likelier to win admiration and affection for the arguer when all weaknesses are openly displayed. Just so, I will myself show you one poem, trivial but attributed to Tennyson, that some might construe as hospitable to Memory. There's only one, but I will not hide it. It's "Ode to Memory," published in 1830, a juvenile effort I see no reason to call trashy. After all, Tennyson's son said his father "considered this one of the best of his early and peculiarly concentrated Nature-poems" (Ricks, p. 210). If I understand correctly (I do) what is meant by "peculiarly concentrated Nature-poems," this is the only poem in that category, so we can understand Tennyson's comment as another instance of his sly ironic humor, a twitting of his none-too-clever son. Still, the comment is there in the *Memoir*, and I do not deny it. The poem itself is medium-sized (124 ll.) and seems actually to ask for Memory to keep itself fresh and to work on him; he pretends to believe it will strengthen, enliven, and that sort of thing. Now, if we look closely, we will see that the poem is actually telling memory to come only if it cannot come as Memory at all: "Come not as thou camest of late" (l. 8) and that, therefore, all the vigorous commands—"Come forth, I charge thee, arise"—are invitations to a Memory that does not exist. But this may seem like special pleading or something, so I will just invite those with the stomach for it to read the poem straight through and see what they think. What I think is that it's a wholly perfunctory exercise in Wordsworthian drivel, tracing connections between the child, memory, divinity, nature, and whatnot, connections that never did hold for Tennyson and that he regarded as inane. It's probably a parody poem, come to think of it; but you are welcome to make up your own mind, feel free.

SEXUAL PLEASURE

I know very well that some of you have been reading along only so as to get to this part, which is fine by me. It is undeniable (trust me) that Tennyson's assault on Memory is conducted for reasons that are as deeply erotic as they are ontological, actually more. Desire feeds on desire, on pure possibility and not constrained materiality: emptiness is bliss. Thus, a memory capable of sending up any image, playing any drama, offering any part is one uncorrupted, vacated. What in Tennyson is deserted is always unclothed, available for *jouissance,* as we say. Note the play in "The Deserted House":

> Close the doors, the shutters close
> Or through the windows we shall see
> The nakedness and vacancy
> Of the dark deserted house.
> —ll. 9–12

Pretending to be shocked by what draws him, he asks that we screen what we are in fact peeking at, that we take our pleasure at the same time we play at shunning it. From the bushes we look in at the fully exposed, naked luxuriance of emptiness.

More elaborate and thus worthy of extended quotation are the exquisite and prolonged delights offered by "Memory [Ay me]." Here the "Blessed, cursed Memory" (l. 5) sends forth, in nonoperation, "subtle shafts of pierceant flame" (l. 4). I haven't a precise idea of what "pierceant" means, but eroticism is often hazy and gauzed-over, so the intensity of the line is actually heightened. Against this joy, Tennyson plays what I believe to be (and I should know) his most elaborate extended simile. Since it is extended indeed and also somewhat indecent, I will explain it before quoting it, since there's a chance you will become distracted in reading it. Tennyson speaks here of the only eroticism offered by memory, which is an unsatisfying, unwilled excitement much like that of, shall we say, nocturnal emissions? And who wants that sort of thing, over and done with, caused by some external agency, finally empty and frustrating? In Tennyson's simile, we have a snake (get it?) so locked into Memory that it cannot detach its sexual desires from the material agency of the sight or sound (smell too, we can bet) of a buffalo, the slightest hint of which sends the snake into some kind of unwelcome and ugly dry heaving against a tree, all very disgusting, even to friends of masturbation. You probably do not believe that Tennyson wrote of such things, so I'll quote at length, offering only the further (clinching) comment that Sir Charles Tennyson (Ricks, p. 262) was so upset by the pornographic nature of all this that he tried to disown it, calling it a "fragment" (which it isn't) and saying it was "very hastily written" (was it? so what?). I won't keep you waiting any longer:

> Why in visions of the night
> Am I shaken with delight
> Like a lark at dawn of day?
> As a hungry serpent coiled
> Round a palm tree in the wild,
> When his baked jaws are bare
> Burning in the burning air,
> And his corky tongue is black
> With the raging famine-crack,
> If perchance afar he sees
> Winding up among the trees,
> Lordly-headed buffaloes,
> Or but hears their distant lows,
> With the fierce remembrance drunk
> He crushes all the stalwart trunk
> Round which his fainting folds are prest,
> With delirium-causing throes
> Of anticipated zest.
> —ll. 32–49

That's what "remembrance" does for you. On the other side of the coin, look at what comes to the lotos-eaters in the way of passion when they agree to forget. Enough said.

NOTHING WILL COME OF NOTHING

A distrust of all binaries, not just the one formed by the play of forgetting and remembering, runs deep in Tennyson. One thinks (do it for me now!) of all the poems on mingling, of "Song [Every day hath its night]": "All is change, woe or weal;/ Joy is Sorrow's brother;/ Grief and gladness steal/ Symbols of each other" (ll. 23–26). Or of the distrust of stable distinctions that figures so importantly in *In Memoriam*: "The very source and font of Day/ Is dashed with wandering isles of night" (XXIV, ll. 3–4). Or of the blunt epigram from 1864:

> The cursed will be blest,
> And the blest will be cursed,
> And great things turn into small things;
> And the worst is the best
> And the best is the worst,
> And topsy-turvy go all things.
> —Ricks, p. 1228

And not just topsy-turvy either. The deconstruction of the forget-remember binary, in particular, does not rest with reversing the hierarchy, throwing parties for forgetting, but proceeds to examine the cooperative enterprise supporting the binary in the first place and to subvert the material protected by memory, working or not. And what is protected (as I guess I have already given away) is the material, substance itself. One forgets or remembers *something*; Tennyson drives us to a land where there is no something, where what we find is so much nothing that there may be no *we* to experience it.

Losing the material, then, evacuates being of threats, precursors, but runs the courageous risk of evaporating it altogether. What is being without origins, a desire without memory? One answer is silence:

> No more? A monster, then, a dream,
> A discord.
> —In Memoriam, LVI, ll. 21–22

Or:

> Swallowed in Vastness, lost in Silence . . .
> What but a murmur of gnats in the gloom, or a moment's anger of bees in their hive?
> —"Vastness," ll. 34–35

Tennyson does not flinch from the possibility that a rejection of definition for the self could land one where there wasn't any "one," in a self-less abyss.

But deconstruction doesn't really land one anywhere; it's a cruise, not a device for reaching destinations. Rather than substituting one *form* of being for another, the deconstruction of memory's powers provides joy in the doing, a way to glimpse rather than grasp further possibilities of being and making, of exciting and being excited. Take "The Lotos-Eaters," a poem which gives us an experience in being suspended, in trying to decide, in floating between one spot and another. The lotos-land might be a ghastly place were we to set up housekeeping there, but we never actually do that, we just glide in that direction. We are allowed to desire that state, to open ourselves up to the possibility of nothingness, enticing ourselves with the glories of falling and ripening and ceasing, of moving toward that state of *seeming* wherein it would be rich to die. As we move and keep moving, never resting and never dying but distancing ourselves more and more from the pounding waves, from the familiar, from the traps of memory, we discover within ourselves voices, we hear the "music" that our own hearts make (l. 36) and finally, at long last, fly close to the heaven of emptiness where we may "harken what the inner spirit sings" (l. 67). We waltz toward poetry, swaying always within desire. The only mistake, and it is a fatal one, is to stop, to stop and remember.

7

Tennyson, Hallam's Corpse, Milton's Murder, and Poetic Exhibitionism

with Buck McMullen

LEGEND, THAT BEST of authorities, tells us that Tennyson hated to be seen. Once, he ran from a herd of sheep that his poor eyesight construed as a mob of day-trippers come over to the Isle of Wight to gaze at him. Exhibitionists, on the other hand, love to be seen; without a gaze they wither and die. They are people like P.T. Barnum, Sally Rand, Oscar Wilde—not like Tennyson. It's ridiculous to think of Tennyson as an exhibitionist, but that doesn't bother us. It's ridiculous to think about exhibitionism at all. Exhibitionism is funny, maybe sad, too, and certainly threatening. One look at any MLA convention or faculty meeting or classroom (yours, not ours) will tell you that we aren't so far beyond the "look-at-me-ma" stage. Exhibitionism is ridiculous, available to ridicule, precisely because it lies so deep in most of us. We laugh to avoid confronting the fact that ma isn't looking, isn't even interested, has gone away, was never there. Exhibitionism asserts that there is an origin. Thus, in its own way, exhibitionism is a merry, hopeful act, defying the facts, denying all evidence of absence. Floating free on the center-ring trapeze, we hang gracefully by one leg, and we are not ignored. The exhibitionist, more acrobatic than regressive, doesn't go off on a sad hunt for origins but loudly asserts and thereby seeks to construct that origin. I exhibit, therefore I am.

Such prancing constitutes a very fragile and daring sort of fictionalizing, of course, but where would we be without such strip-tease-like novel writing? We would not be at all. As George Eliot notes at the beginning of *Daniel Deronda,* "Men can do nothing without the make-believe of a beginning.... No retrospect will take us to the true beginning; and whether our prologue be in heaven or on earth, it is but a fraction of that all-presupposing fact with which our story sets out."[1] Like this passage and like Tennyson's own beginning in *In Memoriam,* our starting point is a "make-believe," a huge whopper we will treat as an "all-presupposing fact."

Our fiction goes like this: three weeks after the death of Arthur Henry Hallam, and a mere five days after news of the death had been received, Tennyson had begun to write the poems that would become *In Memoriam A. H. H.* Section IX, the earliest dated, apparently was composed on or by October 6, 1833. Sections XVII and XVIII were also composed very early for sure. But we want more than these three lyrics, so we'll assert, not really unconventionally,[2] that sections IX through XIX belong to this early phase, as a lot. This cluster has an important function: it clears a space, lays a claim for the right to poetic utterance, makes the entire poem possible. Our "all-presupposing fact," then, is that these lyrics, describing the imagined progress of the ship bearing Hallam's body from Trieste to England, are crucial to fabricating an origin, a location for the speaker.

At the time these poems were being written or imagined, word of Hallam's death was known to Tennyson, but Hallam's body ("my lost Arthur's loved remains") was being transported by ship to its ultimate burial at Clevedon. Hallam was doubly absent from Tennyson: from life, and from the fixed location of an earthly grave. Although these first poems are concerned with Hallam's absence in spirit, they are even more preoccupied with the transit of his body. That body, as we shall see, is terribly important.

But we might well wonder why we are drawn through extended and repeated fantasies of shipwreck, drowning, and floating corpses. After all, Hallam's death had nothing to do with the sea, except for the fact that the body was shipped back to England by boat. Still, one might as easily imagine other mishaps: fire, rat-attack, or various land disasters; the body could have been mislaid, mistakenly swapped for another, snatched and sold for scientific research. So, why all this about water? Why this glaring irrelevance?

The irrelevance is, in a way, the point. Tennyson, we might say, did not manufacture these outlandish fantasies about sea disasters out of an anxiety to get Hallam secured at Clevedon. As a matter of fact, he didn't bother to visit the grave for years and carelessly mistook its location in section XVIII. The fantastic poetic energy expended here proclaims the real origin of the poem and of himself. First, Tennyson must murder Milton, and Hallam's corpse gives him just the weapon he needs.

To begin to express grief elegiacally is no easy task. As death and grief are not new to the world, Tennyson knows, neither is the elegy. Looming behind him, inevitably impressing their lambent shadows on his page, are many prior elegies from a tradition of thousands of years. The darkest antecedent shadow is that cast by the colossus of English elegies, Milton's *Lycidas*, which nearly eclipses Tennyson's page.[3] *Lycidas* is *the* English elegy about a deceased Cambridge schoolfellow poet, and it is already there, written, before Tennyson even takes up his pen. As Edward Fitzgerald wrote to W. B. Donne, "A.T. has near a volume of poems—elegiac—in memory of Arthur Hallam. Don't you think the world wants other notes than elegiac now? *Lycidas* is the utmost length an elegiac should reach."[4] *Lycidas* is already standing where *In Memoriam* wants to be; Milton is the exhibitionist Tennyson needs to displace.

It is interesting that Hallam himself seems to have had some uncanny premonition of the battle his death would provoke. He wrote to Tennyson a few months before his death saying that the Cambridge Union was debating the question: "Tennyson or Milton: which the greater poet?" Robert Bernard Martin, who reports this, notes that the Union minutes are mum as to any such debate, and he suggests that Hallam's report was probably a fabrication invented to "console Tennyson" for the hostile reviews his poems were receiving. Martin calls Hallam's letter "a kindly fiction."[5] Doubtless so, but nevertheless one wonders how Tennyson regarded the notion of such a competition, the ultimate matchup with the champion of poetic showmen.

In any case, the fight that had been brewing between Tennyson and Milton was not long delayed; and we can hardly understand its progress without attending to our premier analyst of poetic pugilism, Harold Bloom.[6] Bloom's brilliant recounting of the ways in which a poet struggles with the shadow of a precursor and the methods of misprision by which an ephebe attempts to constitute a poetic identity are generally familiar by now, and we gingerly adopt the basic model. Our own swerve from Bloom comes with the proposition that something as audacious as exhibitionism can be a subversive response to influence. In addition, we have a different view of language. For Bloom, stylistic choices made by the ephebe poet are matters of indifference in the struggle with the precursor's poem; they are "just something that happens."[7]

Bloom argues that "all criticisms that call themselves primary vacillate between tautology—in which the poem is and means itself—and reduction—in which the poem means something that is not itself a poem. Antithetical criticism must begin by denying both tautology and reduction, a denial best delivered by the assertion that the meaning of a poem can only be a poem, but *another poem—A poem not itself*" (*Anxiety*, p. 70). These distinctions of primary (and nonprimary) and tautology and reduction will be avoided here by eliding Bloom's central term "meaning." Instead of discussing meaning and its location, we will concentrate on how certain verbal elements of *In Memoriam* came into being within a context of repression induced by an anxiety of influence. We propose to reread Bloom, imposing upon his already superimposed structure of the Freudian "family romance" another Freudian structure, that of voyeurism-exhibitionism. Jacques Lacan, in his rereading of Freud, indicates that voyeuristic-exhibitionistic behavior may be understood not only as visual phenomena but as textual ones. The truth value of the Freudian-Lacanian psychology is not at issue here; we adopt it for its focusing power. By this model, "Poetic exhibitionism" becomes a strategy that Tennyson can and does employ to counter the inhibiting pressure of *Lycidas* and the elegiac tradition generally. Such exhibitionism, further, has stylistic consequences in the production of the trope of apostrophe, evident throughout the poem but particularly emphatic in our group, sections IX through XIX.

Simply stated—and the poems state this simply—Tennyson's greatest anxiety in these early lyrics is that the ship bearing Hallam's body will sink. Should this happen, and Hallam's body be lost at sea, the small marginal space left to Tennyson by the long tradition of elegy will be dangerously reduced, subsumed into the then-too-close similarities between his situation as Hallam's elegist and that of Milton as the elegist of the drowned and bodily absent Edward King. Thus, Tennyson's preoccupation in these early poems with the imagined progress of the "fair ship."

Here Tennyson employs, cagily and tentatively, several strategies to evade Milton's influence. He focuses on Hallam's body, both as the corpse now being borne over the seas and as its remembered, animated form, insisting on a rich particularity of the physical to contrast to Milton's abstracting and etherealizing of King. Hallam's body is to be buried on land, a point Tennyson reiterates and distinguishes as elegiacally preferable to the comfortless loss of a body at sea. A land burial and a real cadaver, he arrogantly suggests to Milton, are necessary to the poem: without them, the poet is in cloud-cuckoo-land. Further, just as Milton o'erleaped the bounds presented to him by the factual matter of King's death through imagining a terrestrial funeral for him in the famous flower passages in *Lycidas* (which Milton describes as a "false surmise" that will "interpose a little ease"[8]), Tennyson, directly inverting the sense of Milton's lines, describes his own false surmise in section X, calling it "idle dreams" to imagine that

Hallam's ship is lost and that the body, gulfed "fathom deep in brine;/ And hands so often clasp'd in mine,/ Should toss with tangle and with shells."[9] Tennyson exposes Milton's attempt to manufacture artificially the natural ingredients he is lacking: a body and a grave.

This is not, however, merely an inversion of Milton's false surmise. Slyly, the contrast also implies that Tennyson is more courageous than his precursor, in that Milton's false surmise brings ease, whereas Tennyson's idle dreams speak of the courage to face the deeply feared loss of Hallam's body. Tennyson's charge is that Milton is faking it. Without a body, a burial, a grave, he has no real poem at all. Tennyson enters this anxious Oedipal wrestling match with an elaborately unconcealed weapon, Hallam's corpse, and he batters Milton to death with it.

No poetic or neurotic strategy can actually be this simple, of course, and Tennyson masks his anxiety with a variety of screen devices, chief among them the pose of humility. Tennyson seems to have toyed with the strategy of hiding from Milton entirely by claiming he was working in a different mode or genre; he seems to have considered dodging his poetic genealogy. His muting of the trappings of pastoral and piscatorial elegy can be seen as evasions of the central semantic and formal space occupied by the tradition. Similarly, the long period of composition and the avowal that he was not *intending* to write an elegy for Hallam and, in fact, was surprised one day to find that all those little scribblings he'd been squirreling away just happened to arrange themselves into—not an elegy, exactly, but—"Fragments of an Elegy," can be viewed as Tennyson's way of avoiding the centrality of Milton and the tradition.

Unable to run and hide, however, Tennyson shrewdly turned all this modesty into weaponry. He revised his private title from the self-deprecating "Fragments" to the grandiose "The Way of the Soul," and issued the poem (in an anonymity that fooled no one and acted to accentuate the importance of his authorship) under a title that merely played at deflecting the focus from the actual exhibitionistic center: In Memoriam A. H. H. *Obit MDCCCXXXIII.*[10] All this skittering around humility amounts, finally, not to modesty or an evasion of Milton, or an admission of belatedness, but to a defiant claim to originality, to origins. There is only one subject at which to gaze—Tennyson—and the genre of elegy is subsumed in him. His is the only authentic lament for the dead, the only poem in the *true* tradition.

In specific terms, the extended apostrophe to the "fair ship" in the first poem implies that Tennyson is possessed of mighty poetic powers, mightier, in fact, than his precursor's. Apostrophe is employed as a direct response to the anxiety of influence and as a strategy for deposing the precursor. Though he does not possess the puissance to return Hallam to life (as if that were desired), Tennyson does have the power to invoke the ship, to speak to it, and, by speaking to it, bring it over the water and safely to port: "and my prayer/ Was as the whisper of an air/ To breathe thee over lonely seas" (XVIII, ll. 2-4). This, of course, like malt, does more than Milton can. It is not everything, Tennyson allows—it won't restore Hallam (if, again, that's what we want, which, it turns out, it isn't)—but it's something:

> 'Tis well; 'tis something; we may stand
> Where he in English earth is laid,
> And from his ashes may be made
> The violet of his native land.
> —XVIII, ll. 1–4

And this is better than the merely imagined violet strewn on the imagined site of Lycidas' interment. Tennyson can create ships, talk to them, and the ships obey. He commands the "unhappy bark" carrying Hallam to "Spread thy full wings, and waft him o'er" (IX, l. 4), and lo!, the bark does just that. Unlike Milton, who can only abuse "that fatal and perfidious Bark" (l. 100) which sunk with King aboard, Tennyson's poetic breath can keep Hallam's bark afloat, get him back to Clevedon churchyard (or somewhere in the vicinity, anyhow), bury him securely, and then get on to the real business of the poem: the display of the awe-inspiring beauty of the poet. To accomplish this, Tennyson shifts the focus of these early poems of *In Memoriam* from the hollowness being dictated by the irremedial fact of Hallam's death and by the fact that Milton has already written the poem. The use of apostrophe helps hide the emptiness by flashing before us first the ship, then the corpse, then the poet.

Tennyson's quick-traveling here is, however, impelled by Milton's map. Milton had, after all, executed a brilliant exhibitionistic maneuver in *Lycidas*, displacing King as poetic object and making room for himself. Tennyson is forced to supersede such brilliance, and he does so with a sleight-of-hand that exposes and criticizes Milton's strategy while simultaneously adopting it. Behind the scenes, effected so that we will not notice, Tennyson makes both Hallam and Milton disappear by using many of Milton's own tricks.

Milton's presto-chango (King into Milton) is, from an exhibitionist's point of view, a masterpiece of cunning and tact. After announcing his subject at the opening of the poem, Milton invokes the Muses not, as we might expect, on behalf of Lycidas, but for himself: "So may some gentle Muse/ With lucky words favor my destin'd urn,/ And as he passes turn,/ And bid fair peace be to my sable shroud" (ll. 19-22). After imagining his own elegy, Milton proceeds to sing that elegy, or, more accurately, that paean to himself. First, however, he joins his voice and being with those of Lycidas: "For we were nurst upon the self-same hill" (l. 23). The next verse paragraph (ll. 25-36) batters us with these unifying plurals: "Together both," "we," "both together," and "our," culminating in a poetic coalescence: "And old *Damaetas* lov'd to hear our song" (l. 36). It has become a duet, two joined inseparably into one. Take one part away and there is nothing left: the act collapses and there is no song.

But, in fact, there is quite a song, proceeding because of and not in spite of this fracturing. Milton disengages himself artfully from the loss, first by insisting on its finality—"Now thou art gone, and never must return!" (l. 38)—and then by transferring the mourning activity from himself to nature: "Thee Shepherd, thee the Woods, and desert Caves,/ With wild Thyme and the gadding Vine o'ergrown,/ And all their echoes mourn" (ll. 39-41). The blight is on nature, associated with the speaker only through the remote figure of a simile: "As killing as the Canker to the Rose.... Such, *Lycidas*, thy loss to Shepherd's ear" (ll. 45, 49). The first singing "shepherd," King (l. 39), has been replaced by another of the same name, Milton (l. 49); and the act goes on as a solo. But Tennyson, while adopting Milton's tactic, affects the stance that Milton's pathetically fallacious displacement of grief onto a mourning nature is callous and insincere posturing. In *The Life of Milton*, Samuel Johnson had railed against the dubious sincerity of the pastoral trappings of *Lycidas*: "We know that they never drove a field, and that they had no flocks to batten.... He who thus grieves will excite no sympathy; he who thus praises will confer no honour."[11]

To Tennyson as well, the grief that is expressed in figures of cankered roses, frosted flowers, inelegant taint-worms, and hazel copses that sympathetically fan their leaves in tune with rural ditties is a hopelessly inferior, and unexciting, form of exhibitionism that he will replace with a superior one. Rather than distance nature to a set of feeble pastoral clichés, Tennyson absorbs nature. In sections XVIII and XIX Tennyson reverses Milton's subtle distancing techniques, calling attention to what he wants us to regard as his disdain for magic, his almost outrageous refusal to distance himself from Hallam's body or from a nature willing enough to mourn in both poets. He needs to open the curtain hiding Milton's magic, exposing its shoddy, egocentric, and callous mechanics, meanwhile accomplishing the same ends. With true exhibitionistic flair, Tennyson will cause two bodies to vanish, not just one. Section XIX is an extended and pointed identification of Tennyson's grief with nature, in particular, with the tidal movement controlling the river Wye. There are no similes, no approximating, hands-off *as* or *like* counters to play with. Section XIX is preoccupied with the sound and silence of nature, which Tennyson appropriates as his own:

> The salt sea-water passes by,
> And *hushes* half the *babbling* Wye,
> And makes a *silence* in the hills.
> The Wye is *hushed* nor moved along,
> And *hushed* my deepest grief of all,
> When filled with tears that cannot fall,
> I brim with sorrow drowning *song*.
> —XIX, ll. 6–12; emphasis added

To proclaim that this is not mere hackneyed diction, Tennyson appends the note: "Taken from my own observation—the rapids of the Wye are stilled by the incoming sea." His nature, unlike Milton's, is not based on poetic convention but empirical fact.

Nor does he so unceremoniously as Milton shove the corpse out of the way. He takes possession of the body, imagining himself in an embrace that is, as it turns out, aiming to get much more than it gives:

> Ah yet, even yet, if this might be,
> I, falling on his faithful heart,
> Would breathing through his lips impart
> The life that almost dies in me.
> —XVIII, ll. 13–16

This CPR, however, revives not Hallam but Tennyson, who rebounds from this "almost death," within the space of a line, with a will "That dies not, but endures with pain," and "slowly" (lots of, sections still to come!) "forms the firmer mind," resolving to treasure "the look it cannot find,/ The words that are not heard again." We haven't long to wait for a replacement speaker. Section XIX begins, misleadingly enough, with a focus on Hallam ("the darkened heart"), introduced by way of water (the Danube, the Severn, and the Wye). But this very water, so threatening to Milton, Edward King, and Hallam, is shrewdly put to use by Tennyson; and it allows him, at the end of XIX, to come on stage: "And I can speak a little then." Milton and Hallam have disappeared and the hollowness left by their absence is now filled up. There are words on which to gaze and the promise of many more to come. We are invited to look our fill.

In his 1915 "Instincts and Their Vicissitudes," written immediately prior to the essay "Repression," Freud examines repression through one of its most puzzling effects, the "reversal of an instinct into its opposite."[12] Freud deals with such reversals in reference to sadism/masochism and scopophilia (voyeurism)/exhibitionism. In both cases, the fundamental instinct originates within the subject: in sadism, as the impulse to master another through violence; in voyeurism, to gain mastery through vision. Both maneuvers seek to control by objectifying, turning the other into literal object.

But how does the primary impulse toward giving pain shift to a pleasure in receiving it? Why does the looker shift to wanting to be seen? In both cases, under pressure from what Freud calls "self-preservative instincts" (or ego-instincts), this secondary impulse may displace the sexual instinct (sadism or voyeurism). In the case of voyeurism, this leads to an abandoning of "the object and a turning of the . . . instinct toward a part of the subject's own body; with this, a transformation to passivity and setting up of a new aim—that of being looked at" ("Instincts," 129). In other words, the fear of losing the object, the risk of investing so much of one's being in another-as-object, may lead the originally active subject to transform himself into passive object. The sadist throws aside the whip and kneels at the block; the Peeping Tom comes out from behind the bushes and takes his place at the window.

In the activity of what might be called "ordinary seeing," shifts between subject and object occur continually, for seeing is not just a single position but a process of movement in which the subject, as part of the process of seeing, possesses the object by relinquishing visual mastery, by momentarily *becoming* the object. In "normal" seeing this activity, in order to register in our understanding, necessitates an ongoing repression of the position we were in a moment before and an elevation of the substituted position we are in now. It is as though the conscious mind will only tolerate or recognize one position or the other. So, at any moment, because one position or the other is being repressed, there is consciousness only of looking *or* of being looked at.

There are, however, extremes, deviations from "normal" seeing, which Freud labels the "perversions" of voyeurism and exhibitionism. These extremes resist the ongoing, alternating repression necessitated by "giving up" the object of vision, and refuse to acknowledge the metaphoric system of shifts by which consciousness of one position or the other is repressed. Voyeurism is, thus, a rigid insistence on maintaining the first position—visual mastery of an object—and a refusal to be seen as an object, thus negating the temporary loss of self (or subject) demanded by the system of substitution that occurs in normal seeing. In exhibitionism, the lost object-position is occupied by the former subject, with the illusion of permanence; the threat of object loss, therefore, is obviated by positioning the former subject as the occupant of the vacant position. If I become the object, once and for all, there is no danger of it getting up and walking off. I also, easily and safely, guarantee my identity.

Both of these extreme responses to the lost object-position (voyeurism and exhibitionism) have clear and unhappy behavioral consequences. Voyeurism not only concentrates on the position of seeing, but also on avoiding the opposite position, being seen. Voyeurism requires seeing from a position of concealment, because the voyeur fears that being seen by another would overturn the carefully manipulated and protected power equation and would make the voyeur the object of the new viewer's mastering vision. The exhibitionist, by occupying the vacant object-position, is always to be looked at and insists on not looking—to be seen but never to see. The exhibitionist is as blind as the voyeur is invisible. To see or to be shown *something* would squeeze the exhibitionist out of the object-position he has moved into precisely because he feared there was no permanent object for him. Forced back, willy nilly, into the subject-position, the exhibitionist might locate in his vision not so much a superior rival (though that would be no treat) but his greatest fear: nothing at all. The exhibitionist, we may say, fears that if he does not occupy the object-position, nothing or no one else will; and his insistence on not being a seeing subject is an avoidance of the feared role of being a subject whose vision finds no object, only the negation of absence.

Like most of Freud's explanations, this one is elegant, tragically engaging, and satisfying. For all that, it has an explanatory exhibitionism about it, a stability and a claim to permanence characteristic of the usurpation of the object-position he discusses. Implicit in the exhibitionistic display, Freud's included, is a role and a fixed set of responses for the audience: admiration amounting to awe, intense desire. Ridicule, cold disdain, rude questioning are strictly forbidden.

But Lacan and his followers deliberately pose such irreverent questions in order to destabilize the Freudian structure. To Lacan, consciousness itself is a part of an ongoing process of marking and repressing differences, a process that was seen by Saussure as the basis of signification. Consciousness, then, is the manifest level of a discourse of repression and substitution, and can no longer claim the privileged status accorded to it by Freudian ego psychology. Robert Con Davis explains this reorganization imposed by Lacan on Freud's theory of seeing: "Lacan has shown that seeing's true aim cannot be visual in any immediate sense: seeing is but a function in a largely unconscious discourse that can be glimpsed in what Lacan calls (extending Freud's discussion), the 'Gaze'—the functioning of the whole system of shifts. . . . The Gaze . . . encompasses the voyeuristic wish not to be seen, and the exhibitionistic wish not to be shown, and the relationship of these 'perversions' (as Freud calls them) points up rather directly the positionality of visual experience *as a text*."[13] Thus to Lacan any conscious text (written or otherwise) is but a part of a textual system of reciprocity and substitution—discourse—between conscious production and unconscious desire.

What Lacan has done, then, is not only to decenter and deprivilege the surface or manifest text but also to call to our attention the existence of an unconscious text, which is also decentered and marked by difference, and that must be simultaneously inscribed within the inscription of the conscious text. For Lacan the words of the surface text are simply the conscious extrusion of signifiers that stand in metaphorically for signifiers from another chain. Though this manifest text presents the illusion of solid centrality, the discourse "is always centered elsewhere in an 'Other' desire. If we look closely at the manifest text, we see something else, a hollowness that inhabits the text—a mere inscription— through and through" (Davis, p. 992).

Tennyson has a multiple difficulty. First, he seems to have no subject; worse, Milton is there. Milton always presented himself to Tennyson as a problem, as a pest that refused to go away. Tennyson tried throughout his career a good many escape strategies, ranging from solemn admiration (freezing Milton into a conventional ministerial irrelevance) to light mockery. He did, it is true, speak in respectful tones of "Milton's Latinisms, and delicate play with words," of the terror he could evoke with his "vague hell," and, more to our purpose, of his *Lycidas* as "a test of any reader's poetic instinct."[14] More common, though, are Tennyson's displays (maybe suspicious displays) of nonchalant indifference.

Tennyson somehow is not very convincing as a Whitman figure, parading around in a stained undershirt in order to demonstrate his disregard for decorum. Tennyson's attempts to use the narrow range of conventional reverence for Milton in order to make some jokes may seem strained. In "Milton's Mulberry," he turns the old sage into a talking tree with nothing better to do than be peevish about undergraduates. But in such incarnations, Milton is merely the vehicle for some anti-intellectual yucks; his presence is so incidental that its inappropriateness calls attention to itself (like Mother Theresa doing a cameo bit in a Mel Brooks movie). Tennyson would have us believe that Milton's presence certainly does not make him nervous; sometimes Tennyson even pretends that he finds it useful, for such things as the experiment in classical form he calls "Milton: Alcaics." The speaker in that poem adopts a pose of mock humility, contrasting the Titanic, organ-voiced Milton with his own tame preference for murmuring bowers. The poem is a gag, taking the form of what Freud called humor: a witty exaggeration of our deepest fears in the hopes of exorcising them. Here,

Tennyson is sticking out his tongue at the anxiety of influence by writing a burlesque, creating an absurd image of poets trying to squeeze out between the toes of the past giants. To all this might be added Tennyson's real-life imitations of Milton's Satan as a toad (a big hit at parties). Again, Milton is used as the basis for raucous, perhaps transparently defensive jokes.

The same uneasy, strutting tone and attitude are apparent in Tennyson's direct comments on Milton printed at the end of Hallam Tennyson's *Memoir* as "My father's talk on Milton's 'Paradise Lost' to me when a boy at Marlborough" (II, 518-23). The remarks appear studied in their casualness, with no sense whatever of apprehension, mystery, or reverence. Tennyson's tone seems consistently familiar, even jovial: "What an imagination the old man had!" His criticisms are bold and sometimes recklessly sweeping: "Certainly Milton's physics and metaphysics are not strong."

This is not to say that Tennyson did not often use Milton, but such direct allusions never seem to be very consequential.[15] And besides, Tennyson's habit of evoking the Miltonic presence in poem after poem seems mainly to demonstrate its considerable irrelevance.[16] In *The Princess*, for instance, he disrespectfully inverts Milton's *Paradise* epics and parodies the notion of the fortunate fall. Princess Ida challenges the heavenly community and, by the strength of her defiant will, erects a rival. This act disrupts the natural order (causing women to attack men and men to dress as women), and provokes what appears to be the comic equivalent of the fall of men and angels: antipathy between the sexes and mock war. But Ida is rescued, much against her will, and pulled back into Eden (or heaven, here much the same), where she evokes not awe but laughter, and achieves not damnation but forgiveness. A little peevish about the whole thing, even at the end, the Princess is asked to see her tragic isolation simply as a comic mistake. Her fall is presented as an ascent to the lonely mountaintop; she descends to the Edenic valley. One falls upward here; ascends down. It is the fall that seems unnatural and absurdly strenuous. Eden is Ida's natural state, so natural that she cannot escape, even if she tries with all her might. So, drawn by sex and love, she returns home. It is as if Satan and his band were pulled upward, kicking and complaining all the way. Ida is both a Satan who is not allowed to rebel and an Eve who is not allowed to fall.[17]

More generally, Tennyson's early attitude tilts precariously toward a bullying bravado. A learned and habitually allusive poet, Tennyson knew much better than to make naïve claims for originality.[18] He could not prove that Milton never wrote, so he anxiously shifted from one foot to the other, trying on various costumes and roles: the superior thunderer who could out-shout Milton; the small rural rhymer who could escape Milton's notice through his insignificance; the gracious and unquestionably secure host at a party for many minor poets, Milton included, to be noticed in passing with a bland, patronizing smile.

Though he didn't completely abandon this last position, with *In Memoriam*, Tennyson clearly needed something much more dramatic. *Lycidas* swam across his orb and threatened to eclipse him.[19] The maneuver Tennyson executes, an exhibitionistic replacement of Milton by Hallam's body and then by himself, builds shrewdly not only on his own skill but also on a critical tradition that suspected *Lycidas* of being insincere. Dr. Johnson, of course, was more than suspicious; and Tennyson slyly feeds the rumor, seeking out that reader of *Lycidas* who wants to know more about Edward King and to see Milton weeping over him—and feels cheated by the result. Not only do we get plenty of Hallam in *In Memoriam*, but plenty of grief as well. As A. C. Bradley says, the movement from grief to triumph in *Lycidas* is "felt by the reader to occupy but a few hours of concentrated experience," whereas in *In Memoriam* we are provided with "a period of some years." Not only that: the apparent four-part structure of *Lycidas* is laughed into puniness by the 131 sections of *In Memoriam*, each "felt to be the expression of the thought of one particular time" (*A Commentary*, p. 23). Each, we might say, is felt to be a view of Tennyson in 131 different positions on 131 different (lugubrious) occasions: rather like an exquisite family album—a family of one.

The inception of *In Memoriam*, then, against which pressed so strongly the priority of *Lycidas* and the fact of Milton as "the great Inhibitor, the sphinx who strangles even strong imaginations in their cradles" (*Anxiety*, p. 23), elicited from Tennyson a strong poet's strongest misprision, so that, like the infant Hercules, he could strangle *from* his cradle. Tennyson elects to answer Bloom's question "what makes possible the incarnation of the Poetical Character?" just as Bloom does: "Desiccation combined with an unusually strong oceanic sense."[20] Tennyson's plan to incarnate himself while banishing Milton to impotent irrelevance is, like the Biblical Creator's, to separate dry land from the sea, claiming *terra firma* as his charted territory. Dry land is, he says, the superior place for elegy, and Milton is welcome to the wash of the undifferentiated thalassic sense, because no true poet would want it. Requisite to a real elegy, Tennyson insists, are the presence of a body and an earthly burial. No "wat'ry bier" for A. H. H.—he will "rest beneath the clover sod" (X), the grasses of which become the instrument for poetizing (XXI). Milton, having neither grave nor grave-grown grasses, has, you see, no legitimate poem and no business singing his insincere monody.

The danger here for Tennyson is that to get Hallam buried, he first must get him across the sea, the territory that belongs to Milton (Hallam unluckily having dropped dead on the continent). That very danger, though, once overcome, redounds to Tennyson's glory: he has bested Milton in the contest between land and sea, and not just in the game of "false surmise," but in an actual sea-crossing. He is able to take credit for this corporeal presence, which mocks the corresponding absence afflicting his would-be precursor. For it is not simply felicitous accident that provides Tennyson with a body, and thus a poem, in contrast to the embarrassed Milton's lack of both. Tennyson claims, through a superior poetic vocation, personal responsibility for transporting Hallam's remains across the water, and, in this, his divinatory prowess is greater than Milton's.

In section XII, Tennyson describes his successful Orphic journey to save Hallam from the Miltonic ocean. In his imagination, Tennyson visits the ship at sea to inspect its progress. This excursion is made "as a dove," a figure that recalls both Noah's dove and Jonah, whose name means "dove" and who sought to evade his calling by returning to the all-embracing sea. But Tennyson is to be a successful dove and a bolder Jonah, one who does not flinch from the rigors of his vocation. He returns from the imaginary visit to the ship and lands Hallam securely on shore, vying with and ultimately triumphing over Milton's ocean realm. Vico, who as Bloom tells us, "identified the origins of poetry with the impulse towards divination (to foretell, but also to become a god by foretelling), implicitly understood . . . that a poem is written to escape dying" (*Map*, p. 19). In this twelfth section, Tennyson refuses the damp poetic mortality offered him as an ephebe and asserts the rarified, godlike authority of foretelling. He reiterates this assertion of authority in the addition to section XIII of a final stanza, not present in the Trial Manuscript of 1850. Rather than ending with the line "Mine eyes have leisure for their tears" and its note of grief, the added stanza, beginning "My fancies time to rise on wing,/ And glance about the approaching sails," shifts the emphasis from grief to the divinatory powers of the poet, from brine to bird.

Tennyson does not beseech the winds and the ship to bring Hallam home (or, like the empty-handed Milton, ask indirect questions of the waves and "Felon winds"); he commands inferiors. In our group of eleven sections, Tennyson's apostrophic addresses to the ship (and through the ship to the natural forces of winds, waves, and time) include seventeen injunctions cast in the imperative mood, his most frequent illocutionary mode. When, as in stanza 3 of section XVII, he addresses the ship without commanding, it is to affirm that the ship has been obedient to his imperatives and, as is the prerogative of divinity, to grant to it "Henceforth, wherever thou mayst roam,/ My blessing" (ll. 9-10).

That Hallam's body is more an instrument for poetically vanquishing Milton than a talisman of personal grief is underscored by the historical record, which strongly suggests a dramatic diminution of Tennyson's interest in the "loved remains" once they were pushing up violets on shore. On December 9, 1833, Henry Hallam wrote to Tennyson, stating that his son's funeral would be at Clevedon in Somersetshire, and inviting Tennyson's attendance as an honored mourner: "I have a place for you in my carriage" and adding, "I have yet no tidings that the ship has sailed from Trieste."[21] Again, on December 30, the elder Hallam wrote: "It may remove some anxiety from the minds of yourself and others to know that the mortal part of our dearest Arthur will be interred at Clevedon on Friday ... you may have been apprehensive for the safety of the vessel" (*Memoir*, I, 106). That Tennyson may have been "apprehensive for the safety of the vessel" we certainly aver—that being necessary to our thesis—but the evidence denies that Tennyson cared much for the body or the ship once the latter had delivered the former to port. Not only did he not avail himself of the reserved space in the family carriage, nor attend the funeral, but he persisted for nearly fifty years in an error of fact about the site of the ship's landfall. The lengthy conceit in section XIX ("The Danube to the Severn gave ...") is predicated upon Tennyson's belief that the fair ship had put in at Bristol, on the Severn, the major port nearest Clevedon. When, in 1883, Edward Malan sent the poet a copy of his article, "Hallam's Grave," pointing out that the ship landed instead at Dover, across the Kingdom, Tennyson muttered gruffly in reply, "It is news to me that the remains of A. H. H. were landed at Dover. I had always believed that the ship which brought them put in at Bristol."[22] But what, really, does it matter?

If once in England Hallam loses his importance as Hallam, it is because his identity has been incorporated into Tennyson's identity as poet. The coarse claim by Tennyson that he has a corpse and Milton doesn't is subject to further coarsening when we substitute for "corpse" the Lacanian notion of "the phallus in the picture."[23] This play of presence (what Tennyson has) opposed to absence (what Milton does not have) leaves Milton, in Lacan's terms, as "the imagined embodiment of the *minus-phi* $[-\Phi]$ of castration" (p. 89).

How economical of Tennyson: first the dead Hallam is put to use as an instrument to castrate and banish from the virile arena of poetry the bogey precursor Milton, then this same Hallam is effaced in his unwanted individuality by being subsumed to Tennyson's person as his metaphorical phallus. The effect is that thereafter in the poem, whenever Tennyson displays Hallam, he also displays his own perceived strength and beauty, his token of "plus-ultra-phi."

The strong poet, Bloom says, must reconcile himself to the truth that "all things were made through him, and without him was not anything made that was made" (*Anxiety*, p. 99). Tennyson is up to the job. By depicting himself as the generator of his poem, he arranges neatly that when the drums roll and the crowd hushes, he will be alone on the ramp and his the only name on the marquee outside. Not for nothing is Tennyson acknowledged as "the most discreetly powerful erotic poet in the language."[24]

🕮   🕮   🕮

What holds our attention to this Tennysonian act is its unfailing deftness. Even in this preparatory, threshold unit (sections IX-XIX), Tennyson manages not only to throw out Milton but to draw the spotlight to his own rhinestone spangles. He reverses *Lycidas* wherever he can: the wind is not an enemy but a friend (Tennyson, that is, is more powerful than Milton and is not subject to the whims of the elements); the "perfidious Bark" is now "fair," a "sacred bark" (Milton is cursed; he is blessed); weeping is not a "meed" (an easily granted reward) but a blindness that causes insight (Milton is adolescent and neurotic; he is mature and well). As if rubbing it in to the Milton whose Lycidas "never must return," Tennyson anticipates in these poems just such a return—and the return of something insistently made material and concrete. In place of the vacancy at the center of Milton's poem, Tennyson gloats in images of "loved remains," "dark freight," "Hands so often clasp'd in mine," "heart," and "dust."

The traditional authorities can agree on no single direct allusion to Milton in this group. Bradley and Ricks, however, both mention section XIII, where the first stanza's widower, who dreams of his late wife only to grope around and find her place empty, is seen as a version of Milton in his sonnet, "Methought I saw my late espoused Saint," which ends, "But O, as to embrace me she inclin'd,/ I wak'd, she fled, and day brought back my night." Actually the authorities do not quite agree even here. Ricks asks us to "Cp." the two passages confidently enough, but Bradley, who does spot parallels to Aeschylus, Ovid, and Pope in XIII, ll. 1–4, says he finds no Milton here.[25] Never mind. We might as well see what we can see with these two poems ourselves, fancy what this emanation of Milton might do when unfolded.

Here are the two poems in question, Milton first:

Sonnet XXIII

> Methought I saw my late espoused Saint
>> Brought to me like Alcestis from the grave,
>> Whom Jove's great Son to her glad Husband gave,
>> Rescu'd from death by force though pale and faint.
> Mine as whom washt from spot of child-bed taint,
>> Purification in the old Law did save,
>> And such, as yet once more I trust to have

Full sight of her in Heaven without restraint,
Came vested all in white, pure as her mind:
  Her face was veil'd, yet to my fancied sight,
  Love, sweetness, goodness, in her person shin'd
So clear, as in no face with more delight.
  But O, as to embrace me so inclin'd,
  I wak'd, she fled, and day brought back my night.

And Tennyson:

XIII

Tears of the widower, when he sees
  A late-lost form that sleep reveals,
  And moves his doubtful arms, and feels
Her place is empty, fall like these;

Which weep a loss for ever new,
  A void where heart on heart reposed;
  And, where warm hands have prest and closed,
Silence, till I be silent too.

Which weep the comrade of my choice,
  An awful thought, a life removed,
  The human-hearted man I loved,
A Spirit, not a breathing voice.

Come Time, and teach me, many years,
  I do not suffer in a dream;
  For now so strange do these things seem,
Mine eyes have leisure for their tears;

My fancies time to rise on wing,
  And glance about the approaching sails,
  As though they brought but merchants' bales,
And not the burthen that they bring.

Both poems deal with the psychology of grief, particularly the relationship of
a terrible loss to sight and to states of consciousness. Milton's poem seems the
more straightforward of the two, a tragic exploration of hope extinguished,
blackness confirmed. Even the proper and orthodox expectation of "full sight
of her in Heaven without restraint" collapses in the face of the poem's final
brilliant oxymoron. Tennyson's section XIII misreads this poem of terror as a
mere trifle of the "he's his own worst enemy" type. His misprision uncovers or

constructs in Milton's sonnet a subtext of self-luxuriating narcissism, thereby clearing a space for his own poem and promoting, by contrast, his own sincerity, honesty, and good mental health. Tennyson also uses this misreading to avoid confronting his loss, to blind himself so as not to look, and to erect a solid and impregnable foundation for his exhibitionistic monolith.

It's worth visiting the site: the progress of this construction makes for interesting observation. Tennyson begins by insulting Milton directly, abridging his sonnet to a perfunctory introductory stanza, disposing entirely of all the outmoded barbarisms about "child-bed taint" and "Purification in the Old Law." He also replaces Milton's specific (and highly conventionalized) figure—"pale," "faint," "vested all in white," face glowing in "Love, sweetness, goodness"—with a blank and unspecified "form," reading Milton's poem as sentimental and dishonest moonshine, a regular Hallmark card. Finally, Tennyson deflates Milton into a garden-variety "widower," calling attention to Milton's grandiose pose as the favored subject of Jove and his "great son." The word that governs Tennyson's first three stanzas is "tears," not Milton's pompous "I." Here, we are told, is real up-to-date grief, not that old puffery easily got up for miscellaneous occasions.

Milton's poem is governed by a desire for sight. But unlike Milton's widower, Tennyson's does not *fancy* that he sees; he *does* see. And a lot of good that does him. The visual directness brings tears, blinding tears, and silence. The threat of looking is that one may find only the black abyss and no object at all. Such loss without context is only loss; that is, it is unavailable for the comfort available in words. Blank loss has no future, no time. Milton can only postulate a vague heavenly future, one that is extinguished by timeless night. Tennyson's widower Milton is also blocked by that emptiness, that "silence," a silence that threatens to spill over onto Tennyson—"till I be silent too"—if he makes the mistake of looking, seeing.

But Tennyson develops fancies that liberate just where Milton's or the widower's enchain. Milton is extinguished when his "fancied sight" turns to nothing. "*My* fancies," on the other hand, says Tennyson, are free "to rise on wing." The lift for these winging fancies is provided by those tears that replaced Milton's obsessive "I." Caught in the rigid voyeuristic need for visual mastery, Milton lays absolute claim to the vision, and tries to trap it: "*my* late espoused Saint," "Brought to *me*," "*Mine*," "once more I trust to *have*."[26] One might say that the voyeuristic bubble bursts precisely when this object threatens to become the subject, when the vision dares to act on its own: "as to embrace me she inclin'd/ I wak'd." Pure ownership cannot tolerate this sort of threat (nor, one might add, can the enthroned male ego—ours anyhow).

There is, then, a kind of grim poetic justice at work in handing this oral-obsessive child his real possession: not *my* wife, but *my* night, my nothingness. Tennyson, using traditional feminine associations, centers "Tears" in order to dissociate himself from and disavow such sight, such presumptions to ownership. Hallam is not "mine" but simply a "comrade," a "human-hearted man." For all that, he is no mere vision or "Spirit," no phantom of a voyeuristic hunger. Tennyson's loss is great, of course, but it is not a loss of sight (possession)—which he never claimed—but of sound, "a breathing voice." And Tennyson can fill in the silence by relinquishing Milton's voyeuristic possessiveness and becoming the object himself. Those tears that blind still allow him to "glance about" warily and quickly among related and associated objects—though not at the subject (Hallam's corpse) itself—in a way that foregrounds his own evocative power. The effect of all this is to read Milton's poem as an uncouth misogynistic fantasy that through the artifice of self-pity masks the natural consequences of such a neurotic possessiveness. Thus, the manifest text of Tennyson's lyric announces courage, probity, and genuineness.

Tennyson reads Milton's poem as striving for a false comedy, a false liberation, signaled when the strained rhyme words of openness and delight—"shin'd," "delight," "inclin'd"—are cancelled by "night." Tennyson's poem moves toward genuine freedom, the early rhymes of confinement—"reposed," "closed," "removed"—opening out into the beautiful "wing," "sails," "bring." Similarly, Milton's view of time is Utopian, static, futuristic; Tennyson asks Time only for patience, a presence that is fulfilling in itself. He doesn't want to be in a dream with Milton; he wants Time to assure him that he is not in a dream. Milton's is a foolish dream world; Tennyson's is actual. *He* has no reason to hide or be dishonest; he can admit openly that he may simply benumbed by grief, that his release is temporary. All the honest tentativeness, however, clothes the surface of a very bold claim.

In order to make good the fullness of this exhibitionistic claim that his position is natural and wholly sound, Tennyson makes a still more violent sneak attack on the already battered Miltonic presence: he asks nasty questions. Does the voyeuristic collapse in Milton's sonnet really lead to all that much misery? Is there no payoff to Milton for the attitude he takes toward his loss? Sure there is, he insists: the considerable pleasure of neurotic self-absorption. Finally, Tennyson claims that Milton's poem is infantile, self-advertising, happy to wallow in self-pity. Tennyson's poem claims a robust health for exhibitionism, a hearty and forthright participation in what is now antiseptically called "the grief process," whereby tears finally lead out into the world.

But Tennyson's misprision, his adoption of authority, should not blind us to what he is doing with blindness, how necessary it is to him. He *must* be the true blind bard; Milton is only doing a sick child's imitation of Homer. Tennyson needs this blindness. Even his widower does not stare, like Milton, into the abyss, but "feels/ Her pulse is empty": he sees feelingly. That is enough to free the blind Tennyson, the exhibitionist. We must also, however, glimpse the Tennysonian subtext, know that there *must* be feeling and no sight, that this complex movement is available to him only if night does not bring back his day.

This Miltonic presence we have been discussing comes from a single allusion—if, indeed, it is one. The subversion of Milton through allusion, however, is implicit and crucial, not because Tennyson ignores him but because he treats him casually, as one of a host of writers who might or might not serve for a decorative touch here and there. Tennyson assumes a pose much like Chaucer's Franklin: big-heartedly welcoming poets one and all to his fun-for-all elegy. But Milton gets no special invitation, no seat at the head table; he is, in fact, almost forgotten among the hoi polloi.

A frequency list of allusions to various poets in sections IX-XIX, compiled from Bradley's *Commentary* and Ricks's edition, looks like this:

    5: Shelley, Bible
    4: Ovid
    3: Shakespeare, Horace, Virgil
    2: Herbert, Byron
    1: Theocritus, Scott, Samuel Rogers, Aeschylus, Pope, Swift,
       Coleridge, Keats, Marlowe, Thomas Moore, Persius, Milton

Allowing that one reference to Milton (and it's questionable, we remember), we get a tie between Milton and the likes of Samuel Rogers, Thomas Moore, and Walter Scott.[27] It should be noted too that this list omits the big winner, Tennyson himself: even Shelley and the Bible, who do pretty well, have no chance against allusions to Tennyson, numbering at least fifteen. The most important source for Tennyson is Tennyson; naturally enough, since he is here declaring and establishing his origin. He must do so, since there is now no reciprocity for him, no one to see. He is disarmingly and poignantly frank about this. For all his smugness about having a body for his elegy, he knows and says that a corpse is not much. At the center, he fears, is an emptiness: "My Arthur, whom I shall not see" (IX, l. 16), "The dust of him I shall not see" (XII, l. 19).

The Lacanian hollowness that inhabits *In Memoriam*, then, is Tennyson's initial dread that his poem may have no object: Hallam is dead past all power to be resurrected, and grief, as an object, has been appropriated by powerful precursors, notably Milton. Nonetheless, as the poetic subject (the poet),

Tennyson feels a compulsion to poetize: "I do but sing because I must,/ And pipe but as the linnets sing" (XXXI, ll. 23–24). But what is to be the object of this piping and singing? In his anxiety that there is none, Tennyson makes his impulse to pipe and sing itself the object, occupying and investing the lost object-position in a strategy of poetic exhibitionism.

Apostrophe is integral to this strategy. The apostrophes in these early sections do not seem to belong to the same order of signification as the narrated events of the whole poem. Rather, they represent a turning of the activity of seeing (and telling) back upon the subject, the poet. Apostrophe repositions the poet from seeing subject to seen object; in the act of invoking and proving his poetic power, the poet puts himself on camera. We need only recall Lacan's remark that exhibitionism is a "drive that most completely eludes the term castration" (p. 78) to demonstrate the necessity of this ploy to Tennyson. Fearing that his poem is "minus-phi," he substitutes himself as its focus, a "plus-phi" piper and singer.

Apostrophe is the necessary rhetorical figure by which Tennyson can displace Milton and exhibit himself as the focus of his poem. Jonathan Culler has written of this trope as a strategy for denying or recouping loss: "[Apostrophic lyrics] substitute a temporality of discourse for a referential temporality. In lyrics of this kind a temporal problem is posed: something once present has been lost or attenuated; this loss can be narrated but the temporal sequence is irreversible, like time itself. Apostrophe displaces this irreversible structure by removing the opposition between presence and absence from empirical time and locating it in discursive time."[28] The apostrophe to the fair ship allows Tennyson to center "the power of [his] own evocativeness" (*Pursuit*, p. 150). The poet leaps into what he fears is the vacancy at the center of his poem and enshrines his presence there. By insisting on being seen, by making his compulsion to poetize the matter of the poem, Tennyson renders irrelevant all matters of priority and belatedness. The poem has shifted to a plane of discourse beyond temporality in which no precursors exist, and fear is transformed into glory.

Apostrophe, then, is the trope of exhibitionistic poesis, of incarnation, and implied in its divinatory refusal of death is the declaration: "There are no other poets before me." To "O" is to proclaim oneself a god, and only the strongest of strong makers can risk the chance of failing in that assertion. Tennyson, surely among the most arrogant of poets, overcomes all fears and initiates in *In Memoriam* with cool aplomb. There is nothing to look at but Tennyson, and we have no choice but to look. Tennyson, after all, is *there*. No doubt about that. Whatever is *not* in the poem, *he* certainly is, riding high, doing acrobatic tricks, calling, "Look ma!—only one hand, balanced with sublime assurance on the dancing tip of my pen!"[29]

8

The Poem Says
Meredith's *Modern Love*

STORIES WHICH BEGIN "A professor of mine in graduate school once said" are the most unwelcome ever told. They are worse than those which follow on "If you want my opinion" or "That reminds me of a time" or "I have a problem with that" or "Just let me say this" or "I don't want to spoil it for you by giving the plot away, but" or even "I never watch television but last night there was this show on PBS."

A professor of mine in graduate school said that before he started the article he has just published on Whitman he had read every bit of criticism ever written on that poet. The question had arisen because the professor was a medievalist, and, at a party, someone had asked, "How did you come to do that article on Whitman, being a medievalist and all?" It was a question that seemed satiny-hostile, even though it came from a graduate student, and we all understood the subtext right away: "How can you summon the audacity to have opinions on a writer outside your field and then to publish them?" We were all taught—I think you were too—that you should certainly publish, but only on things in your field, because things in your field were the things you should know about and occasionally have new insights into. You would recognize these insights as new because you knew everything that had ever been written in your field and thus could spot what had *not* as yet been written in your field. You would know everything written in your field, I should add, even though there were some writers about whom you would, of necessity, know less at the moment than others, not be up on to quite the same extent, depending, of course, on what you happened to be working on. If you were working on Thackeray, you might not be so up on Newman, for example, but you would, if you take my drift, still know everything. Outside your field you wouldn't. Outside your field you would know, as it were, nothing. There were charming exceptions, professors being what they are: the Dryden man who knew Shaw, the Victorianist who edged over into Galsworthy, the Cooper editor who dabbled in science fiction. But so what?

The point is that my graduate professor was right. He was right in principle, even if he was, as we suspected, lying on this occasion. We regarded it as a good lie, a pedagogical lie of the sort we'd all be lost without: it is the right thing to tell students the proper way to do things. You don't begin the education of young football players by revealing to them how to trip, gouge, and practice illegal holding. Similarly, my graduate professor was right to say he had read everything written on Whitman. Perhaps he had, after all. There were real scholars in those days.

A REVIEW OF SCHOLARSHIP

I have read everything ever written on Meredith's *Modern Love*. Meredith is in my field, so that should go without saying, but you might be surprised what often passes for scholarship these days. When I say I have read everything ever written on *Modern Love*, that of course doesn't mean that I've read *everything* ever written on *Modern Love*, or that I've read every word of what I have read or that I remember much of it. What I have done is this: consulted the MLA Bibliographies one by one (I understand these bibliographies are also on tape or on file or on computers, but I don't know how to use them) starting with the latest and working backward until I had reached a point where enough was enough, the point where the sort of insights I had myself (and needed to be sure nobody who had had them before had published them) seemed very unlikely to pop up. After a while you know these things, know in your gut that people in 1953 simply didn't, even the best of them, notice the same things we do today, and there's no use looking for signs that they did so. You won't find them, and you'll waste a lot of time looking. You might as well look for people who talk like Jacques Lacan or U. C. Knoepflmacher in *Weekly World News*.

So, once I had read everything ever written on Meredith's *Modern Love*, I was ready to assess it. The oldest essay to speak to me—from here on I will use the first-person plural to make things clearer—was Norman Friedman's 1957 piece, "The Jangled Harp."[1] Nothing before that can be recommended, not for insights. But Friedman's essay speaks to us because he emphasizes the elements of discord, the "bizarre mixture" of things in the poem. That he puts them *in* the poem in such a Cartesian-positivist way may not be pleasing to us, but he seems to be on the right track, especially for 1957, which is, after all, 37 years ago at least.

(I forgot to say that I also read the *Critical Heritage* entries,[2] which is more than enough of contemporary Victorian material, you will agree, unless you are a new historicist, in which case I wish you would go away.)

After Friedman, good material comes gradually at first, and then more fully in the 1970s. Here we will find nice insights, but ones that are (oh please) incidental to the insights we've already worked up. The quantity of material levels off at a surprisingly consistent rate, and is also surprisingly high in terms of quality. There are both books and articles, though I haven't room here to pass judgment on all of them. Three items, we agree, rise above even the high level of the rest, and they cannot be passed over in silence. John Lucas's well-titled "Meredith as Poet" in the ridiculously-titled collection, *Meredith Now*, is terrific in pushing at us a shifting, contradictory, centerless poem that "cannot be resolved; it can only stop."[3] But far and away the best work is by Cathy Comstock; no one else comes close. She has a superb essay in *Victorian Poetry* and a chapter on *Modern Love* in her book (see details in the note, of course).[4] For the general reader and those outside the field who haven't time to read everything the way I have but who nonetheless want to read something and only have time for the best, Comstock's work is where they should look, and they need look no further. Comstock is alive not only to the way we can make our critical models cause disorder as well as order, but she shows brilliantly how much pleasure there is in tickling our constructions into displaying themselves and then disappearing. There's nobody like her when it comes to this.

And that's the way we did reviews of scholarship when it was possible to do them: we mastered all scholarship and could thus clear the way properly for ourselves and make sure no one had tread before where we were now going to wend.

THE POEM SAYS

My thesis was to have been that most (actually *all*, one hoped) previous accounts of *Modern Love* were disabled by their reliance on a phrase so simple as to hide its central function from all but the most wakeful. That phrase, "the poem says," I was going to trace through enough existing scholarship to persuade even my most hostile and obtuse readers that "the poem says" reduced the project of criticism and of reading poetry to recording a clear and single voice, a voice speaking language that was somehow also clear and single-leveled. The resulting critic was, I intended to argue with some force, simply that most numbing of modern inventions, the good listener. "The poem says," you see, manages to solve by never addressing all manner of difficult questions about how poems and meanings are constructed, about how listening takes place, about where the poem and the critic are situated. I was going to show this, permitting myself some strong language and biting sarcasm, in small but telling doses.

But in reading ALL criticism ever written on this poem, I found that the phrase never appears. I don't know what your reaction would be, but I found this a pretty complete shattering of my thesis. Setting out to find a thing everywhere, I found it nowhere; thinking to comment on profusion, I located a humiliating absence (potentially humiliating, anyhow). What would you do? Like the scientist who gets funding to prove that oysters speak and then learns that they have neither mouth nor voicebox—in fact, no head, really—here you are flummoxed, out in public, your pants down, you bluff called, your hand in the till.

You look back at what you *have* found and try to make do with that: that's the first thing you do, see if you can, in good conscience, make the best of it. You locate some expressions that might be made equivalent to "the poem says," expressions that suggest that meaning is somehow inside the poem and the critic is simply helping it to get out: "the element of spiritual crisis in," "a close read-ing ... *reveals*," "section XXX *describes*," "the basic contrast of XIII is between," "sonnet 1, then, ironically *comments on*," "the poem seems *to hold out* the promise," and "these passages *propose*" (all emphases, needless to say, are mine).[5] Add to these the ones provided in the wonderfully cranky *Explicator* note by Richard F. Giles, who supplies his own emphases: "modern critics insist on *making* these lines ... much more obscure than they are"; "I think it only fair to Meredith that what he literally intended should be firmly established before other trappings are added"; and "If we insist—as most other critics do—on reading a poem backwards *from* our symbolic interpretation *to* its meaning, we do a great injustice to the poet and the poem."[6]

Put all that together and it doesn't look so bad. It makes for a pretty good parade of positivist floats, or might if you could bring yourself to suggest that you were giving a representative glimpse, like what appears on the eleven o'clock news. But the fact is that the measly few examples above are *all that exist*, all the ones I could find, anyhow, and I read everything ever written on the poem. What then? It's a moral dilemma, but not much of one, since the chances of get-ting caught are not too great.

HE SAID/SHE SAID

But that doesn't mean critics have done it right, not before I came on the scene, or that they have been willing to expose their assumptions and procedures to the open air. What they've done (and I should have anticipated this, I admit) is to hide themselves behind a conception of the poem as a narrative, a plotted narrative and with characters too. Thus, instead of pretending to listen in on a poem, telling us what it says, they are listening in on a narrator and a husband (perhaps one and the same, perhaps not), a wife, their lovers, and a few minor characters as they proceed through a plot. These listening/recording critics can pretend to be unplaced and objective just as easily as those I was looking for, but I still felt both disappointed and somewhat duped, as you would, too.

I should add, just to be fair, that there are some excellent readings of *Modern Love* as a novel. J. W. Marston's review in the *Athenaeum* of May 31, 1862 isn't excellent, but it does take the poem to be a story, even if the story is somewhat hard to grasp: "we think she takes poison."[7] For a better grip on a more exciting story (so long as you aren't fooled into thinking it is *in* the poem), try Cynthia Grant Tucker's essay, or Stephen Watt's subtle analysis of the husband's neuroses, or Philip Wilson's brilliant application of Sheldon Sacks's theories of narrative coherence, or Dorothy M. Mermin's influential and sensitive reading, or, best of all, John Lucas's tracing of a search by the husband for some role he can play in a shifting, contradictory world and in a poem that has no center and can never be resolved, but can only stop.[8]

Such approaches provide a certain pleasure, but they naturalize both the plot and the poem, don't they? They also naturalize the critical procedures at work, make the construction of meaning look a lot like eavesdropping. That won't do.

FIRM READINGS

It's understandable that critics should take some operations for granted and should regard their way of doing things as Nature's own, even though it's a method cobbled together from what they've been taught, what they see others doing, and what's in the air around them. I cannot claim immunity from this, and neither can you. It's only human, and we're all in this together, as Derrida has pointed out, more or less. For instance, I myself was preparing to ridicule confident readings, to show how even the critics I most admire (Alan Sinfield, W. J. T. Mitchell, Eve Kosofsky Sedgwick) will, when they really get their steam up, force a text to sit still and do its monophonic duty, singing its one tune to ears that cannot hear it amiss. When they feel the spirit move within them, even these great critics will treat the decoding of those dots on the page as a matter of the commonest sense. I intended, without endangering friendships I value dearly, to mock these practices and to offset their manic rigidity with some lovely rubberiness of my own.

Reading through the poem, though, in search of an apt occasion for the practice of a game so easy I might have had second thoughts about it but didn't, I came across the following lines from sonnet XII, lines which struck me as very moving, but hell with that, since they also seemed to me to *make my point:*

> Methinks with all this loss I were content,
> If the mad Past, on which my foot is based,
> Were firm, or might be blotted: but the whole
> Of life is mixed . . . .[9]

I couldn't help but notice—I thought it was no more than noticing—that Meredith himself—that's the way I put it; I don't want to hide anything—Meredith himself was saying—get that!—what I was going to say, that we purchase critical contentment by imagining that a mixed and slippery—he didn't say slippery, but that's what he meant—base is firm, "firm" being the very word he uses and then repudiates, you see, just as I will proceed to repudiate my friends (until now) and their ill-considered way of reading poems as if what those poems said were plain as day.

You'll be seeing right away what it took me some minutes to catch, that I was preparing to jeer at firmness by way of some firmness of my own. Of all people, I was reading a poem in order to do something with it and confusing the something I wanted to do with it, you see, with the poem itself. What I was saying through it I was attributing to its own tones; my own warbles I was calling "Meredith." The poem was allowing something (it could hardly do otherwise), and I was taking advantage of it, pretending that the poem's unwilled generosity was compulsion: *Modern Love* made me do it. There's a lesson here for all of us.

ANOTHER LESSON

I've never fully understood—now that I'm involved in what might be taken as confession—what to do with idle associations that enter into our experience of a poem and seem, on reflection, not to match very well with what one ought to be experiencing. Sometimes they are downright embarrassing. Avoiding firm readings is one thing, but here are two examples that illustrate how there may be a whirlpool, a real Charybdis, opposite the Scylla of firmness.

> . . . With slow foot
> The low rosed moon, the face of Music mute,
> Begins among her silent bars to climb
> —XXXVII, 10–12

I first constructed "rosed" as a color or tint, the pinkish hue (or maybe yellow, roses also coming in that shade, as do moons, especially in harvest time) one would commonly associate with "Music mute"; the oddity of the word "rose*d*" (rather that "rose" or "rosey") suggested to me that the color was forced onto the moon (i.e., it wasn't naturally rose-colored but had been made that way, "rosed" by force or perhaps by the odd perception of the viewer, who had taken a perfectly normal moon and rosed it). Then it occurred to me that it wasn't a color at all but a positional reference, an indication that the moon had just come up, was "low-risen"; this construction was reinforced by what I was making of the next line, where the moon climbs its bars. But "rosed" sounded a little folksy to me, and I don't usually find much that is folksy in Meredith, though maybe I don't know how to look. Then it entered my head that "rosed" might be a joke, like the word "riz" in the old Burma Shave roadside signs that said, "Spring is sprung!/ The grass is riz!/ That's where last year's/ Careless driver is!"? (The Dead are buried/ The grass is rosed/If you speed you'll join 'em/ Case Closed!) Burma Shave, I'm sure Stanley Fish would say, would be every bit as relevant as, for instance, a letter of Meredith's in which he said straight out what he meant by "rosed." But I'm still not sure how to handle "rosed," and right now I'm looking out my window at a rose I grew myself, with no help at all from my wife though she said she would, a rose that is moon-colored, come to think of it, a sort of watery-cream-yellow. I think all of these things add up.

I have another example:

> Poor twisting worm, so queenly beautiful!
> Where came the cleft between us?
> —VIII, 3–4

When I read this, it was all I could do not to think of a nightcrawler, one of those big earthworms that used to come out—I don't think they do so anymore—of the Midwestern soil at night during a rain (watering would do it too). You could catch them pretty easily and when you caught them they *twisted*, just as in the poem, and inspired pity—thus, *poor* twisting worm. There's more to it:

the odd thing about these worms was that if you accidentally chopped one in half—*cleaved* it, caused a *cleft*—it didn't matter. These worms (we believed) had eight hearts and could be cleft in eighths and still survive, twisting. In fact, they dared you to divide them, since it didn't hurt them and was a really good and interesting survival technique, all of which explains why they came apart so easily in the first place. But I can't remember thinking of them as "queenly" or "beautiful" or imagining the cleft as between the worm and me ("the cleft between us") rather than a matter confined entirely to the worm.

Those are just two instances of what I am convinced occurs regularly to even the very finest and most disciplined readers, judging by my own experience. I am further convinced that these associations are blocked from making their way into print more by dishonesty and timidity than a proper sense of decorum. I may be wrong about that.

READING VERY CLOSELY

Sonnet III ends, heartbreakingly:

> But she is mine! Ah, no! I know too well
> I claim a star whose light is overcast:
> I claim a phantom-woman from the Past.
> The hour has struck, though I heard not the bell.

I wonder if, reading these four lines in, let us say, an anthology with plenty of explanatory notes, you would look for help at any particular point. No? I must confess that I did, and I'm not sure that makes me a poorer reader than you or says anything at all about you being smarter than me. I made it securely through the first line—"But she is mine! Ah, no! I know too well"—never supposing I needed help from a note, but in the next line, the word "claim" gave me pause. What sort of claim was it, on what basis was a right being asserted? "I claim a star": even if one accepted for a moment that the star was his wife or some image he had of his wife, what demand was he making, what claim was he staking?

I still don't know, but I quickly allowed that confusion to merge into a larger one: the phrase "a star whose light is overcast" struck me in a kaleidoscopic sort of way, throwing out too many patterns, shifting them around, refusing to stand still. Of course, that's only a way of putting it: actually the line itself was doing nothing; it was me shifting and spinning and causing the confusion. Still, I couldn't settle on the overcast-star image, couldn't, to put it more plainly, decide what "overcast" might mean. Most readers might be satisfied with the 10-o'clock-weather-report sense of "overcast" as cloudy or misty, but I'm not "most readers" and neither are you. For one thing, we note in that meaning a convenient but suspicious passivity: the star simply *is* overcast, no one did it. But there are plenty of other possibilities that bring the speaker/husband into the action: overcast also carries the sense of a fishing line cast too far (i.e., he has tried to make contact with his wife but missed); of a covering thrown over (i.e., he has screened his wife from himself or he from her); of a stitch of some kind in which no raveling is permitted (i.e., he has sewn her up in a neat—if sad—unravelable narrative from which there is no escape); of a passage (i.e., the star can in fact be reached, its light offering a tunnel to connect them); of something thrown away, hurled to the ground with violence (i.e., he has ripped her away from him and discarded her like trash); to give birth to prematurely (i.e., their love, like fierce fires, has burned itself out); of overdoing the casting of a play (i.e., they have both been wrong for the parts or perhaps ironically too good at playing roles); of a reckoning over the true amount (i.e., he has been the victim of expecting too much—loyal love maybe); to conquer (i.e., she has won what has always been both a battle and a game between them); to transform (i.e., she has no place now in any drama he can construct, she has moved outside his narrative). And that's only the beginning of our fun.

Looking to the next line—"I claim a phantom-woman in the Past"—we are encouraged to see so much parallelism that it almost seems redundant: "another way to put this is," "let me repeat," "as I said before," "in case you didn't quite catch that." Meredith was very fond of these two images, couldn't decide between them, so he simply put them in apposition—not very economical, but we're not complaining. The wild profusion attending the overcast star business, threatening to stampede right over us and not look back, can be tamed by comparing the star to the phantom, putting them up against one another, mashing star into phantom, as it were, and discarding everything that doesn't fit. We'll use a common-sense notion of "phantom," since if we start into the *OED* on that one, we'll make matters even more frenzied and out of control and that's the opposite of what we want, don't you agree? (Why?) Do you follow me? Let's see the lines again:

> I claim a star whose light is overcast:
> I claim a phantom-woman in the Past.

Before impressing our hundred or so meanings of overcast onto phantom and seeing what fits, though, let's agree about "phantom-woman in the Past." Whoa! I just noticed that the anthology gives us a note at this very point (I noticed earlier, of course, but saved it for now as a surprise). After "Past" it says "4," and "4" says: "He claims, not the woman who is now beside him, but the woman who once loved him, and is now only a phantom out of the past."[10] That seems to solve at a stroke our problem and many another. I didn't know (maybe you did) that the woman was even for sure there, beside him, as he spoke, or that she "once loved him" and doesn't now or that he knows anything of the sort or that he's so sure how he feels or that "a phantom *out of* the past" (our editors' version) is quite the same as "a phantom *in* the past" (poem's way of putting it).

I was, until I saw the note, starting to think that the star and the phantom weren't going to match at all. Neither is present, I guess, though the star may be offering a way to locate presence; but the phantom seems to have been a phantom even in the past, an image that was never there, doubly distanced: he's not claiming a lost love but a lost illusion. In that way of reckoning things—and it's a dismal way—the star and phantom are not in apposition but in sequence, as if the hopeful shadows of overcasting were too much to bear, as if the narrator were searching for an image that wouldn't so readily offer itself for deconstruction.

Let's put this plainly: let's say the first image offers itself as too richly ambiguous, too teasing, too demanding. If there's hope or if the problem is simply in his perception, he'd better do more than think up images; or, put another way, maybe he has hit on an image—the overcast star—which offers him a pathway (a narrative) which will reconnect him to his wife. Stars are distant enough, we might say, and overcasting them ought to double-distance them, make them so remote they can offer nothing in the way of hope—or challenge. But let's say the overcasting actually hints at bringing the star down into his neighborhood, his parlor, his lap. So he (pathetically it seems to me) tries again, since what he seems to want right now is the certainty of a story, and what story is more certain than the self-pitying tale of woman's perfidity. He puts her *in the past* as a phantom even at the time, and that way there's no contact to be regained, nothing to regain contact with. Maybe.

And maybe not. Even if we go in this sad direction, whereby the husband is more attached to the pleasures of a good solid story (a good cry) than to the possible joys of love (a good life), we needn't see him ending with the phantom-woman, needn't see him cementing his attachment to sad stories. There's nothing final about the phantom-woman image, nor need it take precedence over the overcast star. After all, the final line—"The hour has struck, though I heard not the bell"—can be construed as opening things up, right? The ghastly finality of the striking clock plays against his deafness. Maybe he's luxuriating in the image of being tricked, faithful and foolish man that he is (or finds pleasure in thinking himself to be); but *maybe* he's offering a clever, brave thumb-on-the-nose to finality and neatly-told stories. Maybe he's unravelling things right at the end here: he goes on despite striking hours and striking images, goes on to unravel the sad, self-pitying story and keep things open, overcasting backwards and forwards at the same time to claim (maybe) a finer set of possibilities for himself and her.

What's to keep us from imagining a last-minute rebound, a surge of hope, a recasting of the narrative into an optimistic mode? The fact that the hour has struck (if indeed it actually has) and that he didn't hear it (if he didn't) doesn't necessarily mean he was stupid or a dupe (though it might). It could mean that he heroically resisted and thus transformed pathos into comedy, death into new life, or maybe that he fought his way out of the plot of lugubrious self-pity he seems elsewhere so fond of. Away with melancholy! The pleasures of the maudlin, of murky stars, phantom pasts, tolling bells of doom may be enough for you, but I was made for the open air, for larger fields of hope and bright air and creative love.

I think reading the poem that way makes you a better person, but not, I suppose, a better reader.

TIME TO EAT

Others have noticed a few of the references to teeth and biting in the poem, especially the horror-show line, "Had he not teeth to rend, and hunger too?" (IX, l. 4). In noticing such things, though, they have hustled to connect them to coherent patterns that unify the poem, "animal imagery," for instance.[11] About the notion that image patterns act to unify there is no need, I hope, any longer to comment. We could launch one more attack, but what would be served by doing so? Cheap pleasures, of which we have more than enough these days. Even if there were benefits worth garnering from an analysis of the assumptions that guide these searches for unity, would those benefits repay the labor, be worth the time and space we would all have to devote to the job? I prefer to regard "unity," like virtue, as an idea that once served well and now threatens us so little that we can afford to be kind, to wave a nod and a gentle smirk its way.

Besides, it's not "animal imagery" that the line about rending teeth connects to, anyhow, but imagery of transgressive consumption, tearing flesh, cannibalism. That's what we should be talking about. I am ready to listen to objections that would run like this, "You begin by dismissing out of hand image patterns and then, without blinking, haul out a replacement pattern for the one you don't like." That looks cogent, but it's not; for what I am talking about here is not a "pattern" but a "cluster" I happened to notice, and thus is not in the poem but in me: I am the one, and you too, suddenly becoming alert at the mention of cannibalism; *Modern Love* hasn't the slightest interest in it.

Here's how it goes, as we go through the poem. Early on, we are invited—I am inviting you—to consider in a conventional way the possibility of taking bites out of another, pretending to regard it with terror and downright disapproval. In sonnet V "She treated him as something that is tame,/ And but at other provocation bites" (ll. 4–5). Even here, perhaps only the dullest reading would regard the biting as unarousing, but let's say this: we have barely started the poem and haven't left behind our own dull responses. Four poems later we get the line already quoted, "Had he not teeth to rend, and hunger too?" Now we see that the biting alluded to earlier is neither the nibbling of foreplay nor the spiteful (but still cautious) childish chomp of rage; it is full-scale gorging.

But we are wrong to think of this hunger, these rending fangs, this lust to suck blood, crack bones, gnaw forearms in terms of the standard binaries of eater and eaten, marauder and victim, cannibal and dinner. Eight poems later— we are now up to XVII—we get "At dinner, she is hostess, I am host" (l. 1), a deceptively mild, simple-seeming introduction to the joys of mutual dissolution, or perhaps the paradox of consuming by being consumed. Put more plainly, they savor one another and make of one another a feast, devouring what they would preserve and polishing off that which must be left behind for others. This is not the world of masculinist atomism, where an individual can prosper only at the expense of another; we have entered into a realm of feminist unindividualized connectiveness where "making use of" is joined with, inseparable from "being used." They are now one, offering unreservedly their mutual flesh to the single set of big jaws and pointy teeth and unappeasable appetites that now marks their being.

We were at sonnet XVII, with thirty-three poems to go. One would think we would see further changes, some development in this idea and image of what we might call "self-sustaining cannibalism." But I can't see that anything happens from here on out, which means that I cannot think of anything I can make happen from here on, so proud am I of the paradox (powerful) formulated previously. To the extent that you open yourself up to being devoured, just to that extent will devouring be opened up to you. There's no end to the banquet, so long as you don't distinguish between yourself and what's under the coverdishes. Bring your pot to the pot-luck. Eat that you may be eaten. Like the meal of flesh, we can go on forever.

The poem will support us. I take it that "My feet were nourished on her breasts all night" (XXIII, l. 16) is another climax of mutual grazing, her breasts being just as nourished by his feet, you see. And so on, from the rakish joining of their bodies into one sweet dessert—"we'll sit contentedly,/ And eat our pot of honey on the grave" (XXIX, ll. 15-16)—through the "prae-digestive calm" (l. 6) that awaits the spicy festival in XXXVII, and the vampirish "This is my breast, look in"—(You look into mine; I'll look into yours)—of XLIX, to the climactic image of knifing one another up so as to feed "on the advancing hours" (L, ll. 9, 7), the whole world having been turned into a giant body, their body, which swells into the very cosmos as it is consumed.

All of this illustrates advances made on notions of image-patterns and unity, suggesting quite clearly that literary criticism is a cumulative and progessive operation, building on the solid work of the past, moving with slow certainty toward a final state in which everything will be explained to our satisfaction.

IDEAS OTHERS MAY WISH TO PURSUE

I think I have made my point. I will therefore radically condense what I had left to say (points "G," "H," and "I" on my outline), so much so that this concluding section will not really wrap things up but will lend to those things a useful radiation. By that I mean only this: the three subjects touched on here would serve well, each one of them by itself, as a focus for sustained inquiry. Such inquiry, however, will have to wait on others, others fortunate enough to find a publisher with more vision and sense of duty than my own, a publisher who would never dream of saying to them, "This is far too long as it is. Sales projections suggest the best we can hope for is a disaster, and our costs. . . ."

The first topic is "On Writing" and takes up the ways in which we might play with those wild narrations of writing within the writing of the poem. That may not be clear, but it's as good as I can do, laboring under condensation. What I have in mind are those moments where written documents, writers, and what we would call "the circulation of discourse" invade and subvert our smooth-motoring reading of the poem. Here are some clues: her "handwriting" (hand-writing, you see, suggesting, among other things, biting the hand that feeds you [see above] and "writing the body") and the letters in XV; the French novel and the metacommentary in XXV (*is* there a novel? whose novel is it? can it ever be truly written, or only written *on*?); the hidden note uncovered in XXXIII (was it hidden or displayed?); and the faint thin line he drops to us at the very end.

The second topic is "Those In Attendance." Here we deal with the other guests at the feast, the gate-crashers, the voyeurs, and the readers. That's *us*, you see; but what seat do we have at the table? Which window are we looking through as we read? Are we watching or being watched, becoming excited or exciting the poem itself? Think of the "nodding elders" chatting away in sonnet XVI (chatting of what? we know, but does the poem?); of Jack, Tom, Moll, and Meg in XVIII (what brew have they drunk? is it one never brewed?). The idiot who acts like a fly, the friend about to marry, the burly lovers, the innkeeper, the doctor: none of these belong to the poem any more than we do, but what would the poem do without them? What would it do without *me?*

The third topic is XXXI, which seems to be a poem written by Miss Bates or My Uncle Toby, it is so dithering. One could explicate it nicely, since it can be made to talk about interesting things—gender, sexual attraction, philosophy, dogs—and do so in any direction whatever. "I am approved," it ends: "It is not half so nice as being loved,/ And yet I do prefer it. What's my drift?"

What's my drift? Just contemplate that phrase and you'll see what is going on here and almost everywhere else. I'll stop now, as any more words would spoil things utterly, would be screams in the symphony, pee in the stew, sharks in the swim, tacks in the roadway, jeopardy on the horizon.

9

The Canonical Poetry of *The Pearl*

Part I *Pre-Game Ceremonies*

THE MAJOR QUESTION

I THINK YOU should be prepared to explain why you spend so much of your time reading *The Pearl* and publications like it. What is it about such material that makes you fond of it? I will not presume to answer for you or to guess; the question belongs to you. So, you should feel obliged to look within yourself and examine closely your own experiences and motives. Ask how such materials as *The Pearl* found their way into your possession in the first place. Why do you deposit them where you do, hide them or flaunt them, lend them to friends or keep them for yourself, thrill with pride on coming across them or recoil in shame?

What is it that occurs when you read them? Is "read" a term that captures precisely your engagement with these works? While engaging with them, do you find your mind running to matters best termed aesthetic, historical, formal, political, commercial, pedagogical, comparative, gender-specific, rhetorical, or sociological? That is a complete inventory, as far as I can see, so you should choose one.

We'll never get anywhere in this essay unless you make ready your view of your own preoccupations and be honest about it. It does not occur to me that there would be any difficulty here, any reason to experience shyness, nervous titters, bottomless revulsion. How could there be? I have had literary training and am therefore an imaginative person, but the self-loathing in which you find yourself washing is incomprehensible to me.

AND DESIRE

I believe you are sick with shame because your engagement with *The Pearl* and publications like it is penumbraed (fringed, shadowed) with desire. I am guessing here. Because you did not include desire in the catalogue of interests you found your mind running to (see above), it appears that you regard desire and its exercise as shameful things, things you wish you were without. It would be better for you not to feel that way, to admit that, right or wrong, desire forms a part of your makeup and that you really don't mind that it does. Conventional wisdom tells us that it is a healthy relief to see such things within and speak them out. I am suspicious of this nostrum myself, dubious that time or custom can transform depravity into health and allow you to look at a monster in the mirror and cry, "Beauty!"

PROPER SCHOLARLY TREATMENT

To deal effectively with this material, in a manner that will neither cloy nor insult, it is necessary to be unreservedly responsive to it, no question about it. A good measure of that brimming response will, of course, be taken up by a chaste and measured enthusiasm. Those who do not feel it must simulate it; otherwise there is no hope of reading properly. You see at once that while what I have said is true as regards the right way to read *The Pearl*, it is no less true of reading the poems (all of them) of Wordsworth and the plays of Shakespeare, i.e., of all literature, great literature at least, of which, it seems to follow, the poems of *The Pearl* form a part.

A PERSONAL HISTORY

It is natural that I should include a section on my own interest in the subject, since I am writing on it. My interest is the normal one, and I am struck in a normal manner by the way in which others seem to lose control, in one direction or another, when *The Pearl* and her relatives are flashed before them. I mean by that simply that so few seem cool and professional about this literature, either discussing it or, I daresay, reading it. I have not myself lost control, lost sleep, lost weekends, or lost sight of the fact that my interest is scholarly, even when I have been in adult bookstores. I was in an adult bookstore once, and not by accident. I was in Washington, D.C., and I went into this adult bookstore, where there seemed to be many alert people, to ask directions. "Do you know where the N.E.H. is?" "What?" "I'm trying to find the N.E.H. and I don't know where it is." "Oh." "Do you know?" "This ain't it." "Yes, I see that, but do you know where it is?" "No, Mac, I don't."

RELEVANT SECONDARY MATERIAL

My general subject, you understand, is erotica, or the Erotic generally. Of the many indispensable studies and aids connected to this subject and its dissemination, to its history and development, to its reception and cultural effects, none will be cited here. The reasons are clear. To put it negatively, what would be gained? To spin it positively, all this scholarship finds its strength vitiated and its motives contaminated by special interests and, even more, by special needs. There is nothing special about my needs or even my interests, so I naturally am well advised to steer clear of Krafft-Ebing and Ellis and Freud, of Lacan, of Weeks and Marcus, of Dworkin and MacKinnon, and of those others you were thinking of.

DEFINITIONS

The Pearl is a piece of "pornography," by which term we mean that which is received as (a) arousing, (b) improper, (c) welcome. The genre can never be defined in terms of what it is but only in terms of how it is received, because there is no limit to the range of content or treatment which might produce these results and because those interested in suppressing pornography (who quite properly are those with the loudest say in how it is to be defined) are indifferent to content but are convinced that it is not a good thing for material to be received as arousing, improper, and welcome. Other terms will be defined when they come up, unless they are terms being used in the way best suited to my argument, in which case definition would be cruel.

THE QUESTION OF SUITABILITY

This chapter is appropriate for this book and for all others. It accords with the standards and practices we have come to expect and in some cases admire in our discourse. That goes for the subject and for the treatment, too. Standards and practices may change over time, but I am not responsible for that.

GENDER

Once I establish the subject, get it situated firmly and attractively, I will turn to the poems themselves. That will be in Part II. (Part I—I'll add this for clarity—is what we are now in, and it is dealing with more general issues, not the poems themselves). But here in this particular section (*Gender*) of Part I, I *will* intro-duce a few poems, or lines from them, just because the subject of gender is not one that can be hurried past without paying some notice to evidence. It may be too much to say that without gender we would have no evidence, but there's no disputing that without evidence we would have no gender.

And without gender we would have little commentary on pornography these days. Gender is a serious matter: are the poems we deal with from *The Pearl* representing or somehow acting as advocates for a male yearning to dehumanize, then distance, and then attack women? You're expecting me to ridicule the question: does "Leda and the Swan" represent or advocate sex with birds? does *Titus Andronicus* force us into certain baking practices? Will it seem evasive to you if I point out that assertions about what pornography is representing or advocating often (always) ask us to adopt the asserters' bullying contempt for complexities involved in issues of representation or the connection of art and life? You would find that evasive? Assuming, then, that there is nothing dubious (preposterous, criminal!) in treating such complex matters in a no-nonsense fashion, the answer (you remember the question?) is, most often, maybe not.

In a few cases, *The Pearl's* poems will seem vile: discussing women's body parts as if they had been cleavered out and set on a table, mechanizing sex, celebrating father-daughter incest. I am assuming that the tone of joviality attending such poems will strike you as making matters worse, as asking for some kind of com-plicity that you will find repugnant. There is no possibility you would allow for an ironic, layered, or subversive reading of such poems; that's out of the question.

Even if it is (and why is it?), the bulk of these poems, I believe, do not operate in and around violence toward women. The longest poems display no evident interest at all in women, focussing (perhaps a bit too narrowly for some) on the flogging of schoolboys. Others celebrate a sexual reciprocity, both with women who with good-natured passion "meet me half way," but also, perhaps, in homosocial union with the other men who have shared happiness with the same woman:

> Reclined on her breast, and clasped in her arms,
>   With her my soft moments I spend;
> And revel the more in her melting charms,
>   Because they are shared with a friend[1]

Such liberal feeling for women's fervor sometimes extends to allowing female passion a direct lyric voice:

> Oh, when shall I behold, love,
>   Thy noble manly face?
> Oh when they neck enfold, love,
>   Within my close embrace
>   —"Song," pp. 320–21

If this seems uncomfortably serpentining/strangulating, it may be because it is "Translated from the Hindustani" and reflects, naturally, a different culture's *ars erotica.* And perhaps women may find necks stirring in a way shut off to men. I can't say.

You've been pleased so far by the high quality of the verse quoted and relieved by its seemliness, though not all of *The Pearl*'s poems, I suspect, would strike you in the same way. As if in response to the demands of all its readers (not you), *The Pearl* could lower its tone a little now and then, even when it was turning the tables on traditional sexual hierarchies and allowing greater sophistication, power, and wit to the woman:

> There was a young parson of Harwich,
> Tried to grind his betrothed in a carriage.
>   She said "No, you young goose,
>   Just try self-abuse,
> And the other we'll try after marriage."
>   —"Nursery Rhymes," p. 177

One doesn't want to overlook this poem's artful adaptation of the limerick form or the daring rhyme of Harwich and carriage, in which the proper pronunciation of "Harwich" floats a kind of "itch" sound (and suggestion) into "carriage," thus enriching things. Mainly, though, this example suggests how often in *The Pearl* power is assumed to rest with women. Or, even better, it suggests that we needn't be tied to notions like "power" or "gender" in our analyses, neither term being of much use to us.

MY THESIS

I have more than one thesis, but it will help you to follow them all if you agree with me that this poetry is not in the least marginal, does not whistle from the outskirts but sings loudly from the town square. This poetry jumps up, as it were, from all of us, from the center of our literary and life experience. If it is little read and seldom discussed, that is because it is so well known already, so deeply ground into our breasts, and so fervently admired. It is second nature, actually nature itself, nature made literary, we might say, to advantage dress'd in the wardrobe of canonical taste and refinement. These particular poems may not appear in this form in *The Norton Anthology*, but that is because it would be redundant to place them there, a violation of the copyright of the heart.

My thesis, to repeat, is that these poems are produced by a cooperation between our desire and the canon. They are the already-written collaborative works that constitute the core of our heritage, that living cultural throb which William Bennett and Janet Reno both guard and quiver to.

BIBLIOGRAPHICAL HISTORY

The Pearl: A Journal of Facetive and Voluptuous Reading is said (by Grove Press) to have run through 18 monthly numbers, from July 1879 to December 1880, not missing a month. Each number included poetry, usually at the end, effecting, one assumes, a climax. The amount of poetry in each number decreases a little toward the end of the run, but there is really no consistent pattern, as I think of it, in type, bulk, or rhetorical appeals and thus no possibility of monotony setting in.

REFLECTIONS ON CHANGING TASTES

Tastes in these matters have changed little since July 1879-December 1880. I think we are less given to putting our rhymes to music or to finding pleasure in singing them, and thus a poem set "To the Tune of Derry Down" may seem quaint. The decline of learning has decreased our access to classical filth. We flog children more and write about it less. We (males at least) have all but aban-doned the neck as an erogenous area. We may find chamber-pot allusions dated and have less relish for jokes on our body's wastes. Now and then, I will admit, these poems strike one as salty or crude or, let's face it, so vicious that we feel proud to live in better times. Something like "The Old Dildoe," in which the device catches fire during use and grills poor Peg Watkins would never find a reader these days, simply because we have become so much less wild and cruel. Judgments like that come upon one unavoidably in the reading of these poems.

Part II *The Poems*

THE RULES

The poems will be analyzed and displayed according to those methods we have inherited, learned to use, and get paid for employing. We will then apply to these *Pearl* poems the standards we use to screen candidates for admission to the canon. They are: "universality," "breadth of allusions," "formal dexterity and range," "metaphoric deftness," "rhetorical chasteness," "mimetic fidelity," "political acuity," "ability to look backward and forward," and "what Harold Bloom would say."

UNIVERSALITY

The greatest of these poems reach, as great poems will, through time and space to strum the chords of the human heart, set them pulsating to beats felt everywhere and always. For instance, reflections on how life's brevity makes its joys all the more honeyed and available for the swallowing find their way into the distinguished *carpe diem* tradition and into these poems:

> Setting suns may rise in glory,
> But, when little life is o'er,
> There's an end to all the story,
> We shall live and love no more!
> Give me, then, ten thousand kisses,
> Give me all thy blooming charms,
> Give me heavenly, melting blisses,
> Lying naked in my arms!
> —"The Budding Rose," p. 96

Many of these poems, aware of the universality of their subject matter, form, and appeal, are not embarrassed to reflect on it:

> Nature, ev'rywhere the same,
> Imparts to man a lustful flame;
> In Russian snow or Indian fire,
> All men alike indulge desire,
> All alike, feel passion's heat,
> All alike, enjoyment greet
> So that whereso'er you go,
> Still the same voluptuous glow . . .
> —"Love," p. 32

The major test of my thesis—that these poems enjoy canonical or even meta-canonical status—has thus been passed: they speak to and for the all-time-and-everywhere truths of the human heart.

BREADTH OF ALLUSIONS

Every canonical poem, as Eliot reminds us, is on speaking terms with every other canonical poem; indeed, they are joined in a symbiotic network in which the happy interdependence of the parts is signalled by a calling to one another, like yodellers scattered over the farthest ranges of the Swiss Alps who, though separated by hundreds or even thousands of miles and years, still connect by a common song or howl, sending out a melodic beacon signalling, "I am here, and I am also there; I am I, whilst also being You." Just as yodellers not only sing but allow themselves to be *sung through*, as it were, so do poems open themselves up to have written on and into themselves all the poems already or to be written, those that belong in the canon I mean. This is only true of poems in the canon. If a poem is canonical, we will see clearly enough that it is by noting these complex and from-all-directions interpenetrations or, more simply, by hearing how much it sounds like all other poems of its sort, which it should if it really is part of the one very big poem which is the canon.

That the *Pearl* poems all belong in the fold can easily enough be *suggested*, though you'll understand that full proof would occupy too much space. It is also likely that those who demand full proof are those who would be unable to recognize proof if it stuck a pipe wrench up their nose. That is the way it is in every circle you find yourself in, I dare say, be it familial, professional, or sexual. There's another reason why it is futile to go after proof: those who will be convinced by it were already convinced before the proof started to flow. Either way, why bother?

So here's but a glimpse of the allusive reach this collection offers. First, of course, the Bible:

> Grass widows and Princes, a warning I sing,
> Of the sad wicked doings of David, the King;
> With Bathsheba, wife of poor Major Uriah,
> Who was bathing one day, when the King chanc'd to spy her.
> —"Queen Bathsheba," p. 66

Then, a shadowed (artfully) evocation of the Faust legend:

> An age of grief, an age of pain,
> I would endure and ne'er complain;
> To purchase but an hour's charms,
> While wriggling in a maiden's arms.
> —"The Reverie," p. 137

Closer to home, an intertextual folding-in on Richardson:

> Mr. B—was very cruel,
>   "Virtue as at last rewarded,"
> He obtained the mossy jewel,
>   Pamela so long had guarded

And Fielding:

> Even her modest brother Joseph,
>   Joseph Andrews with his Fanny;
> When they once had got their clothes off,
>   Had as little shame as any.
> —"The Budding Rose," pp. 194 95

What started off as a modest "suggestion" of the canonical-level allusion-quotient in these poems has grown now into what I really do think constitutes "proof," despite what I said earlier; and I offer what has preceded in that spirit.

FORMAL SOPHISTICATION

Though the number of poems in *The Pearl* is not great—I believe a trustworthy counting has not yet been undertaken—there are no known poetic forms or styles unrepresented in these eighteen issues. These poems reach out and touch (and thus exhaust) all categories and all possibilities that lie within the range of "the poem" as we understand it. All modes and types and species are here, lyric to epic to dramatic; there are conundrums and epistolary verses, rondeaus and epitaphs and odes and dramatic monologues. There are songs for the rustic folk and practical verses for the middle class, such as "Lines for Valentines." There are playful poems for the chic, such as "Julien's Concert," where (get this!) an entire poem rests on a witty (probably epic) conceit: amorous and erotic things are described in terms of a band concert, with the various instruments and what they do, along with the reactions of the audience being tropes, you see, for a salty second narrative, what we might call a "sub-text."

Just a few illustrations to give you a feel not only for variety (which in itself might not count for much, as we can all with a little practice produce various forms) but a feel for the unbridled excellence of all this.

Even the simplest parts of the simplest "songs" betray to the eye that knows where to look, a high art beneath the artless melodies. Take the chorus of "Adultery's The Go," for instance:

> Adultery's the go.
> The go, the go, the go,
> Adultery's the go!
>
> —"Adultery's The Go," pp. 99–100

The poetic economy is so demanding here that nothing is wasted, with even the punctuation being asked to do a lot of work.

A step up and over from such guileless songs are the limericks written, no doubt, in homage to Edward Lear. Here we do enter into a discourse that may not be for everybody, a range of droll expression and jocular experience that may charm or just as likely disgust. I can be no more explicit, you understand, without actually introducing you to the very expressions and feelings I am anxious to protect you from meeting. You may well conclude that what I have offered does not amount to much as protections go. After all, what with me being so vague, how are you to know whether you wish to be saved from dangers that may turn out to be rewards? How will you know, in this case, whether you wish to swim in the water until you have made the plunge? If that is your (faulty) reasoning, there is nothing I can do:

> There was a young man of Dundee,
> Who one night went out on a spree;
>   He wound up his clock
>   With the tip of his cock,
> And buggered himself with the key.
>
> —"Nursery Rhymes," p. 34

No need to comment on that. Moving to another level, we find the scholarly poems, or at least poems appealing to the scholarly, like the following imitation of Martial:

> To the French, to the Germans and Swedes,
>   Easy Harriet, you give up your charms;
> Italians and Russians besides
>   Have all had their turn in your arms.
>   —"A Taste for Foreigners," p. 98

I will not pretend that I own a classical education penetrating enough to allow me to appreciate fully the resonances in the poem or to know whether Martial is really the classical poet being invoked, for that matter. But I am sure one of the ancients is, and that makes a difference.

Finally, let me set my sites on the most refined poetic form of all, the heroic couplet, the most difficult to employ and the surest test of both the canonical poet and the canonical reader:

> By day experiencing each sweet delight
> And endless transport every night
>   —"The Pleasures of Love," p. 32

This is, I know, only a so-so couplet, if you're thinking of Pope or Dryden: there is an elision of syllables in "experiencing" ("ex-**peer**-yunce-**eeng**) that strikes one as slovenly rather than daring. More important, the day-night formal balance seems wearisome, while the parallel between the adjectives "sweet" and "endless," which should be exact, is wobbly. Still, the couplet is clearly in canonical territory, no doubt of that; it's a big-league couplet. But it is nothing compared to the dramatic, almost ostentatious ease with which the line is managed later in the same poem:

> We pant, we throb, we both convulsive start!
> Heavens! then what passions thro' our fibres dart!
> We heave, we wriggle, bite, laugh, tremble, sigh!
> We taste Elysian bliss—we fondle—die.

One could (and some may) write a long and fascinating essay of appreciation on these four lines alone, on such things as the bold trochaic variations ("Heavens!"), the playful mockery of the stately diction ("wriggle"), and the rich fund of meaning and color opened up in the allusion to "Elysian," which you and I know refers to Elysium, where the blessed dead went in Greek mythology and thus a very happy state, as we also know from allusions in

Massinger, Spenser, Milton, among others, though surprisingly not in Shakespeare, as I recall.

METAPHORIC DEFTNESS

If I had only this category with which to establish my thesis—which is, you know, that these poems are the product of a simple addition of desire to the usual way the canonical greats take shape—I would be worried. It's true that the metaphoric density in these poems is high and so is the originality rate. All the same, the metaphoric effect here is more like a gradual sweep than a quick jab, more like a roller coaster grinding slowly uphill right at the start than a rollicking Tilt-a-Whirl in full roar.

Thus it's hard to illustrate, which means you must take it on trust, though I will identify for you certain recurrent metaphoric clusters. First, there are the metaphors drawn from mathematics: plentiful numbers, weights and measures, calculations, all of which gives the effect of cool precision, I think, suggesting that those writing and reading the poems are deliberate types who will not be rushed into anything. Next in frequency, I believe (I have not gone so far as to commit the absurdity of adding them up) are those drawn from the animal/botanical kingdom, where bees and fruits and blooms and nectar figure prominently. Then there are the references to science, physics especially, to an often surprisingly arcane knowledge of frictions and momentums and velocities, also temperatures, as in fires and ices. And finally, among these clusters, I have identified a strong gathering of geographical metaphors, hills and valleys figuring most noticeably. That ought to do it.

RHETORICAL CHASTENESS

I will give but one example, since I believe rhetorical figures work most exuberantly when they are not identified but proved on the pulses, at which spot we always know whether it is the real canonical thing. I cite therefore, as I say, only one example and here it is, an imposing apostrophe:

> Thou heavenly sun whose golden light
> Displays the hills with verdure bright;
> Sink thee, oh sink thee, in the west,
> And bring the hour I love best.
> —"Before," p. 208

I realize that "rhetoric" includes more than such figures, that it often suggests persuasion or the way any discourse acts within a reader, community, or culture. In those terms, I will say that the discourse here, *The Pearl*'s poetry, acts within a circuit of erotic desire and pleasure, you see, functioning as a form of that pleasure and a stimulus to it (and against it), as a source and recipient of it simultaneously, as an expression and an outlet, as incitement and deflector, as idea and as negation of all thought whatever, even thoughts of desire. But that's only what I think.

AND MIMESIS

One often hears these days of "vulgar mimesis," a kind of replacement for "vulgar Marxism" as a term of abuse, meaning crude and blunt and obvious. The mimesis we are talking about here is not vulgar. If it were, it would be, in the case of this subject matter, very vulgar indeed. But it's not.

Still, much of the humor in the *Pearl* poems is positively Chaucerian in its willingness to go where other poems fear to tread. Take some of the "Lines for Valentines," mentioned earlier. One (p. 605) concerns a man who, having too much to drink, decides that before going to bed he had better first empty his bladder. But it is dark, you see, and he is drunk, and thus he isn't in good shape to look around for "the jerry." Perhaps you have an idea of what's coming. (Perhaps you also have an exact idea of what a jerry is, but I don't.) Anyhow, let's join the poem at this point, as the man is feeling around for this jerry:

> Took up by mischance a big mousetrap instead,
> Which snapped off, alas! his old gentleman's head.

Surely it is not extravagant here to think of "The Miller's Tale," of Sterne, of the better parts of Rabelais. In a similar vein is an Ode on the death of a donkey, which contains stanzas like this one:

> And oh! his fate I do bewail,
> He backed one day against a rail,
> And a long pointed rusty nail
> Stuck in my Ass!
> Whereupon the donkey dies:
> My grief for him was most sincere,
> The pain was more than I could bear,
> So, kind friend, come shed a tear
> Upon my Ass!
> —pp. 221–22

The earlier parts had similar pleasantries about sitting upon, smacking, seeing, kicking "My Ass!" You probably get the point.

The mimetic fidelity of the flogging poems is so intense as to replicate the true beat of the action, along with the sounds and so forth. These poems are actually in thrall to mimesis and thus seem lesser works than those which can pick where to be mimetic and where not. When you have to be faithful to the howling and the whacking and things like "Oh—Oh—Sir—Please—Please—Sir!" there's little room for art of the highest canonical order. I would rank these flogging poems, then, low-canonical, since the very mimetic accuracy which gets them into the canon is finally what keeps them from ascending very high in it once over the border. There's a paradox for you.

POLITICS AND PORNOGRAPHY

That these poems are acutely and shrewdly political is just what we did not expect, but it's true. *The Pearl* seems to have been pluralistic in its position, tolerant of many persuasions; but it did not exclude direct, even fierce statements of opinion on issues of topical concern. There are many instances where contemporary figures or types are ridiculed, perhaps the favorite being lawyers and politicians. In one poem, Gladstone (by name) offers in the name of his country to "bugger the Turk!" (p. 463). Some of the commentary on the national scene is more considered, as in "The State's New Duty" (pp. 159–62), which takes the occasion of a petition to extend the Contagious Diseases Act to the civil population as a chance to expose political corruption, wholesale bribery, and general humbug. It also satirizes patriarchal assumptions about man's sovereignty over women and asserts defiantly a woman's right to the independent use of her own body. In a similar vein, there are poems on birth-control and abortion, like "The Fruits of Philosophy," a reference to Charles Knowlton's highly controversial book on sex, population, and means of using restraints on the former to control the latter.

POEMS THAT LOOK FORWARD AND BACKWARD

That was a rather abrupt pull-up in the last section, I know, but my chapter is getting longer than you want, so I'll rush to the finish. This section is about poems most dear to the canon and its octopuslike way of bringing every work into intimate contact with every other work: poems that carry the past with them and also anticipate the future. One example will suffice, both because, as I say, I'm short on room and also because I could only find one example. Others there doubtless are, but I did not catch them.

I'll tell you about this poem before quoting it and that way you can enjoy it fully. It is based on Robert Burns's "For a' that and a' that" and forecasts the popular song of our own century (though not exactly last year), "Let's Fall in Love" ["Birds do it! Bees do it! . . . "]. Thus it's wonderful canon stickum:

> The licensed by the law do't,
> Forbidden folk and a' do't,
>   And priest and nun
>   Enjoy the fun,
> And never once say nay to't.
>   For they a' do't—they a' do't
>   The beggars and the braw do't,
>   Folks that once were, and folks that are—
>   The folks that come will a' do't.
>
> The wee bit cocks an' hens do't
> The robins and the wrens do't,
>   The grizzly bears,
>   The toads an' hares,
> The puddocks in the fens do't.
>   For they a' do't, &c.

It only remains for me to tell you that "puddock" is an alternate spelling of "paddock," and that a paddock is a frog, most likely, though it could possibly be a toad.

WHAT HAROLD BLOOM WOULD SAY

Harold Bloom would find so many strong poets in *The Pearl* he would think he had found his way into a gym for real big literary artists. Many *Pearl* poets have their eyes on Wordsworth as a poetic father well worth wrestling with:

> Sweet is the memory of the scenes
>   In boyhood I enjoyed,
> Hot vigour thrilling in my veins,
>   By no fruition cloy'd.
> So innocent a child I seem'd
>   That Catherine, Jane, Eliza,
> Would treat me as a girl, nor dream'd
>   That I was e'er the wiser.
> I many a naked frolic spied,

> Nor seem'd a whit to care,
> With changeless glance serene I eyed
> Their sexual members bare.
> —p. 234

The child is father of the man, and this swerve from Wordsworth opens up for *our* changeless glance what was flashing on that Lake poet's inward eye and providing that "bliss of solitude."

And then there's Tennyson. Notice the cocky freedom in such misprisions as "Home they brought the warrior, fed/ To repletion more than just" (p. 173)—a robust revision of the celebrated song from *The Princess,* as I needn't tell you. Tennyson is, just as Bloom says, forced by a powerhouse misreading actually to *write the later poem* through the new poet.

Also taking on one of the Songs from *The Princess,* "The splendor falls on castle walls," an even more mighty *Pearl* poet produces, in place of "Blow, bugle, blow, set the wild echoes flying,/ Blow, bugle; answer, echoes, dying, dying, dying," this:

> Tell me where are there such blisses
>   As the sexes can impart?
> When lips join in heavenly kisses,
>   When they both convulsive start!
>   Throbbing, heaving,
>   Never grieving;
>   Thrusting, bursting,
>   Sighing, dying!
> —p. 138

CONCLUSION

Perhaps you feel that the poetry can do more, soar higher. If you think that way, take another look at the poetry in the canon (of which this is a part) and ask yourself, "Can I do better?" If you can do better, by all means do so. If, on the other hand, you cannot, please consider whether your low opinion of these poems isn't perhaps caused by the fact that you are responding *not to the poems but to that which lies within yourself, a something getting in the way.* To purge yourself of that which is getting in the way, read this essay again and then again. That's my advice.

Interlude II

H. Rider Haggard's The Return of 'She'
An Explication

(THE ESSAY IS ALREADY IN PROGRESS AS WE JOIN . . .)

THUS, AS HAGGARD insists in his "Author's Note," this book, appearances aside, is *not* a "sequel," not a sequel at all but the natural outcome of his "original design,"[1] which was, as I see it, to give us a full taste of the chewiness of returns. After all, "the tale repeats itself" (p. 51), as one hero says, meaning that the plot here is the same as the one in the first book, *She,* to which this is not a sequel, and also that the plot has been played out many times before in history. Quite literally he means that: these are all players doing over again what they have done many times before, under different names.

(And what is that story, exactly? I tried to suggest to you earlier that you needed to tell us. Otherwise all these details are terribly confusing. Who are these heroes? Where do the dogs come in? What about the cat and the ice slope and the volcano and that Khania of Kaloon? What about—)

The plot they are re-playing over and over is a deceptively simple one: the search of two men for a woman. But is She only a woman? Is She a mortal at all or some principle of Nature? A goddess? Isis perhaps? A fallen angel? A demon? Anyhow, these two men, Leo (about forty) and Horace (about sixty), had twenty years earlier located, after some exciting adventures along the way, one She, who was in love with Leo—*again* in love with him, having first loved him back in the days of the Greeks. Back then She had lost him, sort of, to another woman and had, in a rage, killed him, living to regret it, living thousands of years to regret it. So it looks like a triangle: the reborn Leo being loved by She and also by this other woman (reborn in this novel as the Khania of Kaloon), with Horace Holly (Holly is his last name) as Leo's guardian complicating matters by being in love with Leo, too. So it's not really a triangle after all, though it seems to be: two women fighting over a man—that's the surface text—while another man tries to rescue him from women altogether—that's the subtext. The story takes place in Asia, around Tibet, China, and Russia. The dogs you were asking about are death-hounds that the crazy Khan of Kaloon uses to hunt down those he doesn't like, which includes Leo and Holly, only they escape, as they do from many another harrowing danger.

(I see. And what do you have to say about all that? Just judging from the plot, it doesn't sound like *King Lear*.)

Much like *King Lear*, Haggard's *Ayesha: The Return of "She"* is a fable about knowing, about what it means to know and under what conditions we can think we are knowing something. Ayesha (hereafter called She), for instance: she cannot be known at all. She tells us fairly often what she is, or gives some pretty broad hints, but she has too many autobiographies at her disposal, it seems, and tells too many contradictory stories. The narrator, further, says that every one of her explanations of her essential identity are "mere veils to hide the truth" (p. 5). So, the book suggests, each act of knowing, all interpretation, seeks not to uncover but to hide the truth; or, as I'd prefer to put it, construct the truth as something which is always out of reach (tantalizing). Truth would be worthless if we could have it, have it and be done with it; but as something reliably absent (just around the corner), we can be forever driving for it, just as we (and Leo and Holly) are always driving after She.

(Which may suggest that She is the projection of that poor besotted Haggard's silliest fantasies, right?)

She is thus far more (and far less) than a projection of some sexual fantasy. She has no such exact location: her land "is unmarked on any map" (p. 12), though there's no place we'd rather be, if we have the nerve to face her—and our own desires. "Each reader," Holly says, "must form his own opinion of this history, its true interpretation and significance." She is, thus, nothing more than the act of knowing itself, as it *returns*, comes back to us again and again, always offering us the same gifts and asking the same price.

(What?)

What is She? She is what we can bring ourselves to admit to ourselves about our own needs and longings. She is, as she says, "foul when thou seest me foul, fair when thou seest me fair, a spirit-bauble reflecting a thousand lights" (p. 135). Precisely because She is such a pure construction, her power is excessive, threatening to let us in on too much, showing too much, reflecting back on us our own Knowing: "Her loveliness was inexpressible, amazing. . . . It must have caused infinite sorrow had she ever been permitted to display it to the world. It would have driven humanity to madness: the men with longing and the women with jealousy and hate" (p. 144). She is thus never revealed to us as Object but only as the Other who is filled with potential, with promise and peril as well. By seeking to know She fully, we may push past comic recurrence and find the terror of nothingness, not the bouncing ball or the ice-cream truck but the abyss. That way madness lies. She is all veils. Don't make her take her clothes off.

(I still haven't the slightest idea who She is.)

Who is She? That is still our central question.

(That was the central question eighteen pages ago.)

I would have made some headway with it had you allowed me.

(You did say she was all veils; maybe that says it all.)

No it doesn't. And there's not room left now in this essay for any real development of the idea. This is a mess.

(There's plenty of room, and it's not a mess at all. You've done a good job up to now, a fine job. You've made the plot very clear, for instance. Just practice some vigorous economy from here on out. Be terse. Give us old She in a nutshell, what it all comes down to when the veils are lifted, the essence.)

Which is a very serviceable transition line, since She, for all her protean elusiveness, is emphatic about presenting herself as Essence of some sort.

(Good. Now you're rolling!)

Thanks. Others in the novel make the mistake of giving to She a local habitation and a name, but She knows it is more than witchery or magic that makes her take on so many shapes. She can be all things because, paradoxically, all things are the same; She who changes in time is timeless; She is One. She tries to teach this to her lover, telling him that "all great Faiths are the same, changed a little to suit the needs of passing times and peoples" (p. 134). All faiths center in the Oneness that is beyond time and space: "all things are illusions; there exists no future and no past; what has been and shall be already *is* eternally" (p. 135), and *is* eternally in She, "the secret spirit of the World," "that Universal Motherhood" (p. 135). Coming to rest in She, then, is coming to rest in the All That *Is*.

(Yes! That does it. Though it is a little——)

Boring.

(Not boring, but not a fable for our times, you know, a little out of step, all that about the universal **ONE** who also turns out to be Mother.)

But that's only what She is striving to bring into being, the self she is trying to constitute—or sell to others. In fact, no one is buying it, certainly not the reader.

(I see. That's good.)

She cannot stand for long against Leo's need for the One to become one, in the flesh and in the sack. "Flesh and blood are not born of flame" (p. 128), he complains, after another of She's fabulous but noncorporeal son et lumiere shows. Leo has survived several tests and has lived through a repeat of the Wife of Bath's Tale, where he has chosen what looked like an old crone and had her turn ravishing. But he thinks he ought to have, as reward, something more than fireworks; and when told he can have anything he wants—She imagining he'll take immortality or world dominance or the ability to fly or something sensible—he tells her he wants just her: "forget thy greatness and be a woman and—my wife. . . . I ask of thee thyself—now, this night" (pp. 178, 176). That's plain enough: instead of taking on the power of the gods, he wants to hobble and gobble, or, as She puts it: "Oh, then together we might race adown our passions steep; together dare the torrent that rages at its foot, and there, perchance be whelmed or torn asunder" (p. 143).

(I think hobbling and gobbling sounds better than racing adown my passions steep. So what happens?)

She gives him his wish, sort of.

(Do they together dare the torrent that races at the foot?)

She kisses him, with passion.

(Does it whelm them, perchance, or tear them asunder?)

It kills Leo.

(Kills him?)

Yes.

(Why?)

I'll tell you. Leo dies, She would have us believe, because he has tragically chosen love over godhead, or something like that, spirits and mortals being bad matches. She kills him again, you see, as she had in Greek times, in accord with this eternal recurrence pattern the novel displays when it thinks of it.

(But that's not the best explanation.)

Right. The best explanation is this—It requires me going back a little and getting some breathing room and space.

(Go ahead. This is what we've been waiting for.)

The subtext I have hinted at already has to do not with tragic heterosexual but with homosexual love, with Horace Holly's battle to rescue Leo from She, the

Khania of Kaloon, and innumerable mortal females so he can have him all to himself. She, in this rendering, represents the attraction of a banal heterosexual catastrophe that can do no more than screen the true erotic oneness between Leo and Horace.

(That's not clear.)

She represents to Leo a way out of love, not a way into it, a way to plunge into death and avoid recognizing his true destiny.

(He plunges into death rather than into Horace?)

Put it this way. Eve Kosofsky Sedgwick has brilliantly traced in Victorian culture the triangulation of homosocial love that is often expressed in fictions of two males loving one another through the body of a woman they are both pursuing.[2]

(Right. That is good stuff, and I can see that it's exactly what's going on in your book here, *Ayesha: The Return of "She"*.)

But nothing like that goes on here. Instead two women (with some helpers) are battling over one man, not to express their love for one another (though maybe they are, but I don't care about that) but to play out, almost, a male homosexual drama of female self-destruction. The subtext teases us with a tale of She as the female principle that will rid us of females, the doomsday machine that will act as a kind of black hole, sucking all women (at least those in the vicinity of Kaloon) into nothingness with her.

(That's what happens then?)

No, I told you what happens: Leo dies, and Horace Holly does too, later. I'm talking about a shadow text that doesn't quite get itself written.

(But is all the more powerful, more legible for that very reason?)

Exactly.

(And it doesn't bother you that you could say that about any plot that wasn't there?)

What's it mean to be *there*? Besides, I have good reason to trace this shadow plot.

(You're in love with Leo yourself and want She out of the way?)

The shadow plot of desire is the desire of Horace, of the voice of the novel, for the golden boy Leo.

(He's on the wrong side of forty, isn't he? Some golden boy!)

"A more magnificent man I have never met," says Horace, who seems most lasciviously drawn to Leo's hair, "a curling golden mane" which "hung upon his neck" just "as his great beard hung upon his breast, spreading outwards almost to the massive shoulders." That hair is the key, showering gold everywhere and revealing itself shamelessly just as it hides, erotically, the delicate features of the boy, though now, as you say, a boy well over forty: "The face, too—what could be seen of it—was beautiful" (p. 12). Holly cannot do much but watch as two female principles battle over Leo, the mortal (though witch-empowered) Khania and the immortal She. After all, he has had lots of advantages over the more-than-forty years he has Leo all to himself, first as his guardian and then as his sole travelling companion on these endless and exciting journeys. Lots of camping out and shared hotel rooms. Now, however, his only hope is that the female contest—"Yes, I will match my strength and magic against hers, as it is decreed that I shall do" (p. 83)—will end in mutual annihilation. Holly sees the poor crazy Khan of Kaloon as an "object lesson" (p. 57), a man driven mad by the love of women and thus a walking homily on the necessity of avoiding women.

Leo draws women like bad meat draws flies; all the women in Kaloon do "their best to make love to him," which Holly can appreciate but, understandably, resents. He does what he can: "I took care that he was never left for one hour alone. No *duenna* could have clung to a Spanish princess more closely than I did to Leo" (P. 64).

One may say Holly loses, that the transgressive subtext is never allowed to surface, but, as I said before, I think, this lawless homosexual love story is the one that writes itself and finds completion in our own minds and hearts.

(So it's a two-layered love story, the interesting part to you being all underneath, on the bottom layer?)

It's more than a love story, though, and its focus is certainly not wholly or even primarily domestic. Any novel ranging over the plains of Russia and the mountains of Tibet had better be doing something more than one that never leaves an English drawing-room.

(You regard that as a telling argument?)

If not more, than at least something different. And here, sure enough, we find in Leo's dilemma the romance of capitalism figured in unusually naked form, so very naked as to become brazen and grotesque.

(Are there really degrees of nakedness? And why do you find excessive nakedness so repellent? Speaking for myself, there's no such thing as being too naked.)

The truly erotic capitalist romance—erotic because it is part hidden, stripping but never stripped—presents the hero with a choice between love and the world, between the domestic and the businessy, between the home and the imperial realm. According to this prescribed legend, the hero is always supposed to turn his back on the capitalist world and slobber his way into private boudoir bliss; and the audience is supposed to cheer this choice. And this paradoxical rejection of capitalism is capitalism's favorite fable because (a) it suggests that capitalism is so strong it can survive and even promote snubs; (b) it promotes a dualism between world and heart which identifies the capitalistic with the world, makes the ideas of capitalism and imperialism "natural"; (c) it suggests more subtly that these worlds support one another, i.e., without capitalism there would be no love and no heterosexual desire; and (d) it deconstructs the opposition, melting love into money, home into empire. Here, then, the fact that Leo is being asked to choose between world (or galactic) domination and a barrel of fun with She simply recapitulates the same paradoxical self-promoting myth, whereby the world is made one with capitalist imperialism and where there are no choices except those which support that world.

(This is pretty compressed. I guess you mean that movies where somebody leaves the rat race for a nice house in the country, gives up Madison Avenue for the woman he loves: those plots really are deeply conservative. Am I right?)

Leo's choice is, it seems, that of the man in the grey flannel suit, and it appears that once the alternatives are framed in this way, all choices lead to Wall Street.

(I see now.)

But it only seems to be that way in this novel, for Ayesha does not offer Leo the rat race but a form of communist meritocracy. She is, you see, an alchemist, able to take the common iron ore of the mountains they are in, millions of tons of it, and turn it into soft (24k.) gold. Her plan is to make gold so common it will flood the market, drive all bankers and stock brokers to suicide, wash away money altogether, and readjust not only commodity exchanges but standards of power and value: in place of monetary value she plans to set up values of "true worth" (p. 156).

(That'll all happen if the gold standard is disrupted? I don't understand.)

We may find it difficult to see how erasing the gold standard would do all this, but if we do our homework we will soon understand. We can, for instance, study the writings of one of Haggard's contemporaries, William Jennings Bryan, presidential candidate, Bible-thumper, hater of evolutionists, and enemy of the gold standard; it was Bryan who electrified political conventions with his thunderous denunciations of those who would "crucify mankind upon a cross of gold." Ayesha spells out the effects of killing off the bankers and stock brokers even more clearly than Bryan: "What if I uphold the cause of the poor and the oppressed against the ravening lusts of Mammon? Why will not this world of yours be happier then?" (p. 156). Instead of an economy of scarcity, there will be one of plenitude; merit will replace possessing, and generosity will eclipse the desire to hoard. There's something to think about.

(It's my opinion that you don't understand all this about the gold standard at all. A child would know as much.)

So, clearly, the capitalist drama shuts down before the fourth act, blown apart by a riot of anticapitalist metaphors. Ayesha, it is true, holds in place a power-center, occupied either by Leo or herself, so the subversion is certainly incomplete. She envisions a takeover of the world and a kind of tyranny she would not mind operating herself, should Leo have no taste for it. But it's still a twist that manages to expose the politics of the capitalist romance for what they are.

(That's easy for you to say, since limitations of space allow you to get by with that bald assertion.)

Even more subversive here, though, is the decentering of that drama, the ironic insistence that what looks like the climax of the novel is really a distraction, that the grand She is nothing more than a pest, getting in the way of the main story, which is about Holly and Leo and how they learn to acknowledge their love and fulfill it. Thus the grand choice Leo is asked to make is trivial. It's like asking God to hand out the Grammies, like asking King Lear to be a judge in a diving competition. Leo should not be making a different choice but no choice at all, just gliding over to Nature, to Holly and homosexual happiness, which he has, in truth, had all along. There has been no need for choices of any kind, capitalism and heterosexual domesticity being alike unnatural and perverse.

And finally, the politics of Leo's choice, presumably memorialized by the tragic finale—he dies, we recall, when he makes the wrong choice—

(I had forgotten that myself. Did you mention it before?)

Yes, he dies, in what is the by-damn climax of the novel, hardly to be missed by even the dullest reader of the novel—dies, thus apparently casting in cement the right-wing politics of the choice. The choice must have been important, we imagine, or it wouldn't be the climax of the plot. Saying it isn't important is like saying Hamlet's death is a trifle, like saying it doesn't matter how *Dr. Faustus* comes out, like saying who wins between Ahab and the fish can't concern us very much. But what if Hamlet peeked round the corner at the end of the play and said the poison didn't take and he was feeling better by the minute, if Mephistopheles said it was all a joke about selling the soul, if Ahab were one hell of a swimmer? You get the point.

(No.)

The point is that the *return* business guarantees that no death is final, that what looks like the climax isn't, that the true center of the novel is displaced, hidden. This is a novel that ends in mid-sentence and that lets us know several hundred times how it is that these stories will keep getting themselves told and how once again, in a few years or maybe weeks, She and Leo and Holly will be back at it. As the novel is about to be silenced for now, it reminds us: "Think not that Ayesha's strength is spent or her tale is done, for of it thou readest but a single page" (p. 186).

(YIKES.)

What we have read and will keep reading will never be a conclusive tale of the triumph of heterosexual love and imperialist capitalism, not some sublime right-wing tragedy. Instead, we have the never-ending pleasure of returning to the tale that keeps returning to us: the subversive comedy of homosexual love, anarchic recurrence, and abusing She: "Thus he beat her with his words, and, wonderful to say, Ayesha . . . submitted to the chastisement meekly [and] began to cry" (p. 147). So much for She-Who-Must-Be-Obeyed and all She represents. In the end, it's the boys who get to tell the story, the happy boys with their erotic games that never end, that keep coming right back to them.

(And it's the same story, right? Have I got that?)

I'd ended the essay and you keep on going. Yes, they keep telling the same story.

(And old Ayesha only has a bit part in it, right? Despite appearances, she's only a blocking character, adds a little spice to how Holly goes after little Leo and beds him. That it?)

Yes, and the politics, too, which you forgot; they're important. Now I don't have a closing line. You went on past the end and took away all the force of the closing I had and used back there, half a page ago.

(I don't understand the political argument too well, but anyhow that part is— not wearisome exactly but less arresting than the other part—the part about sex, for instance. But I'll give you an ending. The one you have is a little nasty, about beating Ayesha, which seems really not so central in the novel as you make it. I don't think She is a hazard.)

You don't?

(No, I like her. Besides, I think she's integral, part of the whole system you talk about, the system that returns over and over. I mean, where would they be without She? Holly and Leo would be just another musty and dull couple of bachelors sitting around in London being mostly respectable and probably not even interested in sex any more. As it is, they get to go chasing after things, which naturally inspires them to chase after one another and get into strange and entingling spots and eat spicy food. So here's your ending: Instead of tragic finales we have comic recurrence; in place of funerals, a dance, a complex and all-inclusive dance where the conclusion of one set throws everyone into the opening whirls of another. And at the center of this raucous festival, doing a most improper dirty dance and urging others to follow, is an unlikely three-some: an old ugly man trying to get to a young pretty man, who is stepping away—not very briskly—toward a woman so beautiful and so understanding that she can perpetuate the twirling dance of desire, getting what pleasure she [and we] can from keeping the dance and the chase and the story alive. What other pleasure is there?)

Is that where you'd end?

The Third Part
Fictional Strippers

10

Words Cannot Express
Frankenstein's Tripping on the Tongue

𝓘N UNIVERSAL PICTURES' 1931 film *Frankenstein,* the creature, outfitted with a brain that is sadly abnormal, can manage only rather pointless bestial (or motorcycle) noises. Meanwhile, his creator is gabbling on with manic aplomb, spilling even the secret of his resuscitating science (a ray in the spectrum beyond ultra-violet) and letting us know that, however questionable his control over his offspring, he is never at a loss for words, and good ones, too. That's quite a switch from the version in Mary Shelley's novel, where the self-educated creature has made himself into a Demosthenes/Joseph Goebbels figure whose dangerous fluency can very nearly neutralize the senses and trap one within its eloquence. At least that's his creator's view of the matter, a view we may suspect a little, given that Victor Frankenstein is no master of the media himself. Sour grapes? Victor's own mumblings are comprised of stock phrases, wild inclusive adjectives, and verbal equivalents of quitting the game altogether: "words cannot express," "I cannot describe," "inexpressible pleasures," "unspeakable rages." He's the editor, after all, with an authority over the words that's hard to beat; so when we find him throwing in the towel with such phrases as "No word, no expression could body forth . . .", we may just sneer. The creature, after all, locates those bodying-forth expressions readily enough.

All this is pretty strange, this matching of the glib against the dumb, this apparent contest which is not really between words but between that which can be in words, on one hand, and, on the other, that which cannot be in words or which reaches beyond words or which distrusts words or which doesn't know which words would suit or which knows and prefers not to use them or which wants *us* to supply the words or which wants us not to read but to look or which wants us to read signs other than words or which sanctions silence as sacred or which points to but does not name the forbidden—or something. This chapter is a meditation on the book's inarticulateness (if that's what it is, which it probably isn't). I want to propose a series of plain answers to plain questions, a series of answers wholly plausible and wholly incompatible. That's the goal, at least. The point is to say something (profitable) about our customary modes of constructing explanations, about how innocently we center such explanations, and about the happy ease with which such centers may be shifted, juggled, made to disappear. I don't want to say that the book is *about* The Silent or The Inarticulate. I have no idea what the book is *about,* though I do have an idea that such a formulation misplaces the emphasis. I don't even know that there's a contest. Perhaps it's just play, inconsequential play of the greatest importance.

LET ME REVEAL MY TALE: VICTOR'S REVELATIONS

"Hear me; let me reveal my tale; and you will dash the cup from your lips!"(8) says Victor to a bold explorer (Walton) who has gone looking for love among the icebergs. Walton, in no position to be choosy, finds his affection for his guest growing every day, and is happy to settle in and listen to Victor's tale without much regard to the cup. After all, Walton says, this is a man whose very countenance bespeaks "benevolence and sweetness that I never saw equalled," along with a bit of "wildness, and even madness," to be sure, but never mind that. Just hear this man speak, Walton says, and you will love him as he does: "When he speaks, although his words are culled with the choicest art, yet they flow with rapidity and unparalleled eloquence" (Letter 4).

With Walton looking on in speechless adoration, then, Victor launches forth: "I am by birth a Genovese, and my family is one of the most distinguished of that republic. My ancestors. . ." (1). One must indeed be enchanted to regard this as unparalleled eloquence. But perhaps Victor is just taking some warm-up pitches, and we are willing to shuffle irritably beside Walton as Victor slogs through an extremely tedious tale about an exalted family where everyone doted on everyone else but especially on Victor, about a childhood so wearisomely happy as to be marked apparently by no events at all (other than the folks going out and buying the boy a little girl), about his undisciplined reading, and about his school days, which were certainly not Tom Brown's. Meanwhile, we may not be finding Victor all that adept as a story-teller. He mentions, for instance, that the January-May marriage of his parents resulted in a grandfatherly sort of behavior from father to mother "which gave an inexpressible grace to his behaviour to her" (1). If we cared anything about the matter, we might wonder why such grace would be inexpressible; but we don't. Similarly, we are unlikely to want to hear much about his feelings for his toy "more than sister." And not much is what we get: "No word, no expression could body forth the kind of relation in which she stood to me" (1). The smutty metaphor, "body forth," suggests pornography most of us would like to avoid. At least, we are glad to have dodged the many words and expressions that would bring the body forth. We want Victor to get on with it.

The payoff for listening to all that about Albertus Magnus is, of course, the creature, which is what we've all been waiting for. Finally, Victor concocts him and says, "How can I describe my emotions at this catastrophe" (5)? That question, we are glad to find, is not explored, Victor's emotions being a great deal less interesting to us than the twitching body before him. Of that body he asks, "[How can I] delineate the wretch whom with such infinite pains and care I had endeavoured to form?" When he goes on to say that the creature "became such a thing as even Dante could not have conceived" (5) we feel cheated, knowing that Dante would have done just fine and suspecting that Victor sheers off into the ineffable just at the point when we are counting on his unparalleled eloquence to help us out.

Victor tends to lose his dictionary every time things get interesting. Apparently not trusting his ability to cull his words with the choicest art, he lets Justine go hang, though he isn't happy about it: "No one can conceive the anguish I suffered" (7); "I cannot pretend to describe what I then felt . . . words cannot convey an idea of the heart-sickening despair that I then endured" (8). He admits some responsibility for these "deeds of mischief beyond description," but even that confession does not make the words flow with the rapidity and clarity Walton has promised us: "I was seized by remorse and the sense of guilt, which hurried me away to a hell of intense tortures such as no language can describe" (9). Victor confronts the creature a bit later with the accusation that his ungrateful progeny has made him "wretched beyond expression" (10), leaving it a matter of doubt whether the creature might not bear responsibility for his tongue-tying as well. Whatever the cause, things do not improve. Victor reacts to the creature's long monologue by being unable to "describe," being at a loss, "even in my own heart," to find an "expression" for his sensations (17).

He does well depicting trees and rocks from time to time, but repeated shocks throw Victor back into the land of the wordless: on seeing Henry's corpse, "How can I describe my sensations on beholding it" (21); on Elizabeth's, "a sensation of horror not to be described" (23).

Grief, horror, happiness, love (or whatever it is he feels for Elizabeth), remorse, guilt, and even anger—"My rage is unspeakable" (23)—are beyond the reach of this teller of the tale. What's more, his incapacity seems to infect others on contact. Walton, who had heretofore done quite well with words, listens to Victor and is stricken dumb: "All that I should express would be inadequate and feeble" (24). Victor's death does not restore Walton's tongue; leaving the corpse for a moment in order to write to his sister about how he cannot muster words for writing, he reenters to find draped over the body "a form which I cannot find words to describe" (24).

So Victor, seeking a triumph over nature, over Walton, and over us through words, has failed; just as he failed utterly in his debate with his creature. He had hoped to use his award-winning fluency against his un-tutored offspring in order to bring him under control. On first sighting his son, hate and anger "at first deprived me of utterance," but not for long: "I recovered only to overwhelm him with words," namely, "Begone, vile insect! Or rather, stay, that I may trample you to dust!" (10). Unparalleled eloquence maybe, but it does not seem really to overwhelm the creature, who, without missing not a beat, booms out with tragic Romantic control suggest-ing a tranquilly recollected emotion, "All men hate the wretched; how, then, must I be hated, who am miserable beyond all living things!" Victor's sputter-ings cannot hold up against this.

Victor's impotence with words creates the possibility of a good many explanatory centers that are not without their allure. We can connect his remoteness from words to his activities, his unholy or inhuman presumption that removes him from the natural communion, signalled in language, among humans or between humans and nature or God. We can construct any num-ber of general moral fables in this way, or we may turn the argument toward semiotics, toward gender (Victor's maleness), or, more particularly, toward his social and political positioning or his psyche. I am hardly able to keep myself from following the line that as Victor advances toward the truth, toward the real, he must necessarily abandon language, which is powerless in the face of the referent. It's probably just as well for all of us that I do not want to follow any such particular line here, but only want to suggest something about the infinite number of lines we may spot (or draw) and the way they have of erasing themselves before our eyes.

EXONERATING VICTOR: "THESE INEFFECTUAL WORDS"

The first thing that should erase itself is this construction we have called "Victor." Most of us these days will probably be quick to abandon a character-centered explanation of any kind, especially when, as I hinted above, we have the much more enticing territory of language itself. It is, we will say, language itself that is dumb, not Victor. That's a formulation that's more fun even than incest; and we can certainly lay claim to some plausibility (and hope for an audience) by announcing that it is language itself (and the perforations and endless gaps in its fabric) that is foregrounded.

First of all, we have been lying a little: these reachings toward the ineffable or admissions of illiteracy are not confined to Victor but are spread around pretty much everywhere. The creature, Elizabeth, Victor's father, and Walton all use similar formulations. Walton's very first letter, written long before Victor has blighted him, lets Margaret know how excited he is at the prospect of departing on his voyage by telling how he cannot tell her how excited he is: "I cannot describe to you"; "It is impossible to communicate to you" (1). Waiving as inadmissible, crude, and certainly unpublishable the possibility that Mary Shelley simply didn't have very many words at her disposal and was thus stymied, we hasten to the failure of language itself and find the most promising focus not in Walton but in the moving voice of the creature.

An argument based on creaturespeak and the silence at the heart of language or on the connections between words and power might well be rich, rounded, and persuasive.[1] Power is irresistible these days, and we do find the creature hoping that he can find in words the tool to connect himself first to knowledge, then to virtue, and then to love (with the cottagers). He learns to read and speak in the hope that the force of his words will blind all the cottagers, not just the old man, "enab[ling] them to over-look the deformity of my figure" (15). But word-power is ill-equipped to do battle with sight; and the creature's trust in an inferior power and his control of it are turned against him. Victor sternly warns Walton: "He is eloquent and persuasive, and once his words had power over my heart; but trust him not. . . . Hear him not." And Walton, sure enough, obediently tries to deafen himself: "I called to mind what Frankenstein had said of his powers of eloquence and persuasion" (24). In these references to sight is a clue we will pick up later, but there's enough here on power and words to keep us busy for a standard-length essay.

A more purely deconstructive, less political bent would return us to the fascinating section where the creature describes his life-before-language and the effects of mastering it (or letting it master him). Particularly juicy here is the fact that the creature admits to a failure with words only after he has them, not before. Before he has initiated himself into "the science of words and letters," indeed even "before I learned to distinguish between the operation of my senses" (11), the creature speaks an artless, representational prose that sounds like Robinson Crusoe's: "I found that the berries were spoiled by this operation, and the nuts and roots much improved" (11). Even quite dramatic events are described plainly, as if words could connect with things: "The whole village was roused; some fled, some attacked me, until grievously bruised by stones and many other kinds of missile weapons, I escaped to the open country" (11). When the creature says, "I lost sight of her, and in about a quarter of an hour she returned bearing the pail" (11), the contrast with Victor's hyperbolic, on-the-stretch, periodically fumbling prose is quite marked. For Victor, with all his epiphanies and eternities, there are no quarter-hours so carefully noted, and certainly no pails.

But, as soon as the creature begins to acquire language, silence descends: "I can hardly describe to you the effect of these books." And when he breaks the silence he sounds distressingly like Victor, using the same kind of pumped-up, off-the-scale language: "They produced in me an infinity of new images and feelings, that somehow raised me to ecstasy, but more frequently sunk me into the lowest dejection" (15). What has happened to the roots and berries and pails? We do not want to hear the creature whining, "Who can describe their horror and consternation?" (15). We get more than enough of that from Victor.

There is luxurious material here, no doubt, so rich that we will overlook, on one hand, the reverberating power of the creature's direct words, "I shall be with you on your wedding night" and, on the other, the clarity of his writing later on: "You will find near this place, if you follow not too tardily, a dead hare; eat and be refreshed" (24). These things will likely not block us from such pleasantness as connecting speech and muteness, language and illiteracy, power and impotence. Mary Shelley's Preface provides an interesting ironic locus here in its promise to "speak to the mysterious fears of our nature," to speak, that is, to what cannot be recalled or named because "mysterious" or beyond language, to use a foregrounded inadequacy of language to evoke a forbidden semiotics. The motive force of her tale, she says, was not in any referent, not in anything Dr. Darwin "really did," but in "what was spoken of." "I speak . . . of what was spoken of," she says, thus distancing her own language system from any contact with the "really" and dramatizing either its self-supporting, ineffectual artificiality or its mysterious ability to speak to and of the unspeakable, the mysterious fears of our nature.

All of this is extraordinarily attractive, since it can be so easily tied to metacriticism, to a deconstruction of the cautionary reading of the novel. Victor's don't-mess-with-mother-nature sermon, his attempt to persuade Walton and us not to aspire to be greater than our character will allow, is necessarily delivered in a language that promotes what it seeks to censure, that reveals what it attempts to hide, that speaks the unspeakable. From this point of view, it is rather unfortunate that Victor is seized with a blatant and egregious deathbed ambivalence: "Yet why do I say this? I have myself been blasted in these hopes, yet another may succeed" (24). Why did he say *that*? His explicitness may tempt us to psychology and away from language, where the big prizes are stocked. The point is not Victor's waverings but the fact that all prohibitions must be sanctions. We must not trespass, but we must; we must respect the limits of our nature, but we would be fools to do so. How do we know? Language tells us so.

JUST DO AS I SAY

But language determines the book and whatever we say about it, so it's hard to escape some debt to it, some kind of centering. In fact, what we have considered and dismissed thus far will reappear, our dismissals being gentle and not to be taken seriously. In this case, we might note that all the heady talk about gaps, silences, and vacancies can proceed with authority only within some framework of expectation where continuity, sound, and substance are anticipated or even taken for granted. Less abstractly, we note that the novel often directs us not away from but toward speech and substance. The *strange*, the unnameable, here in the form of the first sighting of the monstrous creature, excites Walton to writing: "So strange an accident has happened to us that I cannot forbear recording it" (Letter 4). Instead of the recoil of language before the strange, here we are propelled toward their coordination. Walton goes on to register the strangeness quite exactly: "a low carriage, fixed on a sledge and drawn by dogs" to the north "at the distance of half a mile" with a figure "apparently of gigantic stature" on it. The sight "excited our unqualified wonder," but that wonder, significantly, produces in them not stupefied silence but an itch to close the gap, to track down the strange. This closing of gaps, a foregrounding of the power of naming, can be traced in M. Waldeman's connection of scientific discovery, even Victor's landmark discovery, with the power "to give new names" to old "facts" (3).

We might also note that the words-cannot-express or the I-cannot-describe formulae are often fakes, leading us not to consider language's inadequacy but its ability to do just what it says it cannot. Victor's father says there is no way he can relate the family's misfortune and then proceeds to do so—"William is dead!" (7); Clerval says, "I can offer you no consolation" and then says "a few words of consolation" (7); Victor himself says the creature's "deeds of mischief" are "beyond description" and then describes them; he says he cannot tell us what the creature looks like, a task beyond Dante himself, and then does just that: "His yellow skin scarcely covered the work of muscles . . ." (5).

Such considerations are not likely to stand in the way of reflections on inadequacy or impotence or absence. We have more interesting things to say to one another about these matters than about talk and substance. Still, they might be enough to damage any confident centerings and perhaps to scare us away for a time from pure considerations of language. But we'll be back.

THOSE MYSTERIOUS FEARS OF OUR NATURE

Say we take the phrase from the Preface, "speaking to those mysterious fears of our nature," and attend to the last part of the phrase and not the first, to horror rather than speech.[2] After all, isn't silence terrifying, suggesting that the inability to name marks an inability to control? Speechless, we are at the mercy of that which cannot be reduced to speech; we come face to face with the monster that does not argue, simply rends and tears. Generic studies of a historical kind suggest themselves here, the centrality of the unnameable to terror fiction; psychological or psychoanalytic studies are possible, Freud's uncanny being just one formulation of that which explodes the illusion of rational and linguistic power; studies of horror films are a natural, perhaps connecting the gaps between words not to silence but to the substitution of music, a sound which we cannot ward off and which dramatizes the uselessness of words in the face of mystery.
The last example suggests the weakness of this centering: silence has no privileged connection to horror. "I'm gonna getcha!" or "I shall be with you on your wedding night" or creepy music do just as well.

YOU HAD TO BE THERE

It's not silence itself that is terrifying, common sense tells us, but the experience; the raw, visceral horror can invade only in and through the event. There's no use talking about it, you had to be there. In a novel, which can only talk about it, some rhetoric must be produced which creates the illusion of the experience itself, we might say, and the most obvious form for that rhetoric is the disavowal of the power of words. "Even in my own heart," Victor says, "I could give no expression to my sensations" (17). At the heart of the matter, we find not words but the displacement of words so as to make way for terror or the dramatized inability of words to dislodge a terrifying resident. The contest is often fought openly. Here is Elizabeth in one of those recurrent moments when words cannot console: "Ah! While we love, while we are true to each other, here in this land of peace and beauty, your native country, we may reap every tranquil blessing— what can disturb our peace?" Perhaps like Arnold's girl-friend at Dover Beach, Victor will have none of this ah-love-let-us-be-true-to-one-another, even when it is coupled with Wordsworthian appeals to tranquil blessings from nature. He raises the issue for us quite clearly: "And could not such words from her whom I fondly prized before every other gift of fortune suffice to chase away the fiend that lurked in my heart?" By this point in the novel, we know that words can never win out over experience—"Even as she spoke I drew near to her, as if in terror" (9). Something much worse than a host of ignorant armies is out there in the night, and no hush-a-bye words are going to help us.

Even with milder experiences, like grief, we sometimes find a variation on the words-cannot-express formula that seems to promote the supremacy of experience. Here, it's not that Victor cannot describe but that he "need not describe" the feelings of those who live through the death of a parent, in this case his mother: "Why should I describe a sorrow which all have felt, and must feel?" (3). Indeed, since we've all been there or soon will be, it's a waste of words; experience will show us more plainly than language ever can. Despite the fact that the experience is an unhappy one, there's an easy inclusiveness and authorial modesty about such turns. It seems democratic, this conception of an all-inclusive experience, even when it's put in a snobbish way: "None but they who have experienced them can conceive of the enticements of science" (4). This way of disarming words by pointing to the experience looks at first like exclusion itself, the creation of one of those revolting Mensa groups. Really, though, these "enticements" are made common to any who study science; it is all the same, this scientific thrill, and it embraces any who come near.

Such an argument, as it becomes political, seems to be leading us toward an anti-intellectual populism, an exaltation of common experience over the elitist authority wrapped in words. I wonder if we want to pursue a line which would work very well with Artemus Ward, but which here seems to be leading straight toward the dullest of all readings of the novel: a condemnation of the hubristic overreacher Victor. We seem to have come to an impasse in experience, probably because we trusted in the first place to that most wretched of guides, common sense.

SUBLIME IS AS SUBLIME DOES

But we may have an out, an opening for explanation by way of a more refined view of experience that avoids the merging, anti-intellectual politics we found by pursuing experience in the raw. The sublime, after all, is not a levelling phenomenon; however much it may move us away from petty concerns of self, it does not propel one toward the masses but towards clouds, mountain peaks, and cataclysms. It reaches beyond words, we will argue, into transcendent realms of expansive, soul-swelling ecstasy, realms compounded of the awe-inspiring, the terrible, and the magnificent.

Walton's first letter indicates that he has been launched toward the Arctic by a yen for the sublime: "I feel my heart glow with an enthusiasm which elevates me to heaven." Now, enthusiasm is not the same as sublimity, you'll be saying, but let's not quibble. All we are claiming is that Walton is out for sublimity. When he finds it, presumably he will stop writing letters, having reached consummate muteness. That he doesn't stop writing, even for a minute, simply means that he never completes his quest, never finds the great galvanic sublimity at the pole. It is a novel about the failure to find sublimity, you see.

That argument is guttering out on us, but it's hard to give up easily on the nice idea that the unspeakable is somehow hooked up with the sublime. Not wanting to get sucked into a hapless debate with historical scholars who really know what words like enthusiasm and sublime mean, we can look into the novel for the sublime, for the very word. Not surprisingly, we find it a favorite word with Victor, the novel's equivalent of Ralph Waldo Emerson in his love for vasty-towering words. Victor uses "sublime" a total of four times, by our count, each time in reference to the Alps. A particular valley is "rendered sublime by the mighty Alps," and this particular valley "is more wonderful and sublime, but not so beautiful and picturesque" as some other valley (9). Hopping over the traps embedded in these comparisons, we locate Victor saying in the next chapter that the mountain scenes were "sublime and magnificent" and that they "filled me with a sublime ecstasy" (10). That's perfect. Just enough evidence to work with and the right sorts of details: the elevation produced by the sublime is not exciting to him, i.e., it does not cause him to babble; instead he finds himself "subdued and tranquilized," "the awful and majestic . . . solemnizing my mind and causing me to forget the passing cares of life" (10). That's highly suggestive, very good stuff. Forgetting the passing cares of life, about which he would be tempted to talk, he stands solemnly silent, tranquilized.

Later on, when he is in England, Victor takes a little tour "to view again mountains and streams and all the wondrous works" of Nature (19). In fact, he seems to spend something like four months (not counting another six lolling around London—don't hold us to those calculations) on this sightseeing, all the time aware in a foggy sort of way that the creature may be getting impatient for his promised mate and exercising himself by murdering a few back home. But Victor needs the sublime, we will say, needs to prepare himself for the unspeakably disgusting act before him by some extended bathing in the unspeakably majestic.

And thus we have a novel that somehow connects terror and overarching magnificence to silence by way of sublimity. And we can quit with that. In fact, we had better quit fast, since it would be just as easy to argue that the sublime incites not silence, but talk and plenty of it. People out on the grand tour, looking for the sublime and finding it, were always equipped with pencil and pad. More to the point, Victor's own idea of being tranquilized is, apparently, not our own: he certainly is not silent when he is in the Alps; and his rambles through Oxford, Derbyshire, the Lakes, and Edinburgh spur him to write a compact tourist guide. In the presence of the sublime, Victor's tongue is loosened so much he doesn't even speak about being speechless. The creature's most impassioned words are uttered in the midst of these elevating and, we had thought, tranquilizing scenes.

This idea is a shambles. It seems to be leading, in addition to nowhere, to history, politics, and psychology; and we don't want to travel to those places yet. We somehow got side-tracked from language, which is the field we're used to playing on, one to which we'll now try to return.

IF YOU CAN'T GIVE ME ALL, GIVE ME NOTHING

We fly immediately to the direct negation of substance and, we hope, the disavowal of any efficacy in language, perhaps the indirect or paradoxical disavowal of speech in the act of speaking. All this might be located in the gamey word "nothing," a fierce and nihilistic signal waving to us repeatedly from the text. We recognize as characteristic the pounding negations, the emptyings-out that open Chapter 9: "Nothing is more painful to the human mind than . . . a weight of despair and remorse . . . which nothing could remove . . . a hell of intense tortures which no language can describe." The substantives here—mind, pain, re-morse, tortures—are evacuated or simply swept away by the prominent force of denial: nothing, nothing, no. It is not that these are pretty bad miseries and hard to describe; this is the black, empty maw of the abyss, without substance and without words.

Similarly, when the creature tries to describe himself and his feelings, he does so by making prominent, in fact overwhelming, not what he has but what he has been denied: "If I have no ties and no affections, hatred and vice must be my portion" (17). The lack, the emptiness is made flagrant; all is blackness: "to me," he says, "every country must be equally horrible" (16), since everywhere he will find the same denial, the same wordless rage, the same ironic pointlessness of his carefully acquired eloquence. Black silence is all.

There are several ways to go with this. One is toward the opposition between "all" and "nothing." The creature is especially fond of the word "all," using it, however, with much the same force he gives to the word "nothing": "All men hate the wretched; how, then, must I be hated, who am miserable beyond all living things" (10). The inclusive (or sublime) comforts of *all* are denied here, the solid and affirmative syntax acting not to locate the creature's misery in human life but to place it beyond life, beyond language. Later, after being bashed by the cottagers he was trying to befriend, the creature uses the same ironic formula: "All, save I, were at rest, or in enjoyment" (17).

This odd all/nothing equivalence might lead us toward investigating opposi- tional habits of mind, binary structures that force the characters, at least the male characters, into constructing their worlds and lives into alternatives that are so extreme they meet, crash together, end in disaster. As the creature learns language, we might note, he loses his natural grasp of a graduated scale, where nuts and roots taste *better* roasted than raw, and moves to Victor's absolutist realm, where nuts and berries will be either ambrosial or disgusting beyond all food ever tasted—and, of course, beyond all description. Victor's inability to think in any other terms could be said to lie at the core of his dilemma, and that is the dilemma both of language and of the plot of this novel: why, in seeking for the secret of life, does he turn to death? Perhaps because, in his stretched-out oppositional world, they are not really different: "To examine the causes of life, we must first have recourse to death" (4), Victor blandly announces, as if he were saying, "To have some milk, we must first locate a cow." Why study life through death? Pushing a relational language system to its extreme, Victor recognizes, like Levi-Strauss, stark oppositions, and then, unlike Levi-Strauss, he crushes them into a mad oneness: he examines "all the minutiae of creation, as exemplified in the change from life to death, and death to life" (4). Here Victor's purified language system wins out even over experimental science. One wonders how he located in his microscope those minute creatures changing from death back into life?

But, for all its allure, this attack on binaries has a dated feel to it that makes it boring. Not so boring, however, as the center that old common sense would force on us: that this all-or-nothing business is just a strained way of asserting uniqueness or something special, a tendency of melodrama. No need to look to the countless examples in the speech of Walton, Victor, or the creature, none of whom are satisfied with being the *most* miserable, wretched, or so forth but strain for being the thing itself (like the movie ad: Stallone *is* Rambo) or, even better, something beyond that, something we have never before conceived. And it's not just the characters who are treated this way; such cheap straining after effect extends even to the weather and to grapes: "never did the fields bestow a more plentiful harvest or the vines yield a more luxuriant vintage" (4). It's a crass, braying way of telling us we're hearing something new, experiencing something we haven't before, reading something we should tell all our friends to buy. But this is a crude argument, better left to the lower orders of reviewers, those who talk about rhetoric as "manipulation" and who are on better terms with common sense than are we.

We can, after all, occupy ourselves by destroying our own initial argument, the one about *all* and *nothing* both acting to obliterate substance and language, simply by suggesting that these terms also act to *speak* of what is not to be spoken of, to name what is not there. Sometimes a kind of double negative emphasizes the substance: "Among the lessons Felix had bestowed upon Saffie, geography had not been omitted" (16). Sometimes the emphasis is on the ominously unnamed but clear substance: "no incident occurred from which my rage and misery could not extract its food" (16). Even here, however, while we are likely drawn to considering the incidents which *did* occur aplenty to nourish the creature's rage and misery, the possibility of something else is held open, something that did not occur: welcome incidents which would have fed positive faculties.

It is this capacity of negation to body forth what is not present which deconstructs any neat formulations, such as those with which we began, about negation and silence. Walton begins the novel by announcing what has not happened, thus erasing it and also bringing it into prominence: "You will rejoice to hear that no disaster. . . ." He goes on to deny (and thus affirm) the possibility that his mission is suicidal: "I have no ambition to lose my life . . ." and to enumerate the frozen wonders he has not seen, the "eternal light," "the wondrous power which attracts the needle," and so forth. In his next letter, he continues to bring forth absences to center stage by denying them: "I have no friend"; "Yet do not suppose . . . that I am wavering in my resolution"; "I shall do nothing rashly." The last is particularly interesting, as it denies the rashness that marks his enterprise but, at the same time, announces the ironic truth: he ends up doing nothing and doing it rashly.

COMPARISONS ARE ODIOUS

Having abandoned the possibility of securely connecting negation with silence, we might turn briefly to a relational scheme and look at comparative structures in the novel. We will not, I think, want to look very long. Apparent comparisons turn out almost always to be absolutes: "No guilt, no mischief, no malignity, no misery, can be found comparable to mine" (24). That's the creature, but Victor speaks that way too, entering into unseemly comparisons with the about-to-be-slaughtered Justine—"the torture of the accused did not equal mine" (8)—and often providing us with mock comparisons that turn into the same old self-exaltation: "More miserable than man ever was before" (21). A comparative base is used to exalt the other term into the unknown.

The clash between Victor and his creature turns into a bizarre misery contest. In such a contest, the can-you-top-this prize goes to the one whose unspeakable misery is more unspeakable than his opponent's. Oddly, it is necessary to give voice to this ineffableness in order to advance in the tournament. Once dead, Victor can no longer compete with his creature, who crows over his creator's corpse: "Blasted as thou wert, my agony was still superior to thine" (24). So, comparisons turn to absolutes which are turned back into weapons in a contest that reaches a null point of silence. All of this is possibly interesting, but it isn't leading us into any games we didn't play out and toss aside in the last section.

WOMANSPEAK

Falling back once again, though not entirely daunted, from the idea of language in itself, we look, with very little hope, toward gender.[3] Difficulties pile up fast, especially in distinguishing the genders on the basis of speech. It is true that Justine and Elizabeth seem more articulate than Victor, but nearly anybody would. Besides, they aren't around very long. Worse, the chief males in the story—Victor, Walton, and Clerval—are all specifically feminized in some way. Clerval is attracted to soft Oriental literature, so "different from the manly and heroic poetry of Greece and Rome!" (6); Walton says he has spent his "best years" under his sister's "gentle and feminine fosterage," thus having his "groundwork" "so refined" that macho brutality produces in him an "intense distaste." Victor's childhood has been similarly gentled-up by his angelic mother and the "silken cord" by which he was guided so softly (1). "My mother," he says, "had much desired to have a daughter, but I continued their single off-spring" (1). Aha!

Curiously, the creature, who seems to many readers to be the most lovely and androgynous of the lot, despite his tendency toward violence, is resolutely and conventionally masculine. He makes some passes toward pedophilia, but generally he is active, athletic, self-sufficient, and doggedly heterosexual. He'd be just the boy for Woody Hayes; he wants to be all that he can be, wondering if he should identify with the Satan or Adam portrayed in *Paradise Lost* but never once considering Eve or the angels.

If we push at all this, we are going to end up with some perverse reading of the gentle and connecting masculine at war with the brutal and alienating feminine—and that's no good. We'll just drop it.

I HAVE THAT WITHIN WHICH PASSETH SHOW

Turning to something completely different, how about the possibility that words are prohibited, and prohibited, just to go whole hog, by the most powerful censor of them all, the incest prohibition?[4] Just recall the dream Victor has just after creating the monster: an erotic vision of Elizabeth, embraced and kissed, transmogrifying into the corpse of his dead mother being held in his arms, and then, immediately on awakening, the grinning face of the creature thrust through the curtains surrounding his bed (5). Recall also his oft-expressed resentment of his father, a resentment usually allowed only a mild form but once bursting through in a wild accusation that lays the blame for everything on dad: had he given more than a "cursory glance" to Victor's reading and taken the trouble to explain things to him, all might have been well (2). Then, look at a longish passage in one of those most unwelcome lectures Victor receives from father-intruder:[5]

> "Do you think, Victor . . . that I do not suffer also? No one could love a child more than I loved your brother"— tears came into his eyes as he spoke—"but is it not a duty to the survivors that we should refrain from augmenting their unhappiness . . . ? It is also a duty owed to yourself, for excessive sorrow prevents improvement or enjoyment, or even the discharge of daily usefulness, without which no man is fit for society." (9)

Note that the first sentence raises directly and uncomfortably the Oedipal rivalry in terms of Victor's constant theme: I am the winner in the suffering contest. The second deflects his father's love away from Victor onto a rival, though not the one he is worried about, as it happens. (We'll get to that.) The third sentence is phrased rhetorically—"is it not?"—but then turns into stern and severe hectoring in the fourth—it *is*! Let's say that this passage and others like it sting Victor in a thousand ways. Let's say that Victor is inescapably attached to his mother, especially now that she's dead, and that he harbors murderous thoughts about his father. He certainly doesn't want to hear about his father's "love," since that can only be the love for the impossible prize Victor, too, is after (never mind about the disposable brother). And he does not want to be lectured, treated as a child, regarded as insignificant in the race for the mother's favors. Victor's response to these exhortations is, significantly, silence. The good advice, he says, "was totally inapplicable to my case," so he says nothing. There is that within him which passeth show, but he is forbidden to utter it.

Now, old Frankenstein's closing comments on bucking up, doing your duty, getting back into the social round may remind us of Claudius' attempts to have Hamlet see it his way and let bygones be bygones. I hope they do, since it's the *Hamlet* parallel I wish to suggest. How's this? Victor's Oedipal rages are out of control, especially since his mother's death. His brother's death is a mere trifle or, to put it more exactly, a deflection of Victor's true impulse, an impulse revealed in his erotic dream, where another deflection or screen, Elizabeth, gives way to the true, albeit necrophilic, image of longing: his mother.

The creature pops in, not coincidentally, right at this point. He is a continuation of and an answer to the dream, a psychic double, who declares often enough that he is a "type" of Victor (15), a claim apparently verified in Victor's recurrent ravings about being the killer himself. The double's mission, should he choose to accept it, is to murder the father and revenge Victor for the violation of the mother. Elizabeth, like Ophelia, is both a mask for and a sacrifice to this stark incestuous drama. Victor tries both to carry out this homicidal drama and to avoid it: he creates the creature but he runs away. The father, however, with some versatility plays both the part of Old Hamlet and that of Claudius; he keeps popping in and intruding himself, particularly when he presses for the "immediate solemnization of the marriage" between Victor and Elizabeth (18). By attempting to sort out his son's erotic affairs, i.e., blocking him from the mother, i.e., castrating him, Victor's father evokes what he deserves, silence. How can Victor speak what he feels? And what does he feel? "To me," he says, "the idea of an immediate union with my Elizabeth was one of horror and dismay" (18). No doubt it is, and the father should learn to leave well enough alone.

But he keeps after Victor with his shears, and the son always reacts with anything but pleasure. When he is in prison, in fact, we get more straight-from-the-psyche hysteria: "Oh! Take him away! I cannot see him; for God's sake, do not let him enter!" (21). Of course, there are rational, surface explanations for all these things, but we are not conducting this inquiry on the surface, thanks very much. The line is that Victor, unable to face or articulate his impossible desires, acts on them indirectly through his double, piling up corpses until finally the father is dead (23). Just before the death, Victor has tried to arrange in his mind a convenient transfer of affections, a neat sorting-out of couples, saying that his father "doted on" Elizabeth "with all that affection which a man feels." Such a solution—you take the girl, pa, and leave ma to me—is impracticable on several grounds, so Victor finally kills off the father and then, after a short delirium, has nothing to do but die, not in silence, to be sure, but in a rage of guilt that expresses itself in feeble self-justification: "During these last days, I have been occupied in examining my past conduct, nor do I find it blameable" (24).

Well, there we are, with the most neatly tied package yet.[6] The reason it's so neatly tied has to do, of course, with the neatly tied premises it is using, not to mention the very neat work done on *Hamlet* already by Ernest Jones. Perhaps we aren't bothered that Victor doesn't just die, but hurries off to harangue the magistrate, equips himself for the trip, takes a shot at trying to ennoble Walton's crew, and so forth. But not many readers are going to see the father-son focus as central or sufficiently inclusive; and we have an even better reason for leaving this psychoanalytic formalism: most of what we've been saying does not fore-ground silence. And we're determined to do that.

JUST LOOK AT THAT, WILL YOU?

And there is a way to keep to psychoanalysis while considering silence, namely by way of Lacan's strong misreading of Freud. The connections between vision, language, authorship, reading and conceptions of the self have been outlined and explored so often, we can be relieved of that duty here. Let's just say that if normal reading, like normal seeing, necessitates complex and dynamic shifts between the subject and object position, then an abnormal book like this one might very well flirt with perversion, with voyeurism specifically, both in its characters and its readers. Voyeurism we might locate as the attempt to hold steadily to the subject position, an attempt based on a terrible fear of becoming an object, that is, of being looked at. It is, in one way, an aggressive maneuver, seeking to hold the object in its view; but the fear on which such aggression rests is that of a very weak ego or self. I need to look *so as not* to be looked at. I must control the Gaze, lest the Gaze control and engulf me.

The voyeur (whom I see we are calling "I") will never speak, of course, since the last thing we want is anyone spotting us. The voyeur is silent; the ideal object is blind. Voyeurism, then, has certain obvious affinities with some kinds of reading and with many kinds of criticism (not ours, of course), where a sadistic attempt to maintain absolute power over the looking is exercised. Authorship as well, though in more complex ways, may be figured as an attempt to look out at us, to control the Gaze. The promise of Victor to "reveal" his story is, at least in part, a cozening of Walton and us, a blinding of us so that the looking remains all in the writer's control. Even in his weakened condition, he has edited Walton's manuscript; and it is he, of course, who is managing the creature's narrative, or so he thinks. But he is greatly threatened, by the creature and by us. As readers, we seem to be safe from the eyes of anyone, free to be silent. But any sort of active reading will involve us frighteningly in a complex and mirrored field of vision and words where we not only see and hear but are seen and must speak.

Let's develop this briefly. The general voyeuristic strategy is introduced almost immediately, when Walton and his crew sight the creature: "We watched the rapid progress of the traveller with our telescopes until he was lost among the distant inequalities of the ice" (Letter 4). Safe, concealed for the most part by the ship, equipped with magic eyes the object does not have, these sailors are pure subjects, the type for the Peeping Tom in the bushes and, perhaps, for the reader. But it is, we will find, an ideal type, not to be realized or permitted.

With Victor, we can construct the career of the voyeur. He goes after Nature, one might say, not only to *penetrate* sadistically but to uncover, unveil.[7] Nature is hidden in "recesses," and he wants to "show how she worked in her hiding-places," "to unfold to the world the deepest mysteries of creation" (2). Thus far, science "has partially unveiled the face of nature"; Victor wants to remove the last veils, to show, to unfold, uncover those hiding-places, to direct a strip tease of Nature.

And why? Because, we say here, Victor is so shaky in his own foundations that he is hysterical about being pure subject. He identifies himself as the scientist who has done all this, clearly a matter both for Promethean pride and terrible shame. In any case, that's who he *is*, that's how he constructs himself. But it's a self he cannot locate. Notice how many times he announces that he dates the origin of his problems, i.e., his being, from some point or other. He has so many different origins, so many different constructions of the self, that we begin to feel they are thrown out at random. He is what he is because of his nature, because of his birth or blood, because of his special childhood, because of Elizabeth, because of his father's failure to instruct him, because of fate, because of an accidental brush with Cornelius Agrippa, because of his mother's death, because of the lectures of M. Waldeman, because of Justine's execution, "that miserable epoch from which I dated all my woe" (9). The point is not that the disparate items in this list could not be coordinated, by calling most of them turning-points perhaps; the point is that Victor does not do so. He treats each as a discreet point of origin and thus arranges for himself a being so chaotic it really is hollowed out. No wonder he wants just to look. No wonder he has great trouble speaking.

The creature, from this point of view, is battling a world of perverts, trying to establish normal seeing through the interplay of talk. If his efforts to make contact, to live in a world of shifting subjects and objects, the normal world, fail, it is because the world is not normal. No wonder his speech turns to mere eloquence, to slightly sadistic demagoguery. He had hoped that language "might enable me to make them overlook the deformity of my figure" (15). While the formulation here is cast in terms of power, perhaps even coercion—"enable me to make them"—it is significant that the creature does not want to blind others but to have them "over-look," look but not be spellbound, look *and* listen, be both subject and object. But he cannot locate the normal, even in children: "As soon as he [William] beheld my form, he placed his hands before his eyes and uttered a shrill scream. I drew his hands forcibly from his face and said, 'Child, what is the meaning of this? I do not intend to hurt you: listen to me'" (16). He pulls the hands away from the child's eyes and says "forcibly," "look *and* listen," see and be seen! Be normal, live in the world, love me! It is the creature's tragedy that he is set loose in a country full of monsters. Victor himself interprets all the creature's attempts at friendship and connection as terrifying invasions, as acts of voyeurism, most dramatically when the creature looks through the curtains of his bed and when he watches through the window as the scientist manufactures and then tears to pieces his mate.

The positioning of readers in all this is fascinating but too intricate to be pursued here. The question is whether we join the voyeurs in denying the creature love and, finally, life itself; or risk participating in the positional shifts, risk losing our own selfhood. In a way it doesn't matter, since those most intent on gazing, even Victor, always find the Gaze directed back at them; the voyeur always is put on exhibition: "Although the sun shone upon me, as upon the happy and gay of heart, I saw around me nothing but a dense and frightful darkness, penetrated by no light but the glimmer of two eyes that glared upon me" (21).

The reading here is more difficult to deconstruct, though its Freudian substructure and all the talk about "selves" and "egos" makes it vulnerable. Glaring at us, though, is the obvious fact that, at least as it is sketched here, the relationship between voyeurism and silence is both too obvious and too inadequately worked out. Rather than decenter it, then, we will set it aside as tangential, though in "love" it has provided us with a most dangerous clue we will pick up later.

TOO VULGAR FOR WORDS

Most modern readers are going to find Victor something of a snob, positioning him, possibly, as that anomaly, an aristocratic radical, but certainly a snob. The first noun in his narrative, after "I," is "birth," and he informs us right off that his family "is one of the most distinguished" of the "republic." Though he seems fond of being a member of a "republic," he clearly sees that republic as happily stratified, with himself in the top layer. The child Elizabeth, for instance, is easily distinguished from the other "hardy little vagrants" in "their rude abode" as "fairer than a garden rose among dark-leaved brambles." She is "of a different stock," you see (1). The wife of the turnkey who attends him in prison has a countenance expressive of "all those bad qualities which often characterize that class" (21). Part of Victor's scientific ardor seems class-driven: he is positively appalled that the "most learned philosopher" "knew little more" than "the untaught peasant" (2), and he sets out to correct that impropriety. Thus far, he sounds like Dan Quayle at a country-club membership meeting. But Victor's standards are even more scrupulous; he includes part of the middle-class in his sneers, Clerval's father being nothing more than "a narrow-minded trader" (3).

Such feelings, to be fair, do not seem to be confined to Victor. Elizabeth, in a rather startling passage, gives us a full analysis of the effect of "republican institutions" on class division. Compared to the great monarchies surrounding Switzerland, that republic has produced "less distinction between the several classes," and can be particularly proud of the results as regards the manufacture of servants with "simpler and happier manners." "A servant in Geneva," she proudly claims, "does not mean the same thing as a servant in France and England" (6). One may wonder whether she isn't proudest of the fact that these republican ideas have produced *better* servants, "more refined and moral" (i.e., less likely to spill the soup or steal the silver), especially when she adds an ugly bit of gossip on how the pretty Miss Mansfield has hooked a most eligible English gentleman, while her ugly sister has been lucky to land the rich banker.

Even the creature, who seems to most of us so resolutely proletariat (along with everything else that is good), is not without his touch of condescending haughtiness: "The girl [in the cottage] was young and of gentle demeanor, unlike what I have since found cottagers and farmhouse servants to be" (11).

There are hints that silence is to some extent class-bound, that those in the know have no need to speak, since both knowledge and power are secure and irrational. In addition, those blessed by blood may find speaking inadvisable, the swarm below, doubtless worthy in their way, not having the wherewithal to understand. Victor justifies his silence at Justine's trial and execution on the grounds that his story would simply astonish rather than enlighten "the vulgar" (7). There is also a subversive sense in which those in power rule by silence, by tacit assumption, to such an extent that they have rendered all speech impotent. Justine is wonderfully articulate, though she knows that words will have no effect in a world in which hereditary power rules through muteness: "But I do not pretend that my protestations should acquit me" (8). This is much the same sad lesson learned by the creature, and it is a lesson in politics as much as anything else.

There's no stopping us once we get onto politics,[8] but I think we should remember that silence comes in many forms, some of them quite expressive, and that we read more than words.

READ MY LIPS

Maybe *lips* isn't quite right, but the possibility remains that we should be reading other signs, silence included. There are, after all, times in the novel when silences seem clearly motivated, when they speak. Victor's reticence is often openly defensive; he does not speak of what he "could not endure to think of" (5) and says so. Silence can also express something like aggression, as in Victor's refusal to write to those at home, even when "one word from you . . . is necessary to calm our apprehensions" (6). Connected to this violent silence is the hush his father can always enforce: "I listened to my father in silence and remained for some time incapable of speech" (18). Old Frankenstein is ever the great repressor. But silence can also speak as positive feelings: "A thousand conflicting emotions rendered [Elizabeth] mute as she bade me a tearful, silent farewell" (18). Victor claims that he checks his strong desire for the sympathy he would receive in telling Elizabeth of the creature's threat out of love for her (22), and perhaps we believe him.

In addition to silence, there are a million other mute signs to read, and the reading of them is often foregrounded. Walton, on first seeing Victor, reads "benevolence and sweetness" in his countenance (Letter 4); Elizabeth is read by all as "bearing a celestial stamp in all her features" (1); "Henry said little, but . . . I read in his kindling eye" (3); Justine's devotion "you could see by her eyes" (6); after the first round of murders, the creature's "countenance bespoke bitter anguish, combined with disdain and malignity" (10); the magistrate Victor tardily tries to enlighten does not need to speak: "lively surprise, unmingled with disbelief, was painted on his countenance" (23). Notice how complex these readings often are, and how much certainty is invested in them.

It is true that a few doubts are expressed about this method of communicating. Elizabeth laments that we can have no assurances "when falsehood can look so like truth," but one paragraph later she is back to the same reading school: "Elizabeth read my anguish in my countenance" (9). The creature is an expert countenance-reader, as he shows when he is spying on the cottagers; but, unlike the others, he is unhappy with the incomplete, sterile, voyeuristic (and aristocratic?) system and what he wants most from the cottagers is their fuller, merging game of words.

Reading countenances, we might add, also seems an odd thing to do in the gothic mode we thought we were living in with *Frankenstein*. Victor finds that M. Krempe has repulsive "manners" and M. Waldeman "an air of frankness" (4), but is this a matter of airs and manners we are engaged with? Isn't this a tale of raping nature, and ripping bodies to shreds, and finding the monster right under the bed? Airs and manners, the delicate reading of fragile nonverbal signals, seem more appropriate to a Jane Austen novel than to a horror story. What are we being sucked into, with all these faces painted with this or that meaning, these expressive countenances? What is happening to us?

YOU DO THE TALKING

To simplify the immensely tangling questions about the position of the reader, I'll deal here with only a few possibilities, keeping mainly to the dramatic rhetorical signals that seem to be in the work itself (*in* the work? ha!). The work and its various narrators are uncommonly aware of their various readers and are often telling them to listen-up: "Remember, I am not recording the vision of a madman" (4). We had better attend.

But it's difficult to find the right seat, the right positioning. Rhetorical signals are so many and so diverse.[9] Even in the Preface we are disarmed, especially by the moving passage that relates, or begins to relate, memories of P. B. Shelley: "Its several pages speak of many a walk, many a drive, and many a conversation, when I was not alone; and my companion was one who, in this world, I shall never see more." Since this sometime companion is of interest to us, we settle in to hear more, eager to respond to this quite intimate invitation. But we find ourselves quite suddenly shown the door, given the bum's rush in the very next

sentence: "But this is for myself; my readers have nothing to do with these associations." Well, pahrrr-dunn meee! Who brought up the associations in the first
place? More to the point, why swing us in the door and right out again like this?

This odd and by no means regular rhythm of invitation and ejection, of
disclosure and denial continues throughout, gliding roughly from Walton's
openness to Victor's secrecy, to the creature's eloquent bullying and back again.
Walton is indeed not only the most ardent recorder but the most attentive host
imaginable. He always worries about what we are thinking, feeling, wondering:
"do not suppose," he says to keep us on track; "you will exclaim" or "will you
smile?" he adds to jog us into listening, nudging us in a friendly way, asking us
if we need a refill. He runs the risk of prescribing our response now and then,
but it's all done in the spirit of hospitality, of making his home and his understanding our own.

Victor is another matter. We know, of course, that he is a skilled rhetorician,
or that Walton thinks he is. His speech to the sailors, exhorting them to carry on
through the ice and polar bears, is so deft it makes Walton and even the crew
nearly burst with admiration (24). Never mind that, taking one consideration
with another, they choose to ignore him, he's still good at it. But with us, Victor
is routinely kicking us out, even without having asked us in. He is very seldom
cordial—"it may be imagined that"—and much more commonly exercising his
apparent right to tell us we cannot possibly comprehend—"no one can conceive" or "who shall conceive?" Not us, it appears. Not if he has anything to do
with it. He may even take some delight in frustrating us, working us up to a state
of "eagerness and . . . wonder and hope" with his science-fiction secrets, knowing we want to hear so badly we could spit, and then coldly dropping us: "that
cannot be" (4).

One wonders why Victor speaks at all, since he is so anxious to withhold. A
remote possibility is that, for all the pain it gives him, he is driven to warn
Walton and those of us thinking about similar exploits not to do it. That's what
he says, very often: "I imagine that you may deduce an apt moral from my tale"
(Letter 4) or, again, "Learn from me" (4). But what is one to learn? "Happier
that man is who believes his native town to be the world"? (4) We already know
what Victor thinks of such bumpkins. And what is the moral he imagines we will
deduce? "One that may direct you if you succeed in your undertaking and console you in case of failure." Well, that's all-purpose, but rather vague. Despite all
this talk about stern morals, then, what Victor has to tell us is by no means clear,
probably even to himself. It is not even clear how much he cares to divulge.

The creature, interestingly, learns language in reference to the effects created
by the words—"the words they spoke sometimes produced pleasure or pain,

smiles or sadness"—and develops an affective rather than a mimetic theory—
"the words they spoke, [did] not hav[e] any apparent connection with visible
objects" (12). As we have noted before, his rhetoric is terribly insistent: "How
can I move thee?"; "Listen to my tale . . . hear me. . . . Listen to me, Frankenstein. . . ; listen to me" (10). Not surprisingly, such rhetoric, though certainly
open, is not at all the unbuttoned, friendly persuasion of Walton. With the
creature, we are dared, threatened to listen, to understand, to sympathize.

And what do we do? How are we positioned as we move in and out from this
creature-center? One negative indication is given by the number of readers
inside the novel, and very poor readers they usually are. Clerval, for instance,
seems to have only the dimmest notion that Victor is troubled; he thinks at first
that his delirious and hysterical friend, thoroughly shocked by being peeked at
by the creature, is, in fact, consumed with joy (5). Late in the novel, Victor
evokes an audience of "the shades of my murdered friends" to approve his vow
to hunt down the monster, a vow he utters with a "solemnity and an awe which
almost assured me that [they] heard and approved" (24). If so, the creature's
"loud and fiendish laugh" (24) disrupts their collegiality—and ours.

More detailed are the rhetorical stage directions given with Victor's attempt
to win over the magistrate. Victor addresses him with a manner he calls
"impressive but calm," and it seems to work: the magistrate's signals of
incredulity change to attention, then to horror, then to "surprise unmingled
with disbelief." But it turns out that the magistrate had listened only with "that
half kind of belief" appropriate for supernatural stories, whereupon Victor
changes postures and adopts some rage-sparkling in his eyes and "a frenzy in my
manner," "something," he modestly says, "I doubt not, of that haughty fierce-
ness which the magistrates of old are said to have possessed" (23). But this
magistrate of now, however impressed or cowed, clearly isn't convinced and just
wants Victor out of there. Another rotten reader.

Given that he is recorder charged with continuing Victor's vengeance work,
Walton seems to be the novel's most important reader. But it isn't clear where
Walton's avowed love for Victor leads him, if anywhere. We leave him silent,
like Victor; the last words are given to the creature, who is himself about to enter
into silence—or so he says. Walton is apparently left to trail back ignominiously
to England, not because he heeded Victor's warning but because the sailors did
not heed Victor's rhetoric. Further, we note that Walton does not fulfill Victor's
deathbed plea, does not "undertake my unfinished work," that is, he doesn't
club down the creature on the spot. While it may be justly observed that he can
leave the creature to do that for himself, how can he be sure those lying lips will
be consumed in flame? In any case, we have the strangely washed out, irresolute,

inarticulate Walton at the end, the reader/writer who has heard, seen, and told most and who can only watch as the terrible tragedy works itself out. If he reads at all, he reads in silence.

I LOVE TO HEAR YOU TALK

Rather than end on that dismal note, let's turn to a hopelessly unfashionable notion of connection. Call it love or, less boldly, sympathy. Running through virtually all the centerings we have touched on has been the master-metaphor of power, an implicitly skeptical or negative view of language, narrative, character, rhetoric, the psyche, politics, gender. Everywhere we have seen gaps and lapses and empty spaces, tricks, and subversions, and negations. We can find them here too, if we want to.

But what if we attend to Walton's cry in the second letter: "I have no friend"; "I have no one near me"? What if we take seriously his growing love for Victor and more seriously the creature's demand for alliance? Of course, such hopes are shattered, and one might say they are shattered by silence. The creature searches everywhere for connection; even in his reading he looks for similarity, for contact. Maybe if we spoke to him . . . ?

Isn't it possible that our deconstructive fun might decenter itself into a great shadow novel, one where the link between reading and language and connection is actually asserted by being denied, one where revelation—"Hear me! Let me reveal my tale!"—leads not to alienating, pathetic voyeurism but to sympathetic participation? After all, readers now necessarily look back through a whole host of Cap'n Cuttles and Abel Magwitches and Jims and Queequegs and Rochesters and Heathcliffs, the rough and thorny and the alien and strange who through speech made some sort of connection with their world and with the reader. But maybe it's we who need to make the connection.

I realize that there are a good many dangers inherent in re-centering this slush, this old slop and slurp about affinities, this old humanism. We have spent a good deal of collective energy in the last decade showing the demons that lie within all that and the disguises put forward in the name of such things as connecting language and participatory appeals. We are so alert to them, in fact, that I wonder what price we are paying for our vigilance.

"Still, thou canst listen to me and grant me thy compassion" (10), says the creature. Surely we can. Let's call it more plainly sympathy that we are granting. Let's say even that it's not a matter of a grant. Let's say it is a matter of nature. Let's even call it love. Come back to the raft, Huck honey, please.

11

Anthony Trollope
and the Unmannerly Novel

THE NOVEL OF manners, insofar as there is such a thing, is a menacing genre. Because it has a great deal to protect, it is given to threatening gestures, to warnings and snarls, and sometimes to violence. It offers rewards, of course, to those with good manners—and often even to those whose manners are only so-so; but it will not tolerate those who raise questions about the manners, those who demand to know what basis in reason or nature a set of rules might have. Rule-breakers are one thing; rule-inquisitors are quite another. Malvolio need only be punished, but Falstaff threatens to give the game away and must be banished. Closer to home, Mrs. Proudie is a raucous upsetter of applecarts but can be accepted all the same, since her regularity in attendance at the market shows how deeply she is in accord with its functioning. But the Stanhopes make jokes about the apples, about the orchard and the greengrocers, about the delivery people, about the whole system—so they must be shipped back to Italy. The novel of manners is often liberal and kindly, welcoming the diversifying of its codes, softening the inflexible, including in its sweep nearly everybody. But not quite everybody. The loafer, the fool, the loudmouth, and the incompetent can all be tolerated; but not the incendiary, the woman from Mars, the anarchist: the one who questions the rules.

Actually, this novel of manners I have been discussing (so well that it starts to take form before our very eyes) does not exist. Where is the novel without alien questioners—the Mary Crawford, the Wilkins Micawber, the Lady Mabel Grex—who do more than break the rules: they expose the rules for what they are—artificial, often ridiculous means for maintaining an ideology. I know of no novel of manners that cannot be constructed—I can do it, and you can too—as an anti- or meta-novel of manners; no novel, that is, that does not expose and often subvert the codes of behavior, the habitual practices of the communities with which it deals, and the individuals who populate those communities. The expulsion or silencing of the alien voices may, I suppose, be construed as a means of protecting the ideology of the prevailing manners. But it may also be construed as a device for exposing the raw power, the snarling brute force underlying that ideology. We'll do our construing in the latter way.

Ideologies function in these novels to convert manners into the appearance of nature. Generally, this sleight of hand, this magic change of mere form into substantial habit, is done very subtly, by means of a whole network of implicit assumptions. These assumptions get to be so mighty they can make us used to anything. After all, you wouldn't think we would need a sooth-sayer to tell us that our own manners—codes of dress, modes of making contact with one another, ways of doing business, or religion, or even (why "even"?) seduction— are a little stylized and hollow. We all wish "nice days" to those whose hideous deaths would trouble us not at all, sign ourselves "sincerely" to manifest hypocrisy, and wear, just as we are directed, uncomfortable and unflattering bits of cloth about our necks or skirts whose length is controlled by the profit motive of "designers." We are, as Trollope is fond of pointing out, not fundamentally different from those who paint their bodies blue and wail at the moon. The ideological machine-guns deployed by manners, however, are aimed directly at the very few who, like Trollope, are inclined to blow the whistle on them.

Even the word "manners" has a slippery way of hiding beneath its bland surface a fierce guard designed to police its borders. A walk through the *OED* entry reveals how the liberally descriptive definition—"Customary mode of acting or behaviour, whether of an individual or of a community; habitual practice; usage, custom, fashion"—quickly glides toward the schoolmasterly prescriptive: "*good* manners." These customary modes of acting and behaving are, it turns out, not random or accidental, and they are enforced by customs officials. The word carries the shadow of "in due measure or moderation" (from the old French *maniere*: moderation, measure) suggesting not only the existence of rules for the measurement of the dimensions of the moderate but a Bureau of Standards that keeps things in line. And the rules for the moderate, we note, depend themselves on moderation, on playing the game in an easy, unquestioning way; not causing a fuss, raising a rumpus, deviating from a middle course. Conservative and cozy manners don't seem to ask for much: so long as everyone runs the middle course, which is the normal way after all, no one is going to have breath enough to ask who laid out the course, why everyone is running, or why it might not be more fun to abandon the track and take off through the woods.[1]

All of this is a windy way to suggest that manners—and the novel of manners—do not just happen but are tied to forms of cultural power and control. Further, actual novels of manners are not, as we might expect, acquiescent, but mount pretty fierce criticisms of the system upholding the set of manners in question. No novels, in fact, are more relentlessly political and ideological than these presumably domestic and personal works. (It costs us nothing to say such things.) They resist the dissociation of the personal from the political and see forms of power everywhere—from the codes governing what a woman must say to a man she wants to marry or sleep with (both in a few cases) to those prescribing how one rids oneself of excess nasal mucous. The novel of manners is most interestingly seen as an attack on the novel of manners, centering the subversive Falstaff, not the snug Squire Western.

It must be sadly admitted that most (other) critics have a tendency to settle down with the Squire, using a conservative invention like *novel of manners* to constrain interpretations, to make them mannerly. That is, we sweat to manufacture a formal category, which we call "the novel of manners," then we distinguish it skillfully from other categories, equally hallucinatory, and then expend a lot of labor arguing that these *novels of manners* are as much a natural phenomenon as frogs or peonies (both of which are, you know, equally artificial). We then pack into this *novel of manners* all sorts of features that, lo and behold, we proceed to find there. Once we have the category set in our mind, we round up members to populate it—any will do, *Omoo* as well as *Emma*—to convince us that we actually have something, that we have discovered it, and not just made it up.

So why am I writing this essay, you are asking, since the whole category is a pious fraud and since Trollope has no more place in this bogus tradition than anyone else who ever wrote anything? I'll tell you: because a strongly traditional focus may allow me to expose both the artificiality of the focus and the way in which novels may be made to squirm away from the categories which try to hold them. Trollope is wonderfully handy here because he can so easily be made into a Houdini, escaping in a matter of seconds from tight generic bonds. Terry Eagleton suggests that all resolutely formal commentary amounts to "the protection of private property," securing meanings, intentions, generic properties once and for all in the words of the critic.[2] Perhaps there is a way not to padlock and install alarm systems for meanings, intentions, and generic properties but to release them. The model for the critic is not the keeper of the vault but David Copperfield's friend Mr. Dick, who attaches his most valued words to a kite and offers them to the wind.

Any defense of the instinctive behavior of a culture, any defense of "manners," is bound to be an exposure of the artificial situatedness of that behavior and of the interested power motives that uphold it. Manners can operate efficiently only when they are not seen as manners, not, in fact, seen at all. One might be able to convince one's students to wear purple ribbons dangling from their noses, if one could *assume* that such behavior were natural, proper, and, above all, traditional. The traditional can so easily be made to seem the natural. But one had better not launch into a passionate defense of the cogency of such a system, precisely because it would then be revealed as a system.

And that's just what Trollope does: expose the system as a system, tied to values, historical situations, the protection of position and power. And the system he attacks-by-defending we might as well call the novel of manners, so long as we explain what we have in mind by that term and explore some of its ideological implications. Trollope has long been associated with what convention (i.e., commentators searching for handles) has designated "the comedy of manners," which we'll say, not being too fussy, is the same thing as the novel of manners.[3] Bradford Booth, who for a very long time was the only one writing substantial commentary on Trollope, admitted that his favorite author "rarely attempts more than the comedy of manners."[4] No need to apologize, even if this were so, but our point (and it's a good one) has to do with the alliance between Trollope and the novel of manners. How can we locate Trollope within this tradition? What does such locating say about Trollope and about the tradition? What does it say about our own processes of reconstruction? Later, I will examine one novel, *The Duke's Children*, in some detail; but for now I would like to see what might come of placing a mock-up of an averaged-out (we'll call it, wildly, "typical") Trollope novel within this mythical tradition of the novel of manners. It probably goes without saying (then why . . . ?) that such a tradition, like all traditions, is ideologically conservative—or at least ought to be: it serves the interests of the ascendent powers. Again, however, the novels themselves we will read as ideologically ambiguous, unstable, Figaro-like servants. They make explicit what should be implicit. They talk too much.

Let's begin by assuming that the novel of manners pretends to take for granted a large system of moral and social codings, codings that manifest themselves in enlightened and highly sophisticated behavior. Such behavior is directed from *within*, as it were; it is presumably "instinctive," developed not by referring to theories or elaborated rationalizations but by common sense, reason, nature— i.e., by inheritance and redundancy. These purported instincts are highly traditional, but they exist necessarily without much historical sense; they do not look consciously to the past; they just *are*. Such instinctive behavior, never aware of its base and never justifying or even articulating itself, is, again presumably, a reflex of a cultural norm. Gentlemanly behavior, to take one example, is, in Trollope, always broad-scale social behavior, activity within the culture. Though very seldom public in the explicitly political sense, it is always public (and political) in its assumption that such behavior will be echoed back, that the gentleman is a universal standard.

In Trollope, however, such a system is forced into speech, forced out of hiding and thus, to a large extent, forced out of power. For one thing, there are so few gentlemen around, and there are so many liars, so many swindlers, so many who are selfish, greedy, even lustful or homicidal, so many who are loud, so many who do not know how to go in to dinner or ride to the hounds, so many Americans! Trollope's novels often give the sense that the morality and grounds for behavior are traditional enough but that the tradition is alive only in the narrator and in a dwindling number of elderly characters; that it is about to become extinct, along with the whole class of gentlemen. Because the world no longer seems to support the assumptions held by gentlemen and because those assumptions are implicitly social and communal, gentlemen often appear alien, even ludicrous, creatures who dropped in from the moon.

Worse, even gentlemen sometimes distrust the basis of their gentlemanliness, giving ground that actually lies right under their feet. When Phineas Finn (in *Phineas Redux*) finds himself on trial for a murder he did not commit, he also finds himself without any support from the gentlemanly society whose instincts should tell them that he is innocent. Despite the warmhearted backing of a large group of women (who seem, ironically, to be the only ones true to the gentlemanly code), Phineas must learn to live in a world where even the staunchest of traditionalists, the Duke of St. Bungay, accommodates himself easily to a relativistic, substanceless vision: he "had learned at last that all loyalty must be built on a basis of self-advantage"[5] The innocent Phineas is put through a trial that judges not the man, his innocence or guilt, but the quality of the "evidence," quite a different and impersonal thing—a thing no gentleman should attend to. But this world has become decentered and chaotic, without any governing code whatever. Mr. Monk explains to Phineas that he never lost "confidence" in his friend but that such confidence could not justify "conviction" (ch. lxviii). Why not? A community that cannot translate gut-level confidence into conviction is

one that has lost its hold on the power of its instincts, one in which the dominant ideology has crumbled. The novel of manners, in other words, circles back
on itself when manners become the reflex of nothing whatever.

Similarly, the faith in "civilization" as an independent force that can be trusted
to take care of itself suffers when no one holds the faith or feels the force. The
novel of manners, one might say, holds to a deep-seated irrationalism; it mocks
rationalists, reformers, and systematic thinking of any kind, holding up in their
place instinctive behavior, the force of "experience" (which might also be called
habituation), and, when pressed, the importance of "blood." In the novel of
manners, the emphasis is on gradual understanding and acceptance, not on radical transformation. Such gradual understanding is tied to certain theories of
education, oddly akin to those which guided Tony Weller in his training of Sam:
"I took a good deal o' pains with his eddication, sir; let him run in the streets
when he was wery young, and shift for his-self."[6] Just so, in the novel of manners, one picks things up: one "grows," "soaks in," "comes to understand,"
simply by being around and not pushing too hard. Youth should, in fact, be
mute, satisfied with adding a certain mild liveliness to the proceedings without
presuming to direct or even to play a large part in them: age, grumbled Trollope,
is so much superior to youth "that it may be doubted whether youth is justified
in making public its work by any other consideration than that of the doubt
whether maturity may come."[7]

This early-retirement-in-reverse policy is, I think, so extreme as to function to
give the game away, to show the desperation of those who would sustain a world
now lost. Still, Trollope's irrationalist faith in this power of mature and civilized
manners can take milder forms: "The simple teaching of religion has never
brought large numbers of Natives to live in European habits; but I have no
doubt that European habits will bring about religion."[8] The subtle habits of a
civilization, its manners, are equivalent to its spiritual life, a mystery that cannot
be taught but which, all the same, must be trusted, accepted, and gradually
absorbed. But where is this spiritual life, this religion of manners? Its temples—
drawing rooms and salons—are full of heathens, and the faithful are a dwindling
band. Trollope's smug trust in the power of European manners to create "religion"
among those living in ill-mannered darkness is countered by a recognition that
this gentle civilization can spread only by baring its teeth: it is very difficult, he
sarcastically comments, to make "a wretched savage understand that you intend
to do good to him, when he clearly does perceive that you intend to take away
from him everything that he calls his own."[9]

The values associated with tradition, with the sort of manners the novels
appear to admire, are never just *there* in Trollope. If they survive at all, they

must be formulated anew and somehow, however shakily, established. In the process, too much is made explicit; too much is shown to be manufactured for ideological purposes in these learned "instincts." This subversive stripping away of the trappings of the habitual becomes clearest in Trollope's contradictory defenses of the "gentleman" and of "blood," defenses of the irrational on what masquerade as rational grounds. Though we are told countless times in wonderfully irrational, circular terms that the way to define a gentleman is to be one and then you'll know, such mystery-cult hints are often supplemented by fatal particulars: an unselfishness, a distrust for show, an unconscious yearning for and ability to exercise power over others, an aversion to such vulgar pursuits as gambling (taking money out of another man's pocket), a desire to make others comfortable, and, most of all, a disgust with lying so deep that it would never occur to a gentleman to lie or to suspect others of doing so. This last is especially disastrous, since it is often made central, and since it is so palpably ineffective as a *rule*. The finest gentlemen are often surrounded by liars, and know it; what's more, they often lie themselves when delicacy or even convenience demands it. The principle of truth-telling, in other words, is too absolute to function well in such an intricate world, where so many conflicting codes make so many different demands. One can search for stability in a relativistic world, but by doing so one risks being a fool. The actual gentlemen in the novels often seem quite fluid, adaptable to shifting conditions and willing enough to apply what Ruth apRoberts calls Trollope's "situation ethics,"[10] but the general discussions of "the gentleman" posit a kind of essentialism that comes close to mocking or undermining the concept that is being defended. However beautiful the idea of a gentleman, then, its purity quickly becomes tarnished in use.

So one turns to subtlety itself as a principle, a principle that constitutes one of the strongest weapons in this ideological armory. We are asked to believe that truly expressive speech is always indirect, that the plain speakers are rude, ill-mannered people who, like the American senator, do not ever understand what is going on. According to this code, indirect speech, sly ironic asides, gestures, raised eyebrows, even silence speak loudest and most to the point. The less talk there is, the more one expresses confidence in the mutual understanding, unstated but complete, that underlies the social code. Silence, then, is more than golden, it is brick and mortar. Lots of words lead to confusion, danger, anarchy—and there's lots of talk in a Trollope novel. Those who go by the single phrase, the effective gesture, are likely to be ineffective, to be ignored.

To be fair, though, it's not just the amount of talk but its quality or mode that matters. Talk that slithers around the corner rather than advancing head-on expresses an assurance in what is around the corner: not a mugger or a tiger on the loose, but someone who shares such a wide field of understanding and assumptions that the field need only be touched, not cultivated. Trollope writes to his brother, for instance, on hearing that a child is expected: "The pleasures of paternity have been considerably abridged, since the good old Roman privilege of slaying their offspring at pleasure, has been taken from fathers. But the delights of flagellation, though less keen, are more enduring. One can kill but once; but one may flog daily."[11] But such cozy writing demands an audience, an entire social group or culture that in the novels is, more often than not, absent. Mr. Harding's appeals to the gentlemanly code as an explanation for his behavior fall on the double-deaf ears of the Archdeacon and are mistaken as cowardice; and even the presumably traditional Lord Silverbridge and Isabel Boncassen are forced into blunt "down-rightness" to make themselves understood. And such plain speakers, even the boorish Senator Gotobed, seem to edge more and more closely to the heart of the novels as Trollope's career progresses.

In the novel of manners as we have constructed it, the conservative bias means that any rejection of illusion, any movement toward clarification, is figured as a relaxation into "things as they are." In Trollope, such an education into ease can indeed be accomplished, but not always: there are many who are ineducable or who remain, like Roger Carbury, isolated by their own gentlemanliness. Even worse, Trollope's novels characteristically raise uncomfortable questions about "things as they are." Just how are things? Very often quite awful, which in turn makes it difficult to see how or why a good man or woman can possibly adjust to, or be educated into the worlds of novels like *Is He Popenjoy?*, *The Way We Live Now*, or *Mr. Scarborough's Family*. "Things are very far from being perfect. Things are always very far from being perfect," says Trollope in a lecture on the "Higher Education of Women."[12] This notion of an imperfect world is all very well so long as one does not pay too great a price for accepting things as they are. Many women in Trollope's audience may well have felt that things as they were did not offer them much, in the way of higher education or in anything else. Very many of the women in Trollope's own novels feel this way, certainly, and find that the answers to the blunt and repeated question "What is a woman to do with her life?" are very limited—limited, in fact, to the often dreary, sometimes panicky decision of whether or not to marry. Men sometimes fare little better: "It is sad to say it, and sad to think it, but failure is the ordinary lot of man."[13]

The casting away of illusions may land one in bleak territory, with few protections and very few rewards. An intelligent physician in *He Knew He Was Right* says about a dangerous disease, "The truth is . . . a doctor doesn't know so very much more about these things than other people."[14] This candor puts us all in the same boat, but it is not so much a cruise ship as a leaky life raft. The doctor is not a pompous fool to be deflated but an honest man who reveals that the slogan of *Barchester Towers*—"we are all of us men"—may be a lovely, unbuttoned attitude to take toward clergymen (or to have clergymen take toward themselves) but not much of a protection against failing health. Nor, when we think of it, is the comic devaluation of clergymen all that comforting. Reducing clergymen to the level of civil servants and the like cuts away any pretensions they may have to social prominence, but it also (Trollope's protests to the contrary) removes their ties to the divine. A clergyman who buckles before Mrs. Proudie or the narrator's ridicule would cut a poor figure before the Almighty. As a result, as Lady Chiltern says, the doctrine of the afterlife becomes "so cold and comfortless in the theory that we do not relish the prospect even for our children" (*Phineas Redux*, xxi). So, instead of a conservative affirmation of the harmonious beauty of things as they are, Trollope can leave us with the ironic suggestion that these things as they are are simply all we have, comfortless and disheartening as that may be.

These anomalies in Trollope, his subversive use of the novel of manners, can be smoothed over by a fairly simple maneuver: assert that the emptiness, ironic nihilism, and so forth reside in the public arena and that the true virtues and the true joys are private.[15] If one constructs such a sharp distinction between the public, institutionally or socially defined being and the private one, certain ambiguous twists and turns seem to become straight lines. Money, for instance, and the getting of it can be both applauded and despised; approved in reference to the comfort and freedom it can allow, disgusting in its tendency to corrupt the social and political order at large. The problem with such a unifying device is that it concurs so readily with the ideology (and the ideological contradiction) it is trying to explain. Naturally it works, since it comes off the same assembly line. One must act as if money appeared from nowhere, as if it were nice to have, even essential, but not an active agent in determining one's behavior. One of the marks of the gentleman is the ease with which he gives away, loses, is cheated of his money. A gentleman should certainly marry for love, only that, just love. Yet, many (most?) are circumstanced so that they would be idiots not to look to the financial situations of their prospective mates.

While money clearly invades, even controls, all areas of life, one must operate as if it did not. Those who really operate this way, who fully internalize these matters, do so, of course, at their own considerable peril. Those who get by keep the code of manners at arm's length, treat it as a rule one must never violate— except when one is violating it. Even those who never violate it might be seen to depend on its violation: the seasoning of the Duke's children is all very sweet and moving, but it is, quite emphatically, accomplished by the payment of enormous sums of money to cover gambling debts. We can construe all this ironically with ease: the proper seasoning can be acquired, and one can adjust happily to the status quo—as long as one has the equivalent of several million dollars to dump without missing it. Money, then, cannot be so easily accommodated to the tradition, nor can excuses for it be easily made on the basis of this division between the public and private being.

Ideologies do not divide so conveniently; if anything, they operate more powerfully and more insidiously in the unconscious private life than in public. Mr. Slope is a grasping, rude man in the pulpit and on the sofa making love: he cannot hide his ignorance of the rules, his lower-middle-class origins. Similarly, Mr. Crawley is a self-conscious tragic hero everywhere he goes, not least when he enters the bosom of his family. Marriage and love are for men and, especially, for women so patently affairs of class, politics, and cash that it seems preposterous to think of a private realm safe from these forces and free for the exercise of an idealized virtue.

Finally, there is a parallel tendency in reading the novel of manners, even Trollope's slippery version of it, to see something in the *process,* the experience of a thing, that belies the form in which it appears.[16] Dynamic experience, one might suppose, is what counts, not the abstract structure of justification that lies behind it. Work, we say, was what counted to Trollope, work for its own sake, not the product of that work. Same with politics, where those who believe there must be some*thing* to be done are ridiculed, contrasted with the true statesmen, who are in politics for the work itself, knowing that *things* will come to be done, if at all, by themselves, like spring showers. One does not initiate or plan; one carries through what is initiated, presumably, by itself. Same with marriage and love: "The beauty of the thing was not so much in the thing loved, as in the loving."[17] Same, most importantly, with fox hunting, where the enormous joy of riding seems to have no relation to whether or not a fox is killed or even found, much less to abstract notions about the cruelty of the whole endeavor.

But how can a distinction between the doing and the form in which the thing is done be maintained? It's all very well to say that the old bedesmen at Hiram's Hospital are as happy as larks, even if they are being cheated, or that farmers really welcome hunters trampling down their crops. The point is that such arguments reveal their own needs all too baldly. And this is the way the novels put the arguments: by insisting that the form of the thing is irrelevant to the activity, they reveal how the form makes possible and controls the activity. Form can be distinguished from the activities it yields only by a sleight of hand, exactly the sleight of hand mastered by the novel of manners. It's not that Trollope doesn't use the full array of tricks; it's just that he has a disarming way of showing us what's up his—and the tradition's—sleeve. He points slyly to the fact that right around the corner from or under the bed of the traditional conservative or even feudal politics of the novel of manners are *not* the moderate politics of liberalism but something much wilder—the radical deconstructive anarchy of unbridled questioning. I would like to demonstrate a little of this in reference to one novel, *The Duke's Children.*

❊ ❊ ❊

Here is a formula for the novel of manners, one that Trollope often adopted: take a character about whom we are made to care and whose values and integrity we are, at least in some measure, made to respect; then put him (or her, of course, though in Trollope it is quite often a him) in a situation where he is, for one reason or another, severely isolated from the social group and culture he thought was supporting him. Through this isolation and the problems it causes, raise questions about the values, the behavior, and the manners not only of the individual but of the culture as a whole. Play with the questions and then dispel them by seeming to resolve them into a set of traditional assumptions, made more lively and flexible by including everyone around—except, of course, the scoundrels and the reformers. The Duke's Children, the last of the Palliser series,18 can be construed as fitting this formula in an especially compelling way. It can also be construed as exposing the formula as a formula and thus subverting the assumptions that prop up the code of manners apparently being supported. It is this last construction that interests me here.

As I see it (why not?), the novel concerns the Duke's struggle to reconcile himself to what he perceives as a new and alien world. The radical estrangement is initiated by the sudden death of his wife, Glencora, announced at the novel's beginning; and the sense of having utterly lost his way continues as his children resolutely act in ways the Duke cannot fathom, cannot fit into the codes he has always felt govern the lives of all people—or at least of all gentlemen, or at least of all the aristocracy, or at least of all politically liberal aristocrats who are not debauched or otherwise selfishly immoral. His daughter, Lady Mary, declares her unalterable love for one Frank Tregear, the second son of a country squire and possessed of neither money nor a profession. The Duke's eldest son, Lord Silverbridge, gets himself sent down from Oxford for a juvenile prank; declares that he is, by nature it seems, a Tory; spends most of his time at a rag-tag gentle-man's club and the track, where he manages to bet and lose upwards of £100,000; and worst of all, he forms a kind of half-baked engagement to Lady Mabel Grex and tells his father about it. The engagement suits the Duke fine but, in the long run, does not at all suit Silverbridge, who finds Lady Mabel a good bit too intelligent and mature for comfort and pins his affections instead on Isabel Boncassen, an American nearly as ineligible in the Duke's eyes as is Tregear. The second son, Gerald, is a sweet-hearted, faintly stupid hobbledehoy like his brother but too young as yet to have run the whole course of Silverbridge's follies. To be sure, Gerald is sent down, from Cambridge in this case, and he loses money disreputably, at the card table; but he hasn't come to the point of thinking about politics or marriage. In time, one is led to believe, he will scandalize and hurt the Duke just as much as his elder brother has.

These are the problems, the conditions that act to isolate the Duke and the tradition he holds to. From one point of view, all turns out well. Mary and Tregear, Silverbridge and Isabel are joined, more or less with the Duke's blessing. Silverbridge even switches his parliamentary allegiance back to the old Palliser liberalism, declaring that one's party affiliation doesn't really matter much and that the current leader of the Conservatives is, after all, "a beast." Major Tifto and Lady Mabel are cast aside rather brutally, it is true, but all comic rituals, we may say, contain these little purification gestures, these clarifying acts of identifying and expelling the unfit. There is no doubt that the novel can be read or reported on as a pleasant fable in which everyone, almost, wins. The Duke and all his children do, anyhow, and they represent everything that counts. Even the tendency to psychologize the novel,[19] to treat it as a subtle recording of the Duke's psychic turmoil, suggests the possibility of therapy. Nothing is seriously out of joint except for the Duke, and he needs simply, as Trollope would say, to retrick his beams.

The first sentence of the novel, announcing the Duke's terrible loneliness, can be read as anticipating his cure: "No one, probably, ever felt himself to be more alone in the world than our old friend, the Duke of Omnium, when the Duchess died." [20] The Duke, we may suppose, *feels* himself to be alone but really isn't—or won't be for long. The opening goes on with an elaboration on his desolation that hints at a therapeutic educational course before him: "He did not know how to look out into the world" (but he will learn); "there was no one of whom he could ask a question" (but there will be). The mythic structure controlling the novel seems to rest on the mild and comic conflict between generations, here between fathers and sons: "Fathers never do quite understand the changes which are manifest to their sons" (lxi). But fathers have a way finally of understanding these changes (or adjusting to them even if they don't) and, in the end, giving to the younger generation their blessings.

The odd thing about *The Duke's Children* is that the Duke never does understand the changes, never reconciles himself to them, never is able to decide whether his children are too headstrong and stupid to see the importance of the values he espouses or whether, in fact, those values are gone, the world transformed into a madhouse. The focus throughout is not on any real change in the Duke, any graceful reconciliation, but on his increasingly lonely steadfastness and his bitterness. The Duke's essential isolation increases as the novel proceeds; he does not see the light but is bludgeoned into accepting the darkness. He never loses the pain that comes from the certainty of having been abandoned, even when all is settled: "My opinion is to go for nothing—in anything!" he cries to Silverbridge (lxxi), and again to Silverbridge, "Gerald, I suppose, will bring me some kitchen-maid for his wife" (lxxiv). The celebration dinners he gamely arranges for the young lovers are spoiled by his grim hilarity: "It was the Duke who made the greatest efforts, and with the least success" (lxxiv). Even at the altar steps "he was reminding himself of all that he had suffered" (lxxx), and the last words of the novel are given to his grumbling about Tregear's arrogance and about a world where the unspeakable has become colloquial: "I do not know that one ought to be surprised at anything."

Manners, then, simply are not coordinated, and the Duke is not so dishonest as to pretend that they are. One can, of course, attribute all this to the Duke, his inadequate recovery, his stubbornness, his archetypal role as refuser of festivity. It seems to me more interesting, however, to attend to the way in which his mulish holdout against the allures of the novel of manners manages to expose the somewhat bullying ideology of that genre. The Duke suggests, for instance, that the notion of a smooth modification of manners from one generation to the next may mask considerable coercion, that change may really be disruption rather than flexible continuity, that loneliness may not be curable, that manners may die, that catastrophic models of destruction and disappearance may be as apt as linear models of adjustment. The liberal Duke, that is, ironically uncovers the deeply conservative ideology of the novel of manners, its belief in compromise, small-scale fiddlings, universal human tendencies, and the like. The traditional Duke suggests a cultural relativism and a radical historicism that are potentially anarchic or revolutionary. Unable to pretend that his world and his beliefs have survived, the Duke questions the ideological base on which continuity and survival of the past are enforced.

The Duke, the tradition of the novel of manners, or we readers might, of course, escape this dilemma by doing what all ingenious sorts do when they find themselves cornered: make a distinction. Proposing once again that the public life is sharply divided from the private, we can then protect the stability and continuity of the novel of manners tradition by claiming a sanctity for a centered character or hero and heroine, whatever may be the case with the world at large. Jane Austen is often read in this way: the "world" may be chaotic, ruled by gross materialism and selfishness, individualism run amuck, vulgar ignorance of traditional values and their reflection in manners; but an enclave is established with Elizabeth and Darcy, Emma and Mr. Knightley, even Anne and Wentworth, where the delicate life of manners is known and endures. Such a distinction, one might say, is characteristic of bourgeois idealism; it depoliticizes and elevates the "personal," allowing "the world" to go its way. Such liberal gestures account for the pervasive readings of "romantic love," "the inward turn of the novel," "the rise of complex characterization," and the like. All are impositions of an ideological distinction, one that claims, among other things, a realm of personal loyalties, love, virtue, and dignity, untouched by the sordid issues of power.

The Duke's Children foregrounds for us these distinctions so blatantly that the invitation to accept them might strike us as a little suspicious. We are told at once that the Duke has lost in his wife the "link between him and the world." What "loving and liking" he had managed had been "exclusively political," confined to one or two people; "he had so habituated himself to devote his mind and his heart to the service of his country, that he had almost risen above or sunk below humanity" (i). We read these comments, very likely, as indicating that the Duke had used his wife to make up for personal deficiencies, principally an habitual aloofness and impersonality born of shyness. But what really is "political loving"? And to what "world" was his wife a link?

We probably think, roughly, that the Duke, who was after all Prime Minister, has done very well with the world but is lacking personally. But the passage seems to tell us just the opposite, and it generally sets up very confusing signals as to what constitutes the world, the personal, and the "humanity" that the Duke is either above or below but not "in." The passage, in other words, invites us to separate the private and public but then muddles or deconstructs the basis on which such a distinction might rest. Similarly, the Duke of St. Bungay, uses this distinction in an extraordinarily cagey letter urging the Duke to return to public life. He argues that the Duke should consider public duty ahead of any private concerns because any man so competent and so needed "cannot be justified in even remembering that he has a self" (xxii). This states the ideology in its purest and most revealing form: a person's true self is private, not operated on by power in any form, and is certainly not politicized or publicized. Clearly, however, the Duke's motive for resisting his old friend's appeals are deeply personal. Just as personal are his reasons, announced late in the novel, for returning to the public duty he loves—his eagerness for power and his feeling that he is nothing if he is not engaged in hard work: "But it is the grind that makes the happiness. . . . For myself I can conceive no other" (xxv). The Duke returns to politics for that most personal of all reasons, the pursuit of happiness. By doing so, he suggests an integration, a disavowal of the distinction that seems to be holding the novel together.

Still, he tries to inculcate in his sons the very separation of public and private that he believes sustains both his politics and his personality. As an aristocratic liberal, the Duke is committed to a gradual lowering of the barriers between classes, by which he seems really to mean a squeezing together of the vertical spectrum without at all giving up the lines that distinguish the levels of society. The Duke does not propose to see the rainbow as a continuum but to preserve even more rigorously the illusion that colors are divided and discrete. He simply wants a thinner rainbow in which red and yellow fraternize more under certain circumstances without producing orange. The way this is to be managed is to see that public life (politics, say) is one thing and private life (marriage, say) another: "I should not turn up my nose at the House of Commons because some constituency might send them an illiterate shoemaker; but I should probably find the illiterate shoemaker an *unprofitable* companion for my private hours" (xxvi; emphasis added). After the Duke meets the piteously uncouth Major Tifto, he rebukes his son for associating with a man for "profit," adding that he does not see what Silverbridge can "gain" by such a companionship (xxvii). Why does the Duke use importations from the public world of commerce to explain the intricacies of the sanctity of the private life? Partly, one supposes, because the austere Duke cannot associate the private life with anything so hedonistic as self-indulgent pleasure. He is caught, then, one way or another, in defending the private life with a language and ideology drawn from public morality and duty, again betraying the split he needs to maintain.

What arguments can the Duke use with his children? Perhaps he is successful as regards Tifto: Silverbridge does dump him—after waiting to see what will happen in a couple of big races. But Tifto is a minor matter, and one might wonder whether Silverbridge's obedience is a signal of his coalescence with the Duke or the result of Tifto's role in a public scandal and his utter failure to hand over to Silverbridge a single winner. The real tests come with the mates selected by his children, prospective partners who violate everything the Duke holds dear: "Such drawing-nearer of the classes was the object to which all the man's political action tended. And yet it was a dreadful thing to him that his own daughter should desire to marry a man so much beneath her own rank and fortune." (xxii).

The distance is so great that it threatens a merging, and a very dangerous one. Plus there is the vulgar issue of money: Tregear has none, and Mary will have carloads of it. Deeply in love with Lady Mabel Grex at one time, Tregear has been persuaded by her that the two of them do not have money enough between them to live in the manner to which they would like to become accustomed. They part, Mabel with such pain and reluctance that she can never forget it, Frank with what we might gather is a temporary twinge that slows him down only for a step or two before he is able to get back into the race. We are told right at the beginning and then many more times by the narrator and by Frank himself that he had not sought Mary out because she was an heiress, or because of her ethereal rank, or because of the alluring combination: Frank "was certainly not the man to pursue a girl simply because of her fortune; nor was he weak enough to be attracted simply by the glitter of rank; but . . ." (iii). But what? Surely Frank's reasons for loving Mary, for wanting to marry her, should not be at all connected to wealth and rank. No! "But he was wise enough with worldly wisdom to understand thoroughly the comforts of a good income, and he was sufficiently attached to high position to feel the advantage of marrying the a daughter of the Duke of Omnium." We know, in fact, that, as with Lady Mabel, all the love in the world would not induce Frank to engage himself to Mary were she not oozing with cash.

Where does this leave us? Frank loves her purely, for her very self, and simply finds it pleasant that she comes equipped with these extra features? Hardly; that would be a little like the shorthanded building contractor finding it pleasant that the woman he loves is the best bricklayer in the Western world. All this is not to suggest that a cynical reading of Frank gets us very far; it's just that the issue of money and love, though foregrounded in about every other chapter, is never settled. Further, this insistent equivocation blurs the public/private distinction awfully. We would much prefer to have it all as clear as a bell: love is one thing, worldly position and money another. The Duke would rather have it this way, too: even after he has officially given in, he frets over his own failure to sort out the appropriate roles of men and women, of love and power:

> "A gentleman should not look to live on means brought to
> him by a wife. You say that he did not."
>
> "He did not think of it."
>
> "A gentleman should do more than not think of it.
> He should think that it shall not be so. A man should own his
> means or should earn them."
> —lxxiv

The Duke makes it all lucid. But what he describes is not what Tregear does, and the Duke cannot clarify the world in this way.

The most damaging possibility introduced in the Duke's outline of proper conduct is that Tregear is not a gentleman. A gentleman is . . . well, something ineffable, but something quite certain. What is at stake is not so much the existence of a class to be known as "gentlemen" as the ability to recognize them. It is the mode of perception—irrational, unempirical, hence not to be questioned or subject to change—that is crucial. And certainly the best gentleman-spotter in the novel should be the Duke. But, when his daughter protests that her chosen is, after all, a gentleman, the Duke responds:

> "So is my private secretary. There is not a clerk in one
> of our public offices who does not consider himself to be a
> gentleman. The curate of the parish is a gentleman, and the
> medical man who comes here from Bradstock. The word is too
> vague to carry with it any meaning that ought to be serviceable to
> you in thinking of such a matter."
>
> "I do not know any other way of dividing people," said she. . . .
>
> "You are not called upon to divide people. That division requires
> so much experience that you are bound in this matter to rely upon
> those to whom your obedience is due."
> —lxvii

Although the Duke tries to rescue himself at the last, arguing that the dividing of people is not to be explained in words but absorbed through the skin with "experience" (a splendid and standard irrationalist dodge), he has already thrown in the sponge: "The word is too vague." Mere clerks or curates may (or may not) be gentlemen. The Duke suggests that he knows who is a gentleman, but does he? If he knows, it is on the basis of some internal wisdom that has come to him with age and blood. And if he has the wisdom, why is the application of it "vague"? And what kind of wisdom does he possess? Is Tregear a gentleman, or is he not—or does it even matter? Late in the novel, the Duke admits that there is no reason Mr. Boncassen should respect his view of things, even though Mr. Boncassen doubtless respects him: "That which to me is deep wisdom is to him an empty prejudice" (lxxi), a near-cynicism the Duke regards as natural enough. Gone is the universal intuition that can uphold the private sensation that maintains the external world of rank, class, and wealth. Mere cultural relativism that mixes public and private has crept up and taken over.

Even more overtly, the Duke is forced to use public and political arguments—duty, position, *noblesse oblige*—to address his children at all. He must abandon the distinction between public and private, abandon the tradition that supports both him and the novel of manners. When the Duke speaks, he speaks always with the intense feeling of a public man, especially when he is being most intensely personal. He believes, above all, in calling things by their proper names, and for much of the novel he nurtures the belief that he can train his children linguistically and all will be well. The Duke's language is thus insistently ideological, but it makes no contact with the world and words of his sons. Much of the comedy of the book arises from the enormous gap between the Duke's abstract vocabulary and beautiful long periods and his sons' colloquial and concrete speech. Even when the father strives for crisp directness, the results are no better:

> "Do you ever think what money is?"
>
> The Duke paused so long, collecting his own thoughts and thinking of his own words, that Gerald found himself obliged to answer.
>
> "Cheques, and sovereigns, and bank-notes," he replied with much hesitation.
>
> "Money is the reward of labour," said the Duke.
> —lxv

Ironically, the Duke sees no connection between experience and the explanation of experience. He can use abstract terms only because he is trying to believe that there is a community out there somewhere which will provide solidity, a form of general "reality," to abstraction. The Duke, in other words, speaks from and within a series of assumptions that make no sense to the new generation. Issues are resolved, but only when speech is downright, often brutal: Silverbridge to Tifto, Silverbridge to Lady Mabel and vice versa, Isabel to Dolly and even to Silverbridge.

Silverbridge is, we assume, finally "seasoned," but to serve what menu? Tifto is ruined and pathetic; Lady Mabel is not pathetic, perhaps, but only because her strong bitterness upholds her: "Time is but a poor consoler for a young woman who has to be married" (lxxiii). Silverbridge cannot enter the old world of his father, even if he wanted to and were equipped to do so. There is no real reconciliation of the sort we had imagined, precisely because the reading habits, the tradition we had assumed, cannot be maintained. The private realm is riddled with political forces; it always has been, only now it is shredded much more obviously. What *The Duke's Children* does is to expose the political underpinnings of the attempt to construct an unpoliticized personal realm. It deconstructs its own governing genre, making available to us not so much the weakness of the Duke's assumptions as the weakness of our own. We are shown the ideological base of this "novel of manners," that is, of our own need for such a construction. It is not, finally, the Duke who is caught in the ludicrous position of being a liberal aristocrat, a man of the people with deep-seated prejudices in favor of a very small group of people, a political leveler and equalizing revolutionary committed to the status quo. It is us.

12

The Power of *Barchester Towers*

*T*HE TITLE OF this chapter is meant to mislead you. Don't you hate that? I am trying to mock those who are power-driven themselves and who regard power as something in nature. The title is a taunt, then, mean-spirited and serving no other purpose than to show how self-aware I am.

It is quite true, would that it were not, that the novel is generally seen in terms of a competition or battle of some kind, in terms of power.[1] The overt mock-epic parodies, the ridicule of the devices and ideas of combat are, of course, recognized by all; but they are generally seen as a further exercise of power, a ridicule of one or the other of the "sides" in the oppositional structure. I want to propose a motion, a wave, by which we might experience the novel, a shift from power to play to love. According to this possibility, the intensely competitive framework is not attacked by a satiric battalion, but displaced over into play. That play, however, is seen unsentimentally, seen as "heartless," and must yield finally to love. In terms of the details of *Barchester Towers*, the center moves from the high-church/low-church, Grantly/Slope warfare to the Stanhope circus to the love of the Thornes and Mr. Harding.

The narrator provides us with a clue to this deconstructive operation, not by being tricky but by being absolutely direct. "Our doctrine is," he says, "that the author and the reader should move along together in full confidence with each other."[2] The only requirement is that we trust him and, easier than it sounds, be willing to "move," and to move through not one but two paradigm shifts. He first must induce us to play: to take none too seriously the human failings of clergymen, the tendency of men and women to desire one another, the foibles of the old, the ambition and arrogance of the young, marriages and births and even deaths. The narrator, after all, is willing to horse around with writing the novel: exposing his tricks, telling us what he doesn't understand, worrying about the length and how to end the whole thing. We only have to be willing to horse around with our reading—and perhaps with our life.

The very first chapter provides one guide among many.[3] It opens with some playful jokes about power, about the furor raging in provincial Barchester over who the new bishop might be (a "most important question" the narrator wryly calls it, at the same time reducing it to the level of gossip). Since the question turns, however, on the timing of the death of the old bishop, a potentially serious note is introduced, one that delicately shades the play and allows for the shift into affection and contact. The easy satire yields to the sweet image of the dying bishop blessing his son and old friend Mr. Harding, while Mr. Harding "in fellowship" holds the hand of the son. This affecting scene soon yields to power or to play, as the son finds the hand-holding something of a hindrance to his itch to send news immediately of the death, so as to snatch the position for himself. The son, Archdeacon Grantly, is, of course, too late, which opens the door to the entry of the liberal Proudies, to war, to the plot of the novel, and to the narrator's wonderful close of the first chapter. The passage is very well-known, which robs me of the pleasure of quoting it, but in it the narrator notes that many will find Archdeacon Grantly's fierce desire for power downright "wicked" and then says, with that beautiful and precise quiet we associate with Trollope, "with such censures I cannot profess that I completely agree." He goes on with a series of gentle questions, asking who among us is not, in fact, subject to ambition, to the real love of playing first fiddle. The point and tone are not satiric; they move to establish not ridicule but kindness, affection, tolerance. *Barchester Towers* teaches us to be tolerant even of those who are intolerant, to know how to laugh at power but also when to stop laughing, to form enduring human ties that warm us, ties that are good for us and easy for us and reasonable. It is not a book gone mad with love. It is not, for instance, necessary that we love Mr. Slope, though it wouldn't hurt at all if we sneaked out a little sweet regard for Mrs. Proudie.

Slope, however, would like to imagine that he is at once inside and on top of power. "Let him be supreme who can" (iv), he says, and he enters Barchester determined to fight—over something, virtually anything. He dives into this peaceful world like a shark into a swimming pool, disturbing the serenity of the heretofore very comfortable and snapping violently to the left and right. He takes an especially big chunk out of Mr. Harding, what with his talk about "useless rubbish" (xii), and he does manage for a time to arrange everybody in town onto some kind of angry football field (though there is a little switching of sides). If we allow him to control things—and he is, we are told, very threatening when he is in control—we start to see the novel in Slope's terms (or the Archdeacon's, which amounts to much the same thing). If we are critics or teachers, we may carry Slope's constructions to the point of laying out our whole experience of the novel as a matched set of oppositions, like this:

High Church	Low Church
Grantly	Proudie-Slope
tradition-authority	individual reason
conservative	liberal
age	youth
men	women
gentlemanly behavior (instincts)	virtuous conduct
privilege	competition
country	city
slow, formulaic prose	active, brisk prose
proverbs, sententiae	scripture
similes	metaphors
dry	wet
backward	forward
in	out

Even as I extend that list in order to set out what I want to explode, I find myself almost seduced by it, almost interested enough in Slope's power construction of things to accept it.

But that would be to resist perversely the pull of play,[4] the pull of the narrator, of the old bishop's spirit, of the quintain, and most of all, of the Stanhopes. Any control Slope thought he had, the very control that makes him dangerous, is effectively dissolved by these travelling players recalled from a triumphant tour of Italy. The Stanhopes are not absolutely free from the ravages of power: Charlotte is an M.B.A. sort and La Signora Madeline 'Vesey Neroni—Nata Stanhope has been put through the gin. Still, even with slightly tattered costumes and sets, they put on a dazzling show.

Dr. Vesey Stanhope has managed to evade for many years so much as even "a day's duty" in the pulpit (ix), feeling, quite properly, that he was pursuing a higher duty in dancing with the butterflies in Italy. Though there is, of course, no order to the Stanhope family and no line of authority, Dr. Stanhope sets the tone. He is, above all, "a *bon vivant*" (ix), not about to stoop to the patriarchal: "That he had religious convictions must be believed; but he rarely obtruded them even on his children" (ix). Still, he has served as a family model in some things, especially for his son Bertie, who has made the decision to be open unto life. Bertie has been an orthodox believer, a nonbeliever, a Jew, and a Papist; he has tried his hand at the law, at painting, sculpting, and other of the fine arts. He sounds much like Oscar Wilde—without any plays actually written, to be sure: "He was above, or rather below, all prejudices. No virtue could charm him, no vice shock him. He had about him a natural good manner, which seemed to qualify him for the highest circles, yet he was never out of place in the lowest" (9). A man who charms and who finds life charming, he is, to an extent, outside of class and even outside of time, a perfect player: "one would have imagined from the sound of his voice and the gleam of his eyes that he had not a sorrow nor a care in the world. Nor had he" (xix).

Bertie, with a little help from his friends, nearly displaces power altogether, upsetting the ecclesiastic seriousness by his admiration for the Jews and the Church of Rome and turning even Mrs. Proudie very briefly into a stage player, obedient to her role, engaging in the farce. The following occurs after Bertie has run the sofa over Mrs. Proudie's dress, sundering it and releasing, the narrator mockingly says, "the wrath of Juno":

> Bertie, when he saw what he had done, rushed over the sofa and threw himself on one knee before the offended lady. His object, doubtless, was to liberate the torn lace from the castor; but he looked as though he were imploring pardon from a goddess.
>
> "Unhand it sir!" said Mrs. Proudie. From what scrap of dramatic poetry she had extracted the word cannot be said; but it must have rested on her memory. . . .
>
> "I'll fly to the looms of the fairies to repair the damage, if you'll only forgive me," said Ethelbert, still on his knees.
>
> —xi

Everything—narrator, players, set, action, dialogue—seems flowing here toward engulfing the world of power, rendering it irrelevant, unseen.

The Stanhopes, in other words, move in to cooperate with the mock-epic and with the narrative reflexiveness in order to turn satire into leap-frog and blind-man's-buff. Bertie disrupts not only the powerful seriousness of the churchy struggles but the romantic ones as well, entering into the chase after Eleanor only with the understanding that he doesn't mind running but will have nothing to do with winning or losing, with contests where one enters into "cold, calculated, cautious cunning" (42). All this is alien to Bertie's nature, not because it is immoral but because it attempts to plot out life, to give it a plan, and to bring it under control. That is Slope's way, the way of power, and not the Stanhopes'. Even Madeline, the Signora Neroni, who can hardly be said to be untainted by the lust for authority, enlists her power, when it counts, on the side of play, turning Mr. Arabin over to Eleanor at just the right time and, much more importantly, defending the vulnerable Mr. Thorne from Slope's mean-spirited strikes and sending the red-headed one yowling from the room.

But, like Dickens, Trollope felt an uneasiness about turning his novel or his world over to play, an uneasiness made explicit in the narrator's famous commentary on the Stanhopes' "heartlessness": "The great family characteristic of the Stanhopes might probably be said to be heartlessness; but this want of feeling was, in most of them, accompanied by so great an amount of good nature as to make itself but little noticeable to the world" (ix). They have no love, even for one another; and though a great deal may be said for this overflowing good nature, especially when the alternative is Mr. Slope and his Sunday Schools, there is in the Stanhopes and in play a necessary resistance to bonds and ties that, whether always noticeable or not, leaves behind just what the great humanists were anxious to center.

And that new centering is developed (or we can develop it ourselves) by way of some rather melancholy old people, those who know a great deal about power and about play but who see things differently and do differently. Monica Thorne, for instance, is, just like the Stanhopes, "essentially good-natured" (xxiii), but she is certainly not, also like them, "heartless." She and her brother do not live for delight, though they take a great interest in delighting others; they are careless of their own power but still, unlike pure players, are anxious for consequences, results. Miss Thorne does not bring Eleanor and Arabin together so that they might frolic. She wants them engaged, good and solid.

But the Thornes are much closer to play than to power, and they are subject to Trollope's most subtle rhetorical calculations. They are introduced in a way that invites us to exercise our own power lenses, to read them as Mr. Slope would, to model them satirically. Miss Thorne, we are told, is "a pure Druidess," "very anxious to revert to the dogs" (xxii); and her brother wears his absurd views and nostalgic conservatism on such an out-of-fashion sleeve as to be quite obviously "open to ridicule" (xxii). If we give in to this obviousness, however, we are diving headfirst into a snare, albeit a playful snare. We are missing the counter-signals, the invitations to eschew ridicule altogether and come look through the Ullathorne windows, Tudor windows that show nothing of power: "There may be windows which give a better light than such as these, and it may be, as my utilitarian friend observes, that the giving of light is the desired object of a window. I will not argue the point with him. Indeed I cannot. But . . . no sort of description of window is capable of imparting half so much happiness to mankind. . . ." (xxii). The point is unarguable from the standpoint of power; these are not windows for the powerful but for mere "homely folk" (xxii). More importantly, they provide happiness not just for the owners but for all "mankind." They issue not from an aesthetic need but from a need for love. These windows are a way of life, which is why, we might say, they give more happiness than any other "description of window," an peculiar phrase throwing the weight onto "description" rather than "window." It is not just a matter of looking at or through the divided glass; we must be able to live in the perspective on the world, the description, which gave rise to the possibility of these Tudor windows in the first place. We must inhabit a world where candlepower and even our own sense of pleasure and delight yield to the claims of human happiness.

By the time we reach the Thornes' fête champêtre, we see that what had appeared an insane and embarrassing recreation of a medieval never-never land becomes a charming and well-mannered stage for lovers, opened up by Miss Thorne's "soft heart" (xxiii) and that of her brother. While Miss Thorne's plan to divide the party according to love and not rank, gathering the old people inside and "leaving the lawn to the lovers" (xxxv), is found to be impracticable, the party does manage to sort out the lovers pretty well. The actual play, the quintain, turns out to be a little too consequential in the way of retributive bags of flour and therefore something of a flop. But there is plenty of other play at this open-hearted festival: "Don't be too particular, Plomacy, especially with the children. If they live anywhere near, let them in" (xxxv).[5] More important than the play, there is plenty of love, most compellingly that of Mr. Thorne himself, who gives his heart to La Signora. The love of such a one as Mr. Thorne is, as the narrator says, "real true love" (xxxvii).

This love is there through the novel, if we can but see it, even in the unlikely breast of Mrs. Proudie, where lies a heart, the narrator admits, "not easily accessible," but there all the same, and there for Mrs. Quiverful to touch (xxvi). We may be reluctant to take very seriously whatever it is Eleanor and Arabin feel for one another, the narrator himself being so boisterously unserious on the subject. But there is no doubt about the nature of the feeling between Miss Thorne and her brother, the old bishop and the whole community, Mr. Harding and the poor bedesmen, Mr. and Mrs. Quiverful, even the archdeacon and his wife.

Mr. Harding is the most insistently centered of these lovers, the one who stands finally as the hero of the novel because the author says in the very last paragraph that he is decidedly *not* the hero. Certainly he is not heroic in the usual sense, since the usual sense is connected to power. Mr. Harding exists without reference to power, instinctively drawing away when it comes near. When Mr. Slope comes on the scene, Mr. Harding is simply unable to make any contact with that ethos, unable to see how Slope can go on hurting people. When Eleanor defends Slope mildly, saying that perhaps he felt compelled by his duty, even by God, to speak the truth as he saw it, her father makes it gently clear that in his universe truth has no business superseding kindness: "Believe me, my child, that Christian ministers are never called on by God's word to insult the convictions, or even the prejudices of their brethren; and that religion is at any rate not less susceptible of urbane and courteous conduct among men, than any other study which men may take up" (viii).

It is this standard and this belief which causes this quiet man to have the most beautiful parts in the chorale, even taking over some solo work toward the end of the book. Through all the disentanglements and the rearranging of lovers, we are told that it is he, who had nothing to do either with befuddling things or clarifying them, to whom we should be attending: "But the satisfaction of Mr. Harding was, of all, perhaps the most complete" (xlix). Like Mr. Pickwick, he lives for the happiness of others, a satisfaction that gives both of them untold delight. And like Mr. Pickwick, Mr. Harding's characteristic act at the end is to withdraw. "When it became known to all the world that Mr. Harding was to be the new dean, all the world rejoiced heartily" (lii); but he finds even richer happiness is giving the deanship to Arabin and, especially, in acts of sensitive kindness to Mr. Quiverful, the new Warden. Walking through the hospital gate arm in arm with his successor, he sweetly introduces his fellow-clergyman to the position and the old men he had so dearly loved himself. Mr. Harding gives to his replacement a "friendliness [which] was everything to Mr. Quiverful," a kindliness that is simply the way he is in this life: "He be always very kind," says one of the old men, the existential *be* standing as something more than a grammatical slip. Mr. Quiverful calls it "uncalled for, unexpected kindness" (lii), but that is because Mr. Harding's perspective does not always present itself to him or to us. We are not always looking through Tudor windows.

If we were, we would develop the androgynous wholeness of Mr. Harding, that "nice comprehension" of others' needs and difficulties, a "nice appreciation of the feelings of others which belongs of right exclusively to women" (lii).

But there is no need for such gender divisions, as Mr. Harding shows, no need for exclusive rights or even private "belongings." Mr. Harding's position is a radical one, allowing nothing to the sharp common sense of power or the heartless caprices of play. He is that most precious of beings, "a good man without guile." And in the novel's last paragraph the author relinquishes any right of possession over him, giving him to us: "The Author now leaves him in the hands of the readers." Mr. Harding, pure love, is now ours.

13

Girl-Watching, Child-Beating, and Other Exercises for Readers of *Jude the Obscure*

*M*OST READERS CONSTRUCT *Jude the Obscure* as replete with pain and sex. A few connect the pain and the sex. The ways in which pain and sex are connected doubtless vary some, all of us being different people, but I'd like to propose two broad categories that would accommodate the readerly experiences of most or all of us with this novel: homicidal voyeurism and sadism. Assuming that does not sound insulting or otherwise unpersuasive, I will feel authorized to turn directly to exploring what it is readers do with *Jude*. Briefly, we readers[1] direct both the voyeurism and the sadism toward children, weaving and embellishing patterns of erotic desire that take the form of an unusually violent sort of pedophilia, what today we would call physical and sexual abuse of children. Further, these pornographic projections both build on and subvert (or at least expose) the demeaning, even murderous distancing devices we use to keep desire alive, the ways in which we push people into the next county, into the role of mere objects, into childhood or some other embodiment of otherness in order to lust after them.

If, as we are told repeatedly by those who know, desire has no goal beyond its own perpetuation, no generator other than the drive to find absence, a provocative gap, it may be that *Jude* presents this "lack" in its purest figuring (or we can say it does) and allows the reader the form of erotic activity most devoted to avoiding fulfillments, endings. I suggest that the extreme or "pure" form of this empty-hence-irresistible eroticism can be located in the image of the child being beaten, and that our desire and our repugnance are alerted and fed by being sometimes participant, sometimes spectator. We beat the boys ourselves and watch as the girls are being beaten. With some considerable athletic versatility, we hop from stage to audience, from sadism to voyeurism, depending on the gender of the figure we construct in the form of the child.

Explaining how this reader-as-pornographer/pervert comes into being will take some doing. To help, here are two scenes from the novel I'd like to use as keys. In the first, Jude's aunt tells a story about the twelve-year-old Sue; in the second, we are shown Jude, age eleven, being beaten by Farmer Troutham:

> Many's the time I've smacked her for her impertinence. Why, one day when she was walking in the pond with her shoes and stockings off, and her petticoats pulled above her knees, afore I could cry out for shame, she said, "Move on, aunty! This is no sight for modest eyes!"
> —II.-vi.

> "'Eat, dear birdies,' indeed! I'll tickle your breeches, and see if you say, 'Eat, dear birdies,' again in a hurry! . . .

> . . . Swinging his slim frame round him at arm's length, [Troutham] again struck Jude on the hind parts with the flat side of Jude's own rattle, till the field echoed with the blows, which were delivered once or twice at each revolution.

> "Don't 'ee, sir—please don't 'ee!" cried the whirling child, as helpless . . . as a hooked fish. . . . "I——I——sir—only meant that——there was a good crop in the ground——I saw 'em sow it——and the rooks could have a little bit for dinner—and you wouldn't miss it, sir——and Mr. Phillotson said I was to be kind to 'em——O, O, O!"

> This truthful explanation seemed to exasperate the farmer even more than if Jude had stoutly denied saying anything at all; and he still smacked the whirling urchin, the clacks of the instrument continuing to resound all across the field and . . . echoing from the brand-new church tower just behind the mist, toward the building of which structure the farmer had largely subscribed, to testify his love for God and man.[2]
> —I.-ii.

These (marginal?) scenes I want to take as paradigmatic of the activity not of the novel but of readers, representing something happening not in the book but in us. As John Bayley remarks, in Hardy, "it seems to be our own activities among the constituent parts of the writing that give us our sense of what is going on";[3] And what is going on here, I claim (and you agree), is erotic readerly projection into the scene. Since we are most concerned with the way gender drives these scenes apart, makes different our own participation in the beatings, we will return to some of the details in these passages, after a brief historical and theoretical excursion into Victorian child-flagellation and our own. For now, we should observe that we may read both scenes as slightly comic. Jude's whirling at the end of a man's hand has the look of common and happy adult-child play; and Sue's rebellious assault on adult power—"Move on, aunty!"—and on prudishness—she loves to offend "modest eyes"—has about it a kind of Tom Sawyer mischievousness. True, it sets us itching for the kind of punishment Tom Sawyer regularly receives, but that punishment never amounts to much, right? Fictional bad boys and girls are seldom beaten or flogged. They are "swished," which sounds downright pleasant, "licked," which sounds maternal or erotic (or both), or, as here with Sue, "smacked," which sounds like a funny noise and like kissing. Jude's breeches are "tickled." Makes us think we're doing nothing wrong, nothing very special: it's all a game, all in fun.

But even if it is all in fun (which in *Jude* it hardly can be), what we readers are doing differs sharply in these two cases. Sue's punishments are not dramatized; Jude's are. Sue's smackings are multiple; Jude's singular. Sue's offense[4] is personal, moral, sexual; Jude's is ethical and economic. The episodes with Sue are set in the past, seem remote; the one with Jude is immediate and concrete. We are made aware of Jude's buttocks, not of Sue's. All these details will help us finally to understand why we position ourselves as voyeurs with Sue and as sadists with Jude, girl-watchers and boy-beaters. It will help us to understand, too, how it may be that the first activity is the more damaging of the two, the more insidious, the more perverse. And the moral of that is: beat me if you like, but please don't look, says the wise child; or, as Arabella (and Moses) puts it, "'Then shall the man be guiltless; but the woman shall bear his iniquity.' Damn rough on us women" (V.-viii.).

In the scene featuring Sue, the juxtaposition of beating with the erotic is clear. Sue is often smacked; she has exposed herself audaciously, knowingly. Causing others to blush, she must be made to blush herself, forming the connection between spanking and the enticing erotics of modesty Victorian sexologists posited. With Jude the connections are not so overt, are, in fact, established through the slow-motion retardation of the action and the prolonged focus on the buttocks, through an emphasis on the boy's pain and soreness, and through a positioning of the language within the range of clues associated with pornography. This last is particularly important: we know we should be aroused because we are generically situated in reference to a form of literature we think ought to be erotic. Consider the dialogue. Farmer Troutham's initial expression of anger, couched as an explanation or erotic foreplay, is familiar to us from a long pornographic tradition—{My lady must smart for this. . . . She has been very troublesome lately with these impudent drawings, but this is positively obscene. . . . Send for Susan to bring my birch rod."[5] Not incidentally, this formula from pornography has slithered over into life, as we all know from endless public displays of righteous correction and their self-justifying preludes: "You little wretch. I told you not to do that. Now you're going to get it! You've asked for it! A good, sound spanking!" The child's response in life is not usually so erotically apt as Jude's "Don't 'ee, sir—please don't 'ee . . . O, O, O!" Jude's rhythmic pleas, which exasperate Troutham further, provide an excuse for prolonging the episode and emphasizing the cadence of the blows, the beat of the beating, we might say. The fall of the hand or rod is sometimes made explicit in porn—"'Oh-h! dear—Mama!' Swish! 'Yah-hah-ah-h!! Oh! I-will-be-good!' Swish! 'Ah-h-h! Oh! I-will-never' Swish! . . .,"[6] a form of dialogue given perhaps its highest or at least most anapestic expression in a line from Swinburne's *The Flogging-Block:* "Oh! Oh, sir! Oh, please, sir! Please, please, sir! Oh! Oh!"[7]

The image of the child being beaten, exploited relentlessly, if perhaps unconsciously, by Hollywood and Madison Avenue, is so central to our culture and so vital to our psychic structurings of desire that we may wonder why it is so seldom discussed.[8] One answer is that, here as everywhere, desire really is connected to distance, to absence, to otherness, to silence. If we bring our collective and individual erotic attachments to child-beating up from the cellar, they cease to be erotic. But that they are dwelling down below is certain. Notice how virtually every legislative act directed toward protecting children from abuse is compromised by its contradictory effort also to protect the abusers. We detest abuse, but not enough to abandon the palpably absurd but deeply-held and deeply-needed belief that such abuse has no connection in the world to "normal spanking," the presumed rights of parents, relatives, teachers, baby-sitters, or others from a wide but designated range to beat, smack, whip, fondle, caress the child's defenseless bottom. Children are thus protected only from "excessive" battering, which may sometimes mean that the law can step in to help them only with the funeral arrangements.[9]

But why is this child so erotic in the first place and why would we ever derive such satisfactions from what would seem the pointless (at least non-genital) act of hitting it on the buttocks? The most comforting position for a twentieth-century American is to claim that erotic child-beating is pretty much confined to one of the following: (a) the British, (b) the Victorians, or (c) the perverted. The notion that sexual flagellation is "a vice peculiar to the English" is often repeated, especially by English writers, as if some points of considerable national pride were at stake.[10] Patriotic Americans, and citizens of every other country, will be quick to rise to contest this claim; but tradition is nonetheless clear on the historical-cultural prominence of England. Explanations given for such prominence always include the rise in prestige of the public-school model and its use of flogging as a means of defining itself; the centrality of discipline and physical subjugation to various popular forms of evangelicalism; the effect of sexual repression and the forcing of people into indirect and perverse forms of sexual satisfaction; and the fact that the French were taking vigorous steps to outlaw corporal punishment everywhere, which alone might make the British eager to do just the opposite. While it doubtless is important (for our purposes) that the activity and plenty of talk about it were in the air in Hardy's time, we must be suspicious of all this mixing of causes with symptoms in an attempt to enclose this startling phenomenon within national boundaries and thus deny its pertinence.

If the strategy to protect ourselves by declaring all this exclusively British breaks down, perhaps we can do just as well by locating sexual child-spanking in the past, the unenlightened Victorian past, something not our own. True, we can spot some conservative Victorian speakers who will talk of the child in ways we find grotesquely alien. Some even seem to see this "child" as fairly contemptible, an inferior species altogether or, more moderately, a radically incomplete adult. Such views can happily confirm our distance and our superiority. According to these welcome speakers, one either enters into pitched battle with the child to destroy it and substitute the completed adult or, less violently, one forces the plant into blooming and, meanwhile, subdues it into being as inoffensive as possible. Here is one of those voices, speaking of "correction": "In judicious correction, courage and perseverance are alike requisite. Crying is the defensive weapon of the child, and if this resistance is successful, by the yielding of the nurse or mother, she will often find difficulty in regaining her lost dominion."[11] One can locate similar expressions of resentment of childhood and the felt need to invade and conquer it in the sermons and correspondence of Thomas Arnold. Arnold sees his school, his tutelage as a kind of high-speed conveyer belt, quickly manufacturing adults out of vile children through using the magic machine of flogging. Flogging, Arnold says, is justified "as fitly answering to and marking the naturally inferior state of boyhood, and therefore as conveying no particular disgrace to persons in such a state."[12] The peculiar reasoning here identifies boyhood and flogging in such a way as to make an unbeaten child unnatural: being flogged defines the state of childhood. Such logic may easily be made to seem preposterous and ugly to us and may allow us to think that perhaps this whole business is another freak of those remarkably freakish Victorians.

The difficulty with this strategy for distancing the phenomenon of erotic child-beating is that it breaks down almost immediately. We find, first of all, most Victorian child-rearing manuals speaking not so monstrously, advising pretty strenuously in most cases against beating children, some even recognizing and protesting against the sexual connections established or exercised thereby.[13] More troublesome still is the persistence in our culture of the image of child-beating, particularly in genres we think of as entertaining: popular novels, movies, and comic strips. Watch the movie version of *The Bad Seed* and ask yourself what desires were being catered to in the little coda where Patty McCormack, playing not the bad-seeded Rhoda but simply herself as actress, is spanked. Why does the same practice occur so frequently in *Our Gang* and *Little Rascal* short films, in television sitcoms and feature films, and in comic strips, from the classic "Buster Brown" through "The Katzenjammer Kids" to "Lil Abner," "Winnie Winkle," and "Little Lulu."[14]

So much, then, for these strategies of denial based on historical separation. Our laws, familial practices, forms of amusement all proclaim that this kind of eroticism is with us still. Such an announcement of survival might be titillating, but it will not make us especially uncomfortable, since we have left to us our most powerful defense: the claim that such forms of eroticism are perverse, thus very far indeed from those normal impulses and normal modes of behavior we ourselves experience.

Even Freud, not always our friend in constructing these defensive maneuvers, distances the subject nicely for us. His famous essay, "A Child Is Being Beaten," is subtitled, "A Contribution to the Study of the Origin of Sexual Perversions."[15] It is true that he begins his essay with an unnerving observation on the surprising frequency of this child-beating fantasy among those who seek out help. He goes on, even more unnervingly, to speculate that the fantasy exists among a great many of those who do not seek out help. But he then settles down to sorting out with cool precision the kinds of "perversions" involved in different configurations of the beating scene: sadism in the beating of a rival, masochism in being beaten oneself, masochism disguised as sadism in being a spectator at the beating of others. Freud's analysis is comforting: tough, analytical, strictly empirical in its base, and modulated through distaste. He also speaks with a certainty we may find reassuring, with accents that ring with confidence. But we can also see the confidence as bullying, desperate, hysterical (Freud would have liked that characterization). Does Freud's mapping of the spanking psyche reassure, or act to give the game away by exposing the carnival of question-begging and arbitrary assertiveness going on?

And then there are others meddling around there and diagramming or explaining things differently. Havelock Ellis, for instance, sees the tie between pain and eroticism as commonplace. He has a way of saying the most outrageous things about the subject: "There is nothing necessarily cruel, repulsive, or monstrous in the idea or the reality of a whipping"; even more startling, "the general sexual association of whipping in the minds of children and frequently of their elders, is by no means rare and scarcely abnormal."[16] If this isn't abnormal, we might scream, what is? A question to be asked, perhaps, but one that only points up the insecurity of any protection based on a distinction between the normal and the abnormal. We may try to externalize what we call the abnormal, but it has a way of sneaking back inside when we're not looking and taking up lodging once again.[17]

All these explications tend to support the argument that the powerful structure of desire in *Jude* that winds its way through the torturing of children emanates from the reader, from us. Such projections may, in Ellis's terms, scarcely be abnormal, but they are suggestive of, among other things, the ways in which we tend to construct gender difference. The narrative patterns used to devise these fantasies of child-beating are, in this novel, quite different for boys and for girls. As I have said, we smack the boys ourselves, but watch the girls being beaten.

That gender is involved at all in erotic child-beating is not immediately apparent. From the standpoint of the pedophile, the child's gender is remarkably fluid: the accepted wisdom is that child-love is neither heterosexual nor homosexual, but something else disconnected from gender. Even in the child-whipping pornography, there is nothing settled about the gender of anyone, disguises being used freely and one sex turning into another easily and often. Steven Marcus noted this curious "ambiguity of sexual identity," though he rushed to deny it as well, offering in the place of confusing ambiguity the assurances of bland homophobia: appearances notwithstanding, "the figure being beaten is originally, finally, and always a boy."[18]

Not so absurd as this mechanical brand of Freudianism is Jude's own humanist liberalism, his tragic sense that we are all in this together, that the purblind doomsters ripping us apart indiscriminately render distinctions based on gender (or anything else) irrelevant:

> Still, Sue, it is no worse for the woman than for the man. That's what some women fail to see, and instead of protesting against the conditions, they protest against the man, the other victim, just as a woman in a crowd will abuse the man who crushes against her, when he is only the helpless transmitter of the pressure put upon him.
>
> —V.-iv.

Appealing as this may be—to men—the later course of events exposes it for what it is: a delusory attempt to find comfort through misogynistic comparisons. Jude argues that women, or some of them, fail to see what men, most of them, see so clearly: though women may be elbowed off the path and trodden on (by men), only fools (women) would blame the men. Men are not the villains at all, just fellow victims, even worse off (when you come to think of it) because they realize (as women do not) the absurdity of it all and have to pay double for such acuity through being taxed with brutality by the obtuse (women). Jude's sense that he and Sue, men and women, are mutual quarry is not quite right—not right at all. Jude says here that some women "fail to see." Perhaps that's because the sightings are inaccurate and because men block all the lines of sight, hog them up, anyhow: men like Jude are endlessly busy spying on women, seeing through and for them, positioning all women as objects, blind objects. It is not a question of equal victimization—for anyone—and none of us can claim to be merely "helpless transmitters" of pressures and desires originating elsewhere.

Jude and Sue, men and women, may well be victims and deserving of pity; but they eagerly enough bully one another into torturing games and find ways to torture themselves. And we readers do not simply watch. We are playing with children here, with empty constructions; and we do with them what we will. The child, a recent social and linguistic invention, can be filled in any way we like; in *Jude*, we stuff the child with pain and with desire. We make the child represent, fill it with meaning;[19] and we do so in ways that both confirm and resent the child's distance from us. The child is Other, desired and detested, fawned over and spanked. The woman-as-child is distanced twice over, a double-zero and thus double-denied and double-desired. She cannot come close to us, not even close to our hand or hairbrush or whip. She is merely a creature of fantasy, an actress-victim in a flagellation drama that never ends, the object for the voyeur.

Jude as male child is closer to the pornographic reader. He is the child at the end of Farmer Troutham's hand being whacked a couple of times firmly at each revolution as he wails and pleads helplessly. He is substantial, the object of sadism. Sue is dimmer, more removed into memory, less settled in form and thus even more available to objectification. We look at Sue as she struggles to be; we watch as she is denied that substance, that subjecthood. As voyeurs, as pornographic readers of Sue, we maintain her hollowness and thus her desirability. Her tortures are more subtle or more interiorized because she is never allowed to take shape. Jude is there presenting his buttocks to be whacked. Sue, no matter how high she lifts her petticoats, can never be more than an image in the mind's eye, in our eye. Her act of defiance, her self-assertion, in fact, freezes her. We operate the controls of the freezer.

The proper place to develop this argument is by way of the novel itself, so I will close this section with a case history Ellis cites, a case history that evokes, I suggest, Aunt Drusilla's pornographic picture of Sue, an attitude that in turn suggests the pathological reader of the text—us, that is:

> When about 5 years old I was playing with a little girl friend in the park. Our governesses sat on a bench talking. For some reason—perhaps because we had wandered away too far and failed to hear a call to return—my friend aroused the anger of the governess in charge of her. That young lady, therefore, took her aside, raised her dress, and vigorously smacked her with the flat hand. I looked on fascinated, and possessed by an inexplicable feeling to which I naïvely gave myself up. The impression was so deep that the scene and the person concerned are still clearly present to my mind, and I can even recall the little details of my companion's underclothing.[20]

❧   ❧   ❧

Jude offers us torture, both the spectacle of someone being tortured by a variety of villains and an invitation to lend a hand ourselves. The chief activity engaged in by the novel or, more exactly, the reader of the novel, seems to be the cruel flogging and slow dismemberment of its main characters, Jude and Sue. The site of the tormenting alters according to gender, but, in either case, it is a child being beaten, impaled, shredded. The reader is politely asked if he wouldn't like to direct a drama of kiddie porn, a snuff movie being played in our head, starring two cookie-bakers who act with charming innocence throughout, just "like two children" (V.-v.), as Arabella says. Even after his disastrous marriage, Jude is unspoiled by any grown-up cynicism: "he seemed to be a boy still" (I.-xi.). Indeed, as the narrator insists later, it is not a matter of *seems*; Jude acts "like the child that he *was*" (III.-x.; italics mine). Sue, despite her sophistication in one or two matters, is, similarly, "such a child in others" (IV-v.) that she can be conveniently fitted into the reader's criminal pedophiliac drama. Though we don't hear any "don't 'ee, don't 'ee, oh, please sir, please sir!" from her, she does react to pain in ways wholly appropriate to this form of pornography, "her mouth shaping itself like that of a child about to give way to grief" (V.-iv.).

But there are differences in the way we project these patterns of erotic abuse, differences shaped by gender. Jude is a Katzenjammer Kid carried to some homicidal limit. One of the features of pornographic child-spanking, really of child-spanking in general, is that it corrects nothing, is meant to correct nothing. If it really put an end to misbehavior, it would put an end to the erotic fun; and no one wants that. Just so, unable to learn, bouncing back fresh and ready for more at the beginning of each episode, Jude, like little Hans and Fritz, keeps asking for it and getting it—from us.

Interestingly, the novel opens with a series of rather subtle persecutions of the boy. Phillotson's leaving is presented as an exercise in half-comic cruelty: "Sorry I am going, Jude?", he asks, getting the response he (or the reader) wants—tears from the infatuated, romantic boy. In another key, Aunt Drusilla's cold detestation—she calls Jude a "poor useless boy" and says he should have died with his parents—seems grimly Dickensian, as does the contempt of the vicious neighborhood women, whose stares fall on Jude "like slaps upon his face" (I.-ii.). Such an attack from "glances," from looks, is highly significant in this novel, another direct, smacking assault.

Jude is hurt, stung, sore, has to eat standing up; but there is a way in which none of this is very serious. Jude can, after all, recover; he can also, more importantly, escape these looks, these stares that are "like slaps." He can slink away: "he did not care to show himself in the village, and went homeward by a roundabout track" (I.-ii.). We should remember, in our sympathy for the sobbing, beaten Jude, that for Sue there is no roundabout track, no escape from the staring eyes, the eyes of the reader.

But Jude has problems of his own, of course, and no small ones. These problems are blunt, insistent, physical. He is hit, smacked, beaten. "All at once he became conscious of a smart blow upon his buttocks" (I.-ii.): this odd, distanced, erotic formulation is paradigmatic for this character. He is always being bent over and whacked, "all at once," his dignity taken down along with his trousers. "On a sudden something smacked him sharply in the ear, and he became aware that a soft cold substance had been flung at him" (I.-vi.). There is the same phrasing, as his bride-to-be enters by way of a pig's penis. His love for Arabella jerks him along "as a violent schoolmaster a schoolboy he has seized by the collar" (I.-vii.): seized and marched off to a good, sound flogging, we may be sure.

All of Jude's punishments, in other words, amount to direct or displaced versions of the spanking of children, highly erotic and infinitely repeatable. Like those children in comic strips—Buster Brown, Perry Winkle, Hans and Fritz—he continues in his provocative behavior, his hopefulness and his idealism, and thus is regularly positioned for a trip to the woodshed. Our pornographic desire is never satiated because it is never fulfilled. The spankings do not halt the misbehavior, rather spur it on. The very same day of his theatrical spanking by Farmer Troutham, he is back in the field he has been warned out of, risking a rerun. He has been brought low by the whipping, it is true, so low that he decides he should find a way not to grow up at all, things being as shudderingly inharmonious as they clearly are in this world. Now to pederast readers, who have greatly enjoyed the spanking, this would be shocking stuff indeed, were it serious; but it is not. Instead of suicide, we get boyish resiliency, the wonderful childish eagerness to continue the erotic game, to be spanked again: "Then, like the natural boy, he forgot his despondency, and sprang up" (I.-ii.). He springs up with comic and erotic elasticity, not just here, but every time he is presumably crushed: when he finds out that the acquisition of Latin and Greek will entail years of grinding work he is floored but not for long, falling under a tree and becoming "an utterly miserable boy for the space of a quarter of an hour" (I.-iv.). The narrative as a whole traces one long rebound from the whipping he receives at Christminster.

Jude does not take these spankings personally. He does not resent them, feels somehow that they are deserved. After Farmer Troutham releases him, he walks away, sobbing and quivering, not, we are told, from the pain nor from any of a number of Schopenhauerean reflections that might comfort him, but from "the awful sense that he had wholly disgraced himself." Like David Copperfield, another object of readerly sadism, Jude takes the sexual spankings as his due, as natural, feeling only a deep sense of shame at having behaved as he has. He harbors no anger for Troutham or for us; he isn't about to tell anyone or phone the authorities. He is the perfect target for sadism.

His life, then, follows predictably enough as a series of physical chastisements, brusque as whacks on the buttocks or flying pigs' pizzles. Arabella and her sexuality are represented as more or less one continual assault on Jude, figured most overtly in the scene where the pig-killing thrusts itself on him not as a farmer's chore, a matter-of-fact little business of life, but as a crushing series of monstrous material facts he cannot, for all his writhing, evade. His attempt to find in suicide a dignified end to it all, a rich tragic finale, is rendered farcical by the thick ice and its refusal to follow the script. Even Jude's mental torments take on a palpable and painful corporeality, as when he conjures up images of the children born to Sue and Phillotson in order to flagellate himself a little (III.-viii.). His actual ending—set in vividly realized squalor, directed by the "rank passions" of Arabella, featuring Jude's drunken (childlike) helplessness—seems a kind of demonic orgy of child-abuse.

But we, the abusers, do all this out of desire for Jude, out of what we might as well call love. The male child is beaten, but the beating is a lovemaking, a fondling, a stroking, the blows themselves being no more than the rhythmic beat of copulation. Thus it is that we pity Jude, extend to him our heartfelt sympathy—and feel no need to "explain" him. The situation, we will find, is very different with Sue. But Jude is directly present to us and is thus coddled in the very process of being whipped. Jude is pitied and gentled, presented as so truly victimized, his fault being only that he is too tender, too sensitive. Just like us. Farmer Troutham, who, if not a surrogate, is at least doing us all a great favor by enacting the pornographic scene, is also a knave. The management of the scene is masterful, Jude being at once a "whirling urchin," the perfect object of pedophile sadism and also a miniature St. Francis. We are allowed to enjoy the eroticism and also flatter ourselves with our superior sensibility, allowed to identify with and take the pleasure of Farmer Troutham and see him as a beast. Our identification with the beater is thus promoted and effectively screened, part of the screen being provided by the gratuitous and laboriously planted satire on the farmer's hypocrisy, the brand new church tower echoing the sounds of the spanking having been erected with the help of Troutham's subscription, "to testify his love for God and man" (I.-ii.).[21]

In similar ways throughout, we are enabled to keep the game going, to adore Jude by spanking him. He is, after all, a likeable sort, filled with superior qualities—a pretty fair mirror, in this regard, for us to look into. And, because he is so much like us, he is not the major pornographic prey here. We can take after him from time to time, like Pip's sister with Tickler in hand, but generally we are not much challenged by him. And desire needs the titillation of remoteness and challenge—the challenge posed, for instance, by the fiercely resistant Sue. We construct Jude, for erotic purposes, as contingent, near-at-hand (and to-hand), docile, familiar, and domestic; Sue is radically distanced, unpleasantly alien, wild, insistently other. No games could be more different than those we play with these two characters, these two genders.

Which make quite strange all the signals we receive on the virtual identity of Jude and Sue. Sue's name enters the novel on the other side of an equals sign from Jude: "His cousin Sue is just the same," says Aunt Drusilla (I.-ii.). The narrator calls them "almost the two parts of a single whole" (V.-v.), a perception seconded by Phillotson: "one person split in two" (IV.-iv.). Arabella, of all people, ends the novel by saying Sue will never find peace "till she's as he is now!" (VI.-xi.). All of this sounds very much like *Wuthering Heights,* like Heathcliff and Cathy, like romantic tragedy. But Sue never is, for us, anything like Jude, a fact that may mute romantic tragedy but makes it easy for us to engage in some remarkable erotic distancing. With Jude, we get close and paddle in the flesh, one might say, only so we can join him in forcing Sue into the faraway, watching her being spanked in the theater of the mind. If Jude is the subject of uninhibited sadism, Sue is caught by the much fiercer monsters of voyeurism.

Jude provides the voyeuristic model for us. Even as a child, he is expert at finding places of concealment from which he can see without being seen. The day of his spanking he sneaks back through the fields to formulate in his gaze the erotic image of Christminster, palpitating and shimmering in the distance. He watches until the lights of the city go out "like extinguished candles": like drawn curtains, the end of lovemaking for a Peeping Tom—for Jude and for us. He whispers to the breezes from the city "caressingly," and in his "romantic" attachment, holds it in his sight "like a young lover . . . his mistress" (I.-iii). He loves from hiding, yearns from behind bushes. He becomes so associated with concealment that even his bakery cart is fitted up with a blackened hiding place, a portable den from which he can send out "longing looks" (I.-iv.). For Jude, or at least for us voyeur readers, all this is perfect. The point is to control the erotic image by denying its physical independence, maintaining it only and always as a captive of the eye, the mind's eye. Thus, Christminster is no closer for Jude when he is within the confines of its gates than when he was at the crest of the hill outside Marygreen.

Christminster, we feel, can take care of itself, can afford to be supremely indifferent to all the voyeuristic perverts using her. Not so Sue. She has had the initial misfortune to be trapped in a photograph, offering "a pretty girlish face" with a "halo" effect (II.-i.) that stirs Jude's juices even more strongly than the "halo" (I.-iii.) he had constructed around Christminster. With that photograph all his own, Jude can display it privately, even kiss it (II.-ii) to his heart's content—if it's his heart he wants to content. Not satisfied with that sort of girlie-magazine erotics, though, Jude takes to looking for Sue herself—or perhaps only a more varied image of her. Sure enough, he soon spots her, unconscious of him and nicely framed by a window in a shop he enters so he can, unseen, steal a glance (II.–ii.). For some time after first fixing her in his sights, "he kept watch over her" by sneaking around to places where he figures he might "gain a further view of her" (II.–iii.). He takes to following her, since "to see her, and to be himself unseen and unknown, was enough for him at present" (II.-ii.). Enough for him! Why it's a regular Peeping Tom's Heaven, a point that Jude (or the narrator) half-acknowledges by saying "his interest in her had shown itself to be unmistakably of a sexual kind" (II.-iv.). Jude goes so far as to start skulking about "often at this hour after dusk" to "watch the shadows" on the blinds of the training school Sue is attending (III.-iii.).

But Jude is no more than a starting-kit, a set of hints to get the pornographic reader going in his erotic projection. And Sue is the main victim of this perverse activity, an activity so cruel it does almost make the sadism of child-spanking seem like love. Sue is deeply wary of being fixed, set, photographed once and for all. She dodges brilliantly, and courageously creates for herself possibilities where we thought there were none.[22] Her oft-repeated "unconsciousness of gender" or, as she puts it, a total absence of any fear of men (III.-iv.) is perhaps her most daring and also most pathetic defense against being set as object, as a halo-round-a-face, as game held in the sites of the voyeur's rifle.

Married or unmarried, copulating or not, Sue is not allowed to come into being, never allowed actuality. "You are often not so nice in your real presence as you are in your letters!" Jude tells her (III.-vi.), providing a very mild form of the truth: Sue is not only much nicer (i.e., more enticing) in letters or at a distance, she only is at a distance. She has no "real presence" for us, no way to break through our mechanisms of alienating in order to control and desire. Part of this pornographic distancing is exposed in the recurrent need to explain Sue, felt both by characters within the novel—from Gillingham to Jude to Arabella— to those without, from Hardy himself[23] and D. H. Lawrence[24] to every recent critic and commentator. Explanation, we might say, is itself a form of control, of fixing and pinning the other on some distant and alluring horizon.

Among the oft-explained differences between Arabella and Sue is that Sue denies and tries to resist the inevitable objectification Arabella stoically accepts and tries hard to exploit. Sue will not live in a world that contains her in photographs and robs her of presence. Arabella practices her fake dimples, arranges her fake hair, mounts the show of fake affection because she recognizes that "poor folks must live" (I.-x.), that women can survive only by making themselves not substantial but "seen." So she arranges to be seen. It is, as she tells Phillotson, "damn rough on us women, but we must grin and put up wi' it!—Haw haw!" (V.-viii.). Arabella sees no alternative, nor, for that matter, does Hardy.

But Sue will not or cannot adopt Arabella's grimly comic attitude, and she is ripped apart, finally, by the most horrible form of child-abuse. For a brief period, she is happy with her children, present to them and they to her. When they are slashed from her, she can find no alternative to succumbing, to giving in, as she says, to the force of the Gaze, to the power of the reader's voyeurism: "We are made a spectacle unto the world, and to angels, and to men!" she repeats twice (VI.-iii. and VI.-iv.). She is even subject to what we gather is a form of physical punishment, as Phillotson apparently puts into practice Arabella's counsel of severity and his friend Gillingham's feeling that all would have been well had Sue been "smacked" regularly.

All this happens offstage, more exactly, on a stage constructed not with nails and planks but with our malefic imaginations in a remote visual area. We control Sue not with our spanking hand but with our powerful eyes. "Many's the time I've smacked her" (II.-vi.) and can continue to do so, in the hazy luxuriousness, the luminous cloudiness of the mind's cinema. Sue is trapped in an erotic nostalgia, in a giant web of repetitious spankings that never vary and never allow escape. We can play over and over the titillating lifted skirt, the saucy come-on. In her parody of exhibitionism, her tragic assertion of independence, she tells Aunt Drusilla not to look at her exposed body, it being no fit sight for "modest eyes." But our eyes are not modest, and we can return again and again to this same scene, snuffing out her independence and brutally misreading her delightful and delicate parody.

Thus Jude is given a sonorous, moving absurdist finale: "Let the day perish wherein I was born, and the night in which it was said, There is a man child conceived." For Sue, there are no grandly expiring days or nights, just a humiliating surrender to Phillotson's punishments, which she, like the child of the comic strips and the well-conditioned child just round the corner or maybe even in the house, believes are deserved. She must writhe on and on, screaming to the readers who have projected her, constructed her beaters, and settled in as directors of this play, "Don't 'ee, sir—please don't 'ee!"

"Afterword"
By Elijah Pogram, Ph.D

"Afterword"
By Elijah Pogram, Ph.D.

I HAVE MADE it clear to the publisher (who has, I assume, informed the author) that my agreement to provide this brief afterword does not constitute an endorsement of any of the positions adopted in this book. It is likewise important to state that I do not stand in any way to benefit from the success of this book, nor will I suffer from its failure.[1] The same goes for members of my family, so far as I know. Further, not only have I no personal ties to or close acquaintance with the author, I believe I had never heard of him until I was approached to do this brief comment.

That said, I may proceed at once to summarize what I take to be the goal of this book (what it set out to do) and to offer as well an assessment of its accomplishments. Those two things, as we shall see, turn out to be rather different. Insofar as his aim can be determined, the author seems to want to produce readings of Victorian novels and poems that we might assume would vex the Victorians, while simultaneously irritating the best of our own contemporary Victorian scholars, or at least the best current practice. In my view, he has succeeded. No one could mistake what we are offered here for a sensitive and informed reading of the Victorians. Indeed, the author seems to despise the very idea of accurately recalling the spirit of the times and the meaning of this literature. For those and other reasons, his work also marks itself as quite distinct from that of the critics and scholars of the Victorian period whom we have good reason to respect. If these estimable scholars attend to this book, doubtless they will be nearly as annoyed as the title of this book predicts.

Is the author justified in seeking such a response? Does he have a worthy end in view? These are questions that could themselves occupy us for volumes; but as my time is short and my honorarium small, I will answer briefly, and my answer is, bluntly, yes. The author here reaches for what we are tempted to call "meta-anguish," a pain that opens doors unto a greater pain. By that I mean that what he calls "bad" criticism, of which he is certainly a master, does indeed (just as he says it will) call on us to respond urgently: it's fingernails on the blackboard. His writing sucks forth from us and thus exposes those traditional and often hidden standards of good writing, good interpretation, and good taste he so adroitly avoids at every turn. He forces us to see behind the curtain, under the table, into the heart of the machinery of our very institutional and professional guts.

But you will recall my saying earlier that his goal and his accomplishment were not quite the same. Let me explain. I take it that the goal of this book is simply to strip naked to the sky some of the artifices of current critical discourse, to suggest some of its absurdities and also some of what has come to be called (unhappily) its complicities with dominant ideologies. I believe I have that right.

In my view, that's what the author thought he was doing; but I think he has accomplished something quite different and quite a bit more important. He has not only made us see the dominant ideology for what it is, but caused us to cherish it all the more dearly. He has given back to us our heritage of traditional critical discourse and sound interpretation, driven us to hug close the practices of our mothers and fathers (those that were literary scholars). He has made us see what we were in danger of losing: the habit of acute and reliable reading. Beyond this, he has shown us, albeit indirectly, how sweet is good writing and rigorous logic, the apt quotation, the telling mot.

There is only one word for a book that can accomplish all this, and we should not hesitate to utter it: brilliant.

Notes

THE PART BEFORE THE FIRST PART

1. This emphasis borrows from Jonathan Culler's discussion of "context" and the danger of forgetting that contexts are "not given but produced," "determined by interpretive strategies." He substitutes the term "framing" to emphasize how literary discourse *and its setting* are something we *do*, not something that is *there*. See *Framing the Sign: Criticism and Its Institutions* (Norman: Univ. of Oklahoma Press, 1988), p. xiv.

2. Eve Kosofsky Sedgwick, "Pedagogy in the Context of an Antihomophobic Project," *SAQ* 89 (1990): 140.

3. Terry Eagleton, *Literary Theory: An Introduction* (Minneapolis: Univ. of Minnesota Press, 1983), p. 201.

4. Eve Kosofsky Sedgwick, *Epistemology of the Closet* (Berkeley: Univ. of California Press, 1990), p. 48.

5. I hope to borrow extra justification and a nice morale boost here from Clifford Geertz's ringing assertion that "the loss of the authority that comes from 'views from nowhere' is not a loss, it's a gain." See his "'Local Knowledge' and Its Limits: Some *Obiter Dicta*," *Yale Journal of Criticism* (1992): 132.

6. P. N. Medved and M. M. Bakhtin, *The Formal Method in Literary Scholarship*, trans. Albert J. Wehrle (Baltimore: Johns Hopkins Univ. Press, 1978), p. 67

7. Boris Eichenbaum, "The Theory of the 'Formal Method'," in Lee T. Lemon and Marion J. Reis, trans. and ed., *Russian Formalist Criticism: Four Essays* (Lincoln: Univ. of Nebraska Press, 1965), p. 103.

8. All of this comes from Barbara Johnson's *A World of Difference* (Baltimore: The Johns Hopkins Univ. Press, 1987), p. 15.

9. Hayden White, *Tropics of Discourse: Essays in Cultural Criticism* (Baltimore: The Johns Hopkins Univ. Press, 1978), p. 263.

10. J. Hillis Miller, "Response to Natalie Zemon Davis and Carlo Ginzburg," *Yale Journal of Criticism* 5 (1992): 183–87.

11. Johnson, *A World of Difference*, p. 16.

12. From Roland Barthes, in order: *The Pleasure of the Text*, trans. Richard Miller (London: Jonathan Cape, 1976), pp. 3, 50; *Roland Barthes*, trans. Richard Howard (New York: Hill and Wang, 1977), pp. 46–47; *The Rustle of Language*, trans. Richard Howard (Berkeley: Univ. of California Press, 1989), p. 177.

13. Culler, *Framing the Sign*, p. 140.

14. The parallels to Gerald Graff's powerful program to "teach the conflicts" are intentional and gratefully acknowledged. Graff argues that "the mistake of traditional educational thinking has been to assume that schools and colleges have to *resolve* disagreements in order to teach effectively," that "students should be exposed to the *results* of their elders' conflicts, but not to the conflicts themselves." See Graff's "Teach the Conflicts," *SAQ* 89 (1990): 52, 55.

15. Paul Ricoeur argues that "the task of interpretation . . . is to allow a text to signify all it *can*, not to signify one thing rather than another, but to 'signify more', and thus to make us 'think more'" : "Rhetoric-Poetics-Hermeneutics," in Michael Meyer, ed., *From Metaphysics to Rhetoric* (Dordrecht, The Netherlands: Kluwer, 1989), p. 147. I am indebted to this formulation, but I wish it weren't put in such a way as to suggest that there are limits to what a text *can* signify, that signification is somehow inside the text, and that interpretation is simply an act of enabling.

16. Victoria Kahn, "Habermas, Machiavelli, and the Humanist Critique of Ideology," *PMLA* 105 (1990): 464.

17. Stanley Fish, "Resistance and Independence: A Reply to Gerald Graff," *New Literary History* 17 (1985): 119.

18. J. Hillis Miller, *The Ethics of Reading* (New York: Columbia Univ. Press, 1987), p. 10; Johnson, *World of Difference*, p. xvii. Hayden White offers valuable probings of these questions surrounding the "status of the text" in *Tropics of Discourse: Essays in Cultural Criticism* (Baltimore: The Johns Hopkins Univ. Press, 1978), p. 263.

19. Culler, *Framing the Sign*, p. 52.

20. David Kaufmann, "The Profession of Theory," *PMLA* 105 (1990): 522.

21. Johnson, *The Critical Difference: Essays in the Contemporary Rhetoric of Reading* (Baltimore: The Johns Hopkins Univ. Press, 1980), p. 3.

22. Culler has a fascinating analysis of the policing of tone, citing William Empson and Kenneth Burke as examples of critics whose manifest brilliance has been largely ignored (or has had far less influence than it should) because they didn't seem always to be "serious." His own "Confronting Religion" (*Framing the Sign*, pp. 69–82) is a wonderful exploration of the way the proclamations and enforcements of seriousness manage to declare certain questions and positions out of bounds.

23. Sedgwick, *Epistemology of the Closet*, p. 12.

24. Peter Brooks, "Response to Charles Bernheimer," *Critical Inquiry* 17 (1991): 877.

25. Johnson, *Critical Difference*, p. xii.

26. White, *Tropics of Discourse*, p. 267.

27. Victor Shklovsky, "Art as Technique," in Lee T. Lemon and Marion J. Reiss, trans. and ed., *Russian Formalist Criticism: Four Essays* (Lincoln: Univ. of Nebraska Press, 1965), pp. 12, 18.

28. Ibid., p. 12.

THE FIRST PART: DICKENSIAN JUGGLERS

Chapter 1: FATTENING UP ON PICKWICK

A version of this essay was once given, I won't say when, as a talk at the Dickens Universe at Santa Cruz. I have disguised the title and changed many things, but not, I want it understood, because of the things said (ugly, small-minded) about the talk at that time. It has since excited admiration among students of mine asked on examinations to summarize its contents and comment on its quality. Enough said.

1. This is a quote from the novel, all editions of it being roughly the same, which is good enough for me. I will tell you that I took this from "The New Oxford Illustrated Dickens" version (London: Oxford University Press, 1948). I am not going to mess up the text with lots of footnotes or with indications of chapters or page numbers every time I quote. For one thing, there are lots of quotes; for another, you aren't going to be fooled into thinking this is the sort of scholarly essay whose accuracy you could depend on anyhow; for a third, I lost the little sheet whereon I had set down the quote locations, most of them.

Chapter 2: LITTLE NELL—SHE DEAD

1. Charles Dickens, *The Old Curiosity Shop* (London: Oxford Univ. Press, 1951), "The Oxford Illustrated Dickens," ch. 71. Further references to the novel will be cited in the text by chapter.

2. In the Preface Dickens says, "In writing the book, I had it always in my fancy to surround the lonely figure of the child with grotesque and wild . . . companions" (p. xii). Master Humphrey later echoes this plan: "It would be a curious speculation . . . to imagine her in her future life, holding her solitary way among a crowd of wild grotesque companions; the only pure, fresh, youthful object in the throng" (ch. i).

3. The definition is Sheldon Sacks's, in his *Fiction and the Shape of Belief* (Berkeley: Univ. of California Press, 1964), p. 46. Sacks does not say that the ridicule of an external object is merely a feature of satire; he says that it is the organizing principle of a satire, what satire *is*.

4. See his *Dickens and the Trials of Imagination* (Cambridge, Ma: Harvard Univ. Press, 1974), pp. 89–113. The characterization of Professor Stewart is one with which he heartily concurs. Indeed it is he who supplied me with it—actually with a much milder version which did not, in its modesty, begin to do justice to his almost feline abilities in the looking department. I guess I should tell you that he has not actually brought himself to recognizing that my more truthful phrasing is the one to go with. He writes, "It's a damned lie what you have! Who the hell are you to say such things, you snorting swine?" So I guess that he really does not (yet) "heartily concur" in the characterization of him I have (in love and admiration) provided, though he should.

5. It was once common knowledge that this happened, more or less, just as it was common knowledge that everyone on both sides of the Atlantic wept bitterly when Nell died. We are now told by the editors of the second volume of the Pilgrim *Letters* (Oxford: Clarendon, 1969) that there is no evidence to support anything of the kind and that there was a much more moderate, mixed response, most people being what we would call indifferent to the whole matter. All I have to say to that is that if that's what evidence does for you, I will do without evidence altogether. The first, common-knowledge story is a better story; and that's what counts.

Chapter 3: VIEWING AND BLURRING WITH DICKENS

1. George Santayana, "Dickens," in *Soliloquies in England* (London: Oxford Univ. Press, 1922), pp. 65–66.

2. This "Dickens" that we're finding things "in" is a concoction devised in order that we can find the things we want and then assign these things back onto some other agency, called "Dickens." It's like an egg hunt where you get to first hide the eggs, then find them, and then declare yourself the winner. We find what we planted in a field (Dickens, or a Dickens novel) we made up. If you say all this is circular and pointless, why then I'll answer that so is a baseball, more or less.

3. All quotations from Dickens's novels are from *The New Oxford Illustrated Dickens* (Oxford University Press). Citations are to chapter numbers.

4. In fact, even this passage is not all that naturalistic, what with the personified and stubborn candle, the pattering and possibly unoccupied boots, and the walking head-dresses—not to mention the implied comparison between the pettitoes and Mrs. Bardell, Mrs. Cluppins, and Mrs. Sanders.

5. George Orwell, *Dickens, Dali and Others* (New York: HBJ, 1946), p. 61.

6. See Dorothy Van Ghent's classic analyses in "The Dickens World: A View from Todgers's," *Sewanee Review* 58 (1950): 419–38, and *The English Novel: Form and Function* (New York: Harper, 1953), pp. 125–38.

7. I am very much indebted to my friend, Professor Jane K. Brown, for many of the ideas on the opening of *Little Dorrit* presented here, ideas which I am shamelessly cribbing from her. The fact that her conclusions as to the interpretive possibilities in this chapter and the novel as a whole differ from mine gives me no little discomfort. I would also like to thank Professors Lesley Brill, Cathy Comstock, and Jeffrey Robinson for many valuable suggestions used throughout.

8. I recognize the parallel here to Charles Lamb's brilliant argument—usually dismissed as perverse—on the inevitably impoverishing and limiting effect that actual productions of Shakespeare's plays must produce. The imagination can entertain many, even contradictory possibilities, enriching possibilities that are narrowed by the interpretive choices actors and directors must make. Hamlet can exist for us in dozens of forms as we read. We are, suggests Lamb, better off not seeing Olivier, or anyone else, reduce that sumptuous banquet to the mere baked beans of "a man who could not make up his mind."

9. Aunt Betsey's victory over the Murdstones is an equivocal one at best, since it gives them just what they want, a relief from any further responsibility for a boy who is only an encumbrance: "Now I must caution you," says Murdstone to Aunt Betsey, "that if you abet him once, you abet him for good and all; if you step in between him and me, now, you must step in, Miss Trotwood, for ever. I cannot trifle, or be trifled with. I am here, for the first and last time, to take him away. Is he ready to go? If he is not—and you tell me he is not; on any pretense; it is indifferent to me what—my doors are shut against him henceforth" (14). Having no more use for David, the Murdstones are free now to run off to other cruel exploitations.

10. The term was most prominently used to mark Biblical and other anti-evolutionary explanations of the earth's development. The catastrophic model was, however, popular also, though never unopposed, in understanding such things as sexuality and child-development.

11. More authoritative and complete psychoanalytic readings of *David Copperfield* and of other Dickens novels are offered in the well-known writings of Mark Spilka, Leonard Manheim, and Michael Steig.

Chapter 4: "ALL THE WICKEDNESS IN THE WORLD IS PRINT"

1. Susan R. Horton, *Interpreting Interpreting: Interpreting Dickens's "Dombey"* (Baltimore: The Johns Hopkins Univ. Press, 1979); see pp. 69–71, builds for us an eight-runged interpretive ladder.

2. The quotation from *Barnaby Rudge* is from the Oxford Illustrated Dickens (London, 1954), ch. 13.

3. This fact was dished to me by Richard D. Altick. I did not find it on my own, nor, to compound the confession, was I able to verify it with the certainty and clarity an historical scholar would require, until Professor Altick sent me also the verification. Still, even had the "fact" been a "fiction" (like all facts), we would simply have construed a larger fiction in which the smaller one about the suicides becomes a fact. See?

4. George Orwell, *Dickens, Dali and Others* (New York: Reynal and Hitchcock, 1946), p. 61; Robert Garis, *The Dickens Theatre* (Oxford: Clarendon, 1965).

5. *Dickens and the Rhetoric of Laughter* (Oxford: Clarendon, 1971), pp. 132–61.

6. All quotations from *Martin Chuzzlewit*, hereafter cited in the text by chapter number, are from *The Oxford Illustrated Dickens* (London, 1951).

7. This is not the only problem lying in wait for those out to create thematic coherence. Is or is not Mrs. Gamp aware of the fictional nature of Mrs. Harris? For the greater part of the novel, she may seem to regard her friend as real or perhaps to dwell in a fictional world containing Mrs. Harris, a world that is more real to her than any other. But in chapter 51, when it suits his purposes to do so, Dickens makes her quite unequivocally aware of the fraud. In the same way, much is made by Dickens—and by critics—of the mysterious location of Todgers's, its mythic nature, and the fact that its whereabouts are known and entrance available only to the initiated. Even postmen wander hopelessly in the surrounding labyrinth, and strangers have no chance. Yet in chapter 10, Old Martin, who would seem hardly to possess the qualities of the initiates, walks straight to the door. How?

8. Lewis Carroll's *Alice's Adventures in Wonderland,* "The Pennyroyal Edition" (Berkeley: Univ. of California Press, 1982), p. 103.

9. Irony is not dominant, of course; one of the problems (delights) is that we cannot locate a reliably dominant tone or mode.

10. Lewis Carroll, *Through the Looking-Glass* "The Pennyroyal Alice" (Berkeley: Univ. of California Press, 1983), p. 62.

11. "When I use a word . . . it means just what I choose it to mean—neither more nor less" (*Looking-Glass,* p. 66).

12. Wayne C. Booth, *A Rhetoric of Irony* (Chicago: Univ. of Chicago Press, 1974).

13. As always with this novel (and any other), there is no flat statement that cannot be contradicted successfully. At one point the word "home" is said not only to have meaning but to have magical meaning: "And though home is a name, a word, it is a strong one; stronger than magician ever spoke, or spirit answered to, in strongest conjuration" (35).

14. Again one is reminded of Carroll, of the White Queen pointing to a hill and remarking to Alice, "I could show you hills, in comparison with which you'd call that a valley" (*Looking-Glass,* p. 20).

Chapter 5: PERFORMANCE, ROLES, THE SELF, AND OUR OWN CHARLES DICKENS

1. All quotations from Dickens's novels are from *The New Oxford Illustrated Dickens* (Oxford University Press). Citations are to chapter numbers.

2. The authority for this oft-repeated, simple (simple-minded) notion is not Dickens but Forster; and even Forster is less than plain, muddying by the passive voice the origin of the decision—perhaps it was the publisher or Forster himself—and stating (plainly enough) that the financial motive was, in any case, secondary: "though it was believed that this resolve, which Dickens adopted as suddenly as his hero, might increase the number of his readers, that reason influenced him less than the challenge to make good his Notes which every mail had been bringing him from unsparing assailants beyond the Atlantic.": See *The Life of Charles Dickens,* ed. A. J. Hoppe (London: Dent, 1966), 2 vols.

3. Even here, Dickens has fun, floating past our minds this interesting syntax and the brief,

impossible possibility that "wetter" is a noun, perhaps something like a cross between a walrus and an otter. All this is grandly irrelevant, of course; but so is the entire episode.

THE SECOND PART: POETS AND PROPRIETY

Chapter 6: FORGETTING TO REMEMBER: TENNYSON'S HAPPY LOSSES

1. Harold Bloom, *Poetry and Repression: Revisionism from Blake to Stevens* (New Haven: Yale Univ. Press, 1976), pp. 151–53.

2. All quotations from Tennyson's poems are taken from *The Poems of Tennyson*, ed. Christopher Ricks (London: Longmans, 1969) and will be cited by line number, or, where necessary, section or part and line number.

3. I am very much influenced here by Alan Sinfield's remarkable and brilliant "materialist decon-struction" (p. 76) of common ways of understanding Tennyson in his *Alfred Tennyson* (Oxford: Basil Blackwell, 1986). Sinfield's procedures can be illustrated by his deconstruction of the posited oppositions between faith and doubt. So long as we are content with (caught by) this binary, we honor and bolster a whole host of assumptions: "Faith and doubt are mutually supporting constructs: they sustain between them the notion that people need an authority beyond the human to make sense of their lives, and thus efface other ways of thinking about the world" (p. 65).

4. *Selected Prose*, ed. John Hayward (Harmondsworth: Peregrine, 1963), p. 110.

5. First published in *University of Toronto Quarterly*; reprinted in John Killham, ed., *Critical Essays on the Poetry of Tennyson* (London: Routledge and Kegan Paul, 1960), pp. 41–64.

6. Even Sinfield, usually the one who charts the land-mines for the less wary, gets knocked about by this one, going so far as to use Lacan to illustrate Tennyson's "deprivation," his "triply determined" anguish for what is not there; see pp. 98–102.

Chapter 7: TENNYSON, HALLAM'S CORPSE, MILTON'S MURDER, AND POETIC EXHIBITIONISM

1. *Daniel Deronda*, ed. Gordon Haight (Oxford: Clarendon, 1984), p. 3.

2. For example, Joseph Sendry deals with sections IX-XVIII as a unit (stopping before XIX, but that's a trifle), a unit possessing "an appreciable degree of internal coherence and constitut[ing] one of the most carefully styled groups in the entire poem" ("*In Memoriam* and *Lycidas*," *PMLA* 82 [1967]: 438). For a very thorough assessment of the chronology of compo-sition using the most currently available materials, see Susan Shatto and Marion Shaw, eds., *In Memoriam* (Oxford: Clarendon, 1982); they adhere to the dating of sections as given in Christopher Ricks's second edition of *The Poems of Tennyson* (Berkeley: Univ. of California Press, 1987), but explain more fully than does Ricks the relationship among the ms. materials. While agreeing with Ricks that only sections IX, XVII, and XVIII are among the certifiably ear-liest written lyrics, they would also agree with Sendry, describing these poems as "the real 'germ of *In Memoriam*'" because "the sections themselves are the nucleii of further growth in the sequence" and "were to be expanded into the series of ten 'ship' sections (9–18)" (p. 10). To further argue a compositional integrity to the sequence, Shatto and Shaw, in their commen-tary, gloss these ten poems as a unit that to them incorporates "elements of the classical rhetor-ical genre, the *propemptikon*, or farewell to the departing traveller" (p. 172).

3. Some have suggested that *Adonais* could be substituted here and made the subject of this essay. Sure it could. A shift in perspective and a little squinting will result in a shift in poetic pater-nity. Our reasons for rejecting the Shelley line are: Tennyson's evident ease in making use of

Shelley (5 times) suggests casual appropriation, not anxiety; Tennyson's own considerable sense of self-importance and the unlikelihood that he would have found the degraded Shelley worth contesting; Shelley's complacency in metaphorizing nature, quite at odds with Tennyson's troubled view. Shelley, finally, seems to us not a false father, just a different and less interesting one.

4. *Letters of Edward Fitzgerald*, ed. William Aldis Wright (London: Macmillan, 1894), v. I, p. 187.

5. *Tennyson: The Unquiet Heart* (Oxford: Clarendon, 1980), p. 173.

6. For a summary of Bloom's position see James R. Kincaid, "Antithetical Criticism, Harold Bloom, and Victorian Poetry," *Victorian Poetry* 14 (1976): 365–82.

7. Harold Bloom, *The Anxiety of Influence: A Theory of Poetry* (New York: Oxford Univ. Press, 1973), p. 71. Further references will be cited in the text.

8. *Lycidas*, in *John Milton: Complete Poems and Major Prose*, ed. Merritt Y. Hughes (New York: Odyssey, 1957), ll. 153, 152. Subsequent references are cited in the text.

9. *In Memoriam, A. H. H.*, in *The Poems of Tennyson in Three Volumes, Second Edition: Incorporating the Trinity College Manuscripts*, ed. Christopher Ricks, Section X, ll. 18–20. Subsequent references are cited in the text.

10. Ironically, *In Memoriam* is sometimes praised for centering its subject (Hallam), unlike the self-centered Milton in Lycidas; see F. E. L. Priestley, *Language and Structure in Tennyson's Poetry* (London: Andrea Deutsch, 1973), p. 121. Also ironically, A. C. Bradley feels called upon to defend Tennyson against charges of "excessive humility" (*A Commentary on Tennyson's "In Memoriam"*, 3d ed. [Hamden, Conn.: Archon, 1966], pp. 5–6). (Further references to Bradley will be cited in the text.) Shatto and Shaw, however, notice that "throughout the poem the interest of the poet centres upon his own grief and his ability to express it through song" (p. 32). They quote, from volume II of Hallam Tennyson's *Materials for a Life of A. T.* (the four-volume early stage of his *Memoir*, privately printed in 1895), Tennyson admitting to his publisher in 1895 that he had written the "Elegies" "for his own relief and private satisfaction."

11. "Milton," in *Lives of the English Poets*, ed. George Birkbeck Hill, 3 vols. (Oxford: Clarendon, 1905), v. I, p. 164.

12. "Instincts and Their Vicissitudes," in *The Standard Edition of the Complete Psychological Works of Sigmund Freud*, ed. and trans. James Strachey (London: Hogarth Press, 1957), v. 14, p. 127.

13. "Lacan, Poe, and Narrative Repression," in *Lacan and Narration: The Psychoanalytic Difference in Narrative Theory*, ed. Robert Con Davis (Baltimore: Johns Hopkins Univ. Press, 1983), p. 987.

14. Quoted in Hallam Tennyson, *Alfred Lord Tennyson: A Memoir* (London: Macmillan, 1897), v. 1, p. 277; v. 2, p. 518; v. 1, p. 512.

15. See James G. Nelson, *The Sublime Puritan: Milton and the Victorians* (Madison: Univ. of Wisconsin Press, 1963); Robert Pattison, *Tennyson and Tradition* (Cambridge, MA: Harvard Univ. Press, 1979); and W. David Shaw, *Tennyson's Style* (Ithaca: Cornell Univ. Press, 1976).

16. Alan Sinfield provides an excellent analysis of the subversive use of Milton's "Comus" in section I of *In Memoriam*, where, he says, Tennyson "identifies himself with the pagan Comus, refusing to have darkness smoothed away" (*The Language of Tennyson's 'In Memoriam'* [New York: Barnes and Noble, 1971], p. 44).

17. *The Princess* is, of course, susceptible to more complex readings and to those that are less misogynistic. We have oversimplified its manifest content in order to emphasize the Miltonic parody.

18. Tennyson's fierce and somewhat comic pride in original observation—being the only one who really knew what the underneath of flowers looked like and so forth—seems to us to indicate how remarkably free from such interests he actually was. Not given to aesthetic pronouncements or, very likely, to what we would think of as theory, he still was seized now and then with the itch to issue justifications of his poetry in terms then current for such justifications,

that is, in terms of originality, fidelity to nature, mimetic crispness. But surely no one who cared about such things would have lit upon such ludicrously trivial examples as the color of a daisy's underside. The attempts to locate his poetry in terms of mimetic naturalism most often reduce critics to equating the power of his poems with his weak eyesight.

19. Sendry's "*In Memoriam* and *Lycidas*" offers a fine example of an analysis in the tradition of influence studies that assumes a liberal, generous, and easy relationship between poets and their "sources." This liberal tradition, its highly dubious ideological base notwithstanding, has a distinguished heritage reaching from Arnold to Eliot to Lowes to Frye. Our method is anti-thetical to that tradition. Sendry says that the object of his study is to offer an interpretation that illuminates so that we may see properly: "In fact, when read in the light of *Lycidas*, *In Memoriam*, or at least significant parts of it, becomes more orderly and intelligible" (437). This drive toward order and the intelligibility it promises is connected to an assumption of interpre-tive power that is able to declare certain readings and certain approaches *wrong*. Such executive authority is justified by a vision of a Utopia of the one right reading, shared by all: "With *Lycidas* in mind, we are less likely to read the poem from the wrong critical perspective or to make unreasonable demands of it" (442). Not knowing ourselves what the rules for reasonable demands might be, we are doubtless breaking them. We have no quarrel with Sendry's notion that the poem might be made intelligible, that is, that it might present itself somehow to our intelligence. We do hope, though, that nothing we say might go to make the poem seem more orderly.

20. Harold Bloom, *A Map of Misreading* (New York: Oxford Univ. Press, 1975), p. 11.

21. Quoted by Shatto and Shaw (p. 179) from manuscript materials at the Tennyson Research Centre, Lincoln Central Library.

22. *Memoir*, v. 1, p. 305. In the *Memoir*, Hallam quotes his father as follows: "I myself did not see Clevedon till years after the burial of A. H. H. Jan. 3rd, 1834, and then in later editions of 'In Memoriam' I altered the word 'chancel,' which was the word used by Mr Hallam in his Memoir, to 'dark church' (v. 1, p. 305).

23. Jacques Lacan, *The Four Fundamental Concepts of Psycho-Analysis*, ed. Jacques-Alain Miller, trans. Alan Sheridan (New York: Norton, 1981), p. 79.

24. Harold Bloom, *The Ringers in the Tower: Studies in Romantic Tradition* (Chicago: Univ. of Chicago Press, 1971), p. 152.

25. See Ricks, II, 331n; Bradley, p. 95. Bradley thinks that a reading of the first stanza that has the widower waking to the "sudden and overwhelming realisation of his loss" represents a frequent misreading of the stanza, that "the fourth stanza shows that this is not so, and that *everything* described in the first stanza . . . takes place in sleep" (pp. 94–95). Milton's waking to his day of night, hence, would be irrelevant. Bradley later admitted his uncertainty as to whether his reading was "right," settling for an uneasy compromise: "It is perhaps as probable that the usual understanding of the first lines is correct" (p. 95). He still does not mention Milton, however. Bradley also detects an echo of "L'Allegro" in section XV, unheard by Ricks.

26. The next line does pick this up—"have / Full sight of"—but note the effect of the enjambment.

27. But it is worth considering that the authorities have fallen here into the practice of ascribing to Tennyson a classical learning he did not come by directly, but that he might have learned at the knee of his fellow Cantabridgian John Milton. The line from many of the Latin poems, for instance, does not run straight to *In Memoriam*, but detours through *Lycidas*. See James Holly Hanford's "The Pastoral Elegy and Milton's *Lycidas*," *PMLA* 25 (1910): 403–7 for a discussion of Milton's appropriation of pastoral, and Watson Kirkconnell's *Awake the Courteous Echo* (Toronto: Univ. of Toronto Press, 1973) for 102 prior elegies that Milton absorbed into *Lycidas*. If we begin to add the source echoes attributed by our authorities to Virgil, Horace, Theocritus, Persius, and Ovid to Milton's tally, we see that a repressed *Lycidas* bulks rather large behind the classical screen that allows Tennyson to avoid acknowledging Milton as a precursor. That the authorities have connived in this is a measure of the strategy's success.

28. *The Pursuit of Signs: Semiotics, Literature, Deconstruction* (Ithaca: Cornell Univ. Press, 1981), p. 150.

29. This phrase is borrowed without permission from our aerialist friend Garrett H. Stewart.

Chapter 8: "THE POEM SAYS": MEREDITH'S *MODERN LOVE*

1. Norman Friedman, "The Jangled Harp: Symbolic Structure in *Modern Love*," *Modern Language Quarterly* 18 (1957): 9–26.

2. They are in *Meredith: The Critical Heritage*, ed. Ioan Williams (New York: Barnes and Noble, 1971), pp. 92–107.

3. John Lucas, "Meredith as Poet," in Ian Fletcher, ed., *Meredith Now: Some Critical Essays* (New York: Barnes and Noble, 1971), pp. 14–33.

4. The essay is "'Speak and I See the Side-Lie of a Truth': The Problematics of Truth in Meredith's *Modern Love*," *Victorian Poetry* 25 (1987): 129–41. The book is *Disruption and Delight in the Nineteenth-Century Novel* (Ann Arbor: UMI Research Press, 1988), with the section on *Modern Love* to be found on pp. 32–39.

5. In order: Michael Lund, "Space and Spiritual Crisis in Meredith's *Modern Love*," *Victorian Poetry* 16 (1978): 376; Hans Ostrom, "The Disappearance of Tragedy in Meredith's *Modern Love*," *Victorian Newsletter* No. 63 (1983): 26; Arthur Simpson, "Meredith's Pessimistic Humanism: A New Reading of *Modern Love*," *Modern Philology* 67 (1970): 347; Simpson again; then another doubling, this time of Renate Muendel, *George Meredith* (Boston: Twayne, 1986): pp. 42, 46; and, alas, Cathy Comstock, "'Speak and I See,'" Victorian Poetry, 137.

6. Richard F. Giles, "Meredith's *Modern Love*, Stanza 50," *Explicator* 40 (1982): 38–40.

7. J. W. Marston, *Athenaeum*, No. 1805, 31 May 1862; in *Meredith: The Critical Heritage*, p. 101.

8. Cynthia Grant Tucker, "Meredith's Broken Laurel: *Modern Love* and the Renaissance Sonnet Tradition," *Victorian Poetry* 10 (1972): 351–65; Stephen Watt, "Neurotic Responses to a Failed Marriage: George Meredith's *Modern Love*," *Mosaic* (17): 49–63; Philip E. Wilson, "Affective Coherence, a Principle of Abated Action, and Meredith's *Modern Love*," *Modern Philology* 72 (1974): 151–71; Dorothy M. Mermin, "Poetry as Fiction: Meredith's *Modern Love*," *ELH* 43 (1977): 100–119; Lucas, in *Meredith Now*, 26–32.

9. Sonnet XII, ll. 11–14, *Modern Love*, in *The Poems of George Meredith*, ed. Phyllis B. Bartlett (New Haven: Yale Univ. Press, 1978), I, 123. Further references to the poem will be from this edition and will be cited in the text by sonnet and line number.

10. Walter E. Houghton and G. Robert Stange, eds., *Victorian Poetry and Poetics*, 2nd ed. (Boston: Houghton Mifflin, 1968), p. 608.

11. See Muendel, *George Meredith*, p. 45.

Chapter 9: THE CANONICAL POETRY OF *THE PEARL*

1. "The Captain's Song," ll. 3, 21–24; in *The Pearl: A Journal of Facetive and Voluptuous Reading* (New York: Ballantine, 1973), p. 515; reprint of 1879-80 journal, complete in one volume. All further references to poems from *The Pearl* will be cited in the text.

INTERLUDE II: THE RETURN OF 'SHE': *AN EXPLICATION*

1. H. Rider Haggard, *Ayesha: The Return of "She"* (New York: Dover, 1978), p. 1; originally published in *The Windsor Magazine* (London), 1904–5. Further references will be cited in the text.

2. Eve Kosofsky Sedgwick, *Between Men: English Literature and Male Homosocial Desire* (New York: Columbia Univ. Press, 1985).

THE THIRD PART: FICTIONAL STRIPPERS

Chapter 10: "WORDS CANNOT EXPRESS": *FRANKENSTEIN'S* TRIPPING ON THE TONGUE

1. A discussion of creaturespeak and a brilliant treatment of language in the novel is given by Peter Brooks, "'Godlike Science/ Unhallowed Arts': Language, Nature, and Monstrosity," in *The Endurance of Frankenstein*, ed. U. C. Knoepflmacher and George Levine (Berkeley: Univ. of California Press, 1979), pp. 205–20.

2. See James B. Twitchell, "*Frankenstein* and the Anatomy of Horror," *Georgia Review* 37 (1983): 41–78.

3. The powerful feminist discussions of the novel seem to have come in two waves. Ellen Moers's important consideration of the novel as female fantasy, as a female myth of childbirth (*Literary Women: The Great Writers* [New York: Doubleday, 1976], pp. 91–99) connects to the more subtle treatment in Sandra M. Gilbert and Susan Gubar, *The Madwoman in the Attic: The Woman Writer and the Nineteenth-Century Literary Imagination* (New Haven: Yale Univ. Press, 1979), pp. 221–47. Later work of significance includes Mary Poovey, "'My Hideous Progeny': Mary Shelley and the Feminization of Romanticism," *PMLA* 95 (1980): 332–47; Mary Jacobus, "Is There a Woman in This Text?" *New Literary History* 14 (1982): 117–54; William R. Veeder, *Mary Shelley and Frankenstein: The Fable of Androgyny* (Chicago: Univ. of Chicago Press, 1986); and especially Alan Bewell, "An Issue of Monstrous Desire," *Yale Journal of Criticism* 2 (1988): 105–28.

4. For a more complete treatment of the incestuous currents see J. M. Hill, "Frankenstein and the Physiognomy of Desire," *American Imago* 32 (1975): 332–58.

5. For an exceptionally artful and witty argument on fathers, see U. C. Knoepflmacher, "Thoughts on the Aggression of Daughters," in *The Endurance of Frankenstein*, pp. 88–119.

6. I do not mean to indicate that there is nothing more or nothing better to be said. See Paul Sherwin, "*Frankenstein*: Creation as Catastrophe," *PMLA* 96 (1981): 883–903; Rosemary Jackson, "Narcissism and Beyond: A Psychoanalytic Reading of Frankenstein and Fantasies of the Double," in *Aspects of Fantasy: Selected Essays from the Second International Conference on the Fantastic in Literature and Film*, ed. William Coyle (Westport, CT: Greenwood, 1986), pp. 43–53; and especially the quite remarkable essay by Gerhard Joseph, "Frankenstein's Dream: The Child as Father of the Monster," *Hartford Studies in Literature* 7 (1975): 97–115.

7. The metaphors of penetration as they cooperate with a conventional cautionary reading of the novel are outlined by Anne K. Mellor, "*Frankenstein*: A Feminist Critique of Science," in *One Culture: Essays in Science and Literature*, ed. George Levine (Madison: Univ. of Wisconsin Press, 1987), pp. 287–312.

8. Readings attentive to the class and political issues in the novel include Anca Vlasopolos, "*Frankenstein*'s Hidden Skeletons: The Psycho-Politics of Oppression," *Science-Fiction Studies* 10 (1983): 125–36; Leo Sterrenburg, "Mary Shelley's Monster: Politics and Psyche in *Franken-stein*," in *The Endurance of Frankenstein*, pp. 143-71; Peter Dale Scott, "Vital Artifice: Mary, Percy, and the Psychopolitical Integrity of *Frankenstein*," also in *The Endurance of Frankenstein*, pp. 172–202; and the excellent book by Chris Baldick, *In Frankenstein's Shadow: Myth, Monstrosity, and Nineteenth-Century Writing* (Oxford: Clarendon, 1987).

9. On this point see the fine essay by Beth Newman, "Narratives of Seduction and the Seduction of Narrative: The Frame Structure of *Frankenstein*," *ELH* 53 (1986): 141–61.

Chapter 11: ANTHONY TROLLOPE AND THE UNMANNERLY NOVEL

1. Interestingly, any chafing against the restrictions of *manners* is found in no definitions of that term, though related words—*mannered, mannerism, mannerist*—often are loaded with

connotations that are negative. It's as if the resistance to the presumption of manners were drained off onto harmless secondary areas, keeping the main ideological territory clean and pure.

2. *Literary Theory*, p. 68.

3. The editors of the volume in which this essay first appeared—*Reading and Writing Women's Lives: A Study of the Novel of Manners*, ed. Bege K. Bowers and Barbara Brothers (Ann Arbor: UMI Research Press, 1990)—presented a sustained argument throughout their introductory material that the comedy of manners should not be confused with the novel of manners, that bad things would result from doing so, and that it would be a shame if, after all they went through to put together that volume, critics still could not rid themselves of their muddle. What I say to that is this: I am not so much confusing the two terms, you might say, as conflating them. That makes all the difference, I submit.

4. *Anthony Trollope: Aspects of His Life and Art*, p. 24. Booth adds that this adherence to the comedy of manners explains why Trollope's novels "do not move us profoundly" (p. 43). Many now would dispute this estimate of Trollope's or the tradition's power. Many also would find Trollope's range much larger than Booth allows, reading the novels in political, sociological, or even formal terms quite alien to Booth's model. They might also cite the large number of novels written in other modes: *La Vendée* (historical romance), *An Eye for an Eye* (melodrama), *The Fixed Period* (science fiction), *The Way We Live Now* (satire), *The American Senator* (anatomy), *The Landleaguers* and other irish novels (tragedies and naturalist fictions), *The Three Clerks* and *The Struggles of Brown, Jones, and Robinson* (Dickensian romps).

5. *Phineas Redux* (London: Oxford Univ. Press, 1973), ch. v. Further references to this novel will be cited in the text by chapter.

6. *The Pickwick Papers* (London: Oxford Univ. Press, 1948) "The New Oxford Illustrated Dickens," ch. xx.

7. "To Alfred Austin," May 2, 1870, in *The Letters of Anthony Trollope*, ed. N. John Hall, 2 vols. (Stanford: Stanford Univ. Press, 1983), i: 515–16; hereafter cited as *Letters*.

8. *South Africa*, The Colonial History Series, ed. D. H. Simpson, 2 vols., 1868; rpt (London: Dawson, 1968) ii: 188.

9. *The Tireless Traveller: Twenty Letters to the Liverpool Mercury by Anthony Trollope, 1875*, ed. Bradford A. Booth (Berkeley: Univ. of California Press, 1941), p. 133.

10. This is one central (and persuasive) strain in the argument she develops in *The Moral Trollope* (Athens, Ohio: Ohio Univ. Press, 1971).

11. To Thomas Adolphus Trollope, Oct. 5, 1852, *Letters* I: 31–32.

12. *Four Lectures*, ed. Morris L. Parish (London: Constable, 1938), p. 77.

13. *Clergymen of the Church of England* (London: Chapman and Hall, 1866), p. 74.

14. "The World's Classics" (London: Oxford Univ. Press, 1944), ch. li.

15. Alas, I have been guilty myself of manufacturing just such an argument: *The Novels of Anthony Trollope* (Oxford: Clarendon, 1977), pp. 57–59.

16. Alas again: *The Novels of Anthony Trollope*, pp. 59–61.

17. *He Knew He Was Right*, ch. xxv.

18. Though there is some controversy as to whether this is or was intended to be a series, it is ordinarily taken as such. The first five novels, in the usual order, are *Can You Forgive Her?*, *Phineas Finn*, *The Eustace Diamonds*, *Phineas Redux*, and *The Prime Minister*.

19. The most influential study along these lines has been John Hagan's "*The Duke's Children*: Trollope's Psychological Masterpiece," *Nineteenth-Century Fiction* 13 (1958–59): 1–21.

20. *The Duke's Children* (London: Oxford Univ. Press, 1973), ch. 1. Further references to this edition will be cited in the text by chapter.

Chapter 12: THE POWER OF *BARCHESTER TOWERS*

1. I have done this myself, arguing in a sort of bullying way not only that there is a kind of battle but that one side (the conservative forces) win: *The Novels of Anthony Trollope* (Oxford: Clarendon, 1977), pp.101–13

2. Anthony Trollope, *Barchester Towers*, ed., James R. Kincaid (Oxford: Oxford University Press, 1980), ch. xv. Further citations will be by chapter number in the text.

3. See U. C. Knoepflmacher's detailed and rich analysis of the first chapter in his "Introduction: Entering a Victorian Novel—*Barchester Towers*," in *Laughter and Despair* (Berkeley: Univ. of California Press, 1971), pp. 3–24.

4. Two critics keenly sensitive to this issue are Joseph Wiesenfarth, *Gothic Manners and the Classic English Novel* (Madison: Univ. of Wisconsin Press, 1988), pp. 41–59, and Cathy Comstock, *Disruption and Delight in the Nineteenth-Century Novel* (Ann Arbor: UMI Research Press, 1988), pp. 8–15.

5. D. A. Miller argues brilliantly that the Ullathorne party can be so open because it has already subsumed the police. The world is so in accord with policing in its free operation that no police are required (*The Novel and the Police* [Berkeley: Univ. of California Press, 1988], p. 110). This figuring of freedom as simply digested policing may seem paranoid, but that be simply because paranoia is the most refined form of power-logic. In any case, Miller's wonderful argument is not to be missed.

    One should also note the equally engaging counter-arguments of Andrew Wright, *Anthony Trollope: Dream and Art* (Chicago: Univ. of Chicago Press, 1983), pp 44–45. Wright says that to locate Ullathorne at the center "is to draw a boundary round a mirage."

Chapter 13: GIRL-WATCHING, CHILD-BEATING, AND OTHER EXERCISES FOR READERS OF *JUDE THE OBSCURE*

1. "Who is this *we*, anyhow?" one might ask. The "we" in this essay is a location, a cultural positioning that is so resolutely mapped for us it cannot be unoccupied. "We" is not a person reading or even a way of reading (much less a position located within the text), but a spot from which we read, a spot that, like a rest-room in a roadside park, may be uninviting but can hardly be unvisited. It is this spot, this cultural position, that makes the sort of reading that we do inevitable.

    To call this "we" perverse, pedophile, sadistic, or particularly male is a maneuver that is not so much "wrong" as a continuation of the same strategy that created the "we" in the first place. Such locating and reading as are described in this essay are made available to us by mechanisms that also allow us to deny that we are accepting them. To call this "we" a bogus "universal" concept is to mistake the armchair where one reads for the universe, to exempt oneself from the fields of power that make possible the strategies of evasion and denial being employed.

    "We" in our culture is not a criminal or hidden place, a deviant or pornographic reading: it is every place, every reading. That claim is preposterous; but without it, we have no place to open our mine.

2. All references to *Jude the Obscure* are to the 1912 "Wessex Edition," reprinted in the Riverside edition (Boston: Houghton Mifflin, 1965); further references are cited in the text by part and chapter number.

3. John Bayley, *An Essay on Hardy* (Cambridge: Cambridge Univ. Press, 1979), p. 118.

4. It is interesting that Sue's offense is a blatant form of exhibitionism, given that she is later on so much the victim of voyeurs. Here, it is almost as if the subversive nature of her self-exposure wrests control away from the looker. The exhibition, that is, so violently assaults expectations

and mocks sexual desire that the exhibiting object ridicules the looker: look if you dare, but I will make fun of your looking. "Move on aunty! This is no sight for modest eyes!" seems a form of a humiliating rebuke I remember (having received) in my own youth—"When you get your eyes full, fill your pockets!", called out derisively by a female fourth-grade classmate, hanging upside-down from the playground trapeze.

5. Anon, "Lady Pokingham; Or They All Do It," *The Pearl*, No. 1 (July 1879); rpt. (New York: Grove Press, 1973), p. 17.

6. Anon, *"Frank"and I* (New York: Grove Press, 1968), p. 233.

7. "Algernon's Flogging," *The Flogging-Block*; from notes to Swinburne's *Lesbia Brandon*, ed. Randolph Hughes (London: Falcon Press, 1952), p. 499.

8. For a longer, torturing discussion, see my *Child-Loving: The Erotic Child and Victorian Culture* (New York: Routledge, 1992), pp. 246–74.

9. On the prevalence of "spanking" in America, the widespread tendency to regard the practice as normal and virtuous, and the great difficulties posed thereby for drafting or enforcing laws protecting children, see Elizabeth Pleck's excellent *Domestic Tyranny: The Making of Social Policy Against Family Violence from Colonial Times to the Present* (New York: Oxford Univ. Press, 1987).

10. For an especially enthusiastic endorsement, see [Dr. Iwan Bloch], *Sex Life in England* (New York: The Panurge Press, 1934). By the way, the author of this ridiculously unreliable book is apparently not Bloch at all, but one Richard Deniston. The idea is common enough and is often repeated: J. Z. Eglinton (also a pseudonym) goes so far as to say that the practice is exclusively British and that it is to be found in "*all* British erotic works" from the 1770s to the 1870s, a claim which, though untrue, does testify to the zeal some bring to the subject: *Greek Love* (London: Neville Spearman, 1971), p. 212.

11. *The Mother's Best Book, Or Nursery Companion; by a Committee of Experienced Ladies* (London: Kent & Co., [1859]), p. 77.

12. Quoted in J. J. Findlay, *Arnold of Rugby: His School Life and Contributions to Education* (Cambridge: Cambridge Univ. Press, 1897), p. 61.

13. The sexual association of flogging or spanking for both parties were clearly recognized: see John Davenport, *Aphrodisiacs and Anti-Aphrodisiacs: Three Essays on the Powers of Reproduction; with Some Account of the Judicial 'Congress' as Practised in France During the Seventeenth Century* (London: privately printed, 1869), p. 113. Indeed, as early as the late seventeenth century a pamphlet appeared protesting the beating of school-children's naked bottoms on the grounds of the "lechery" involved, the "appetite" and "fire" aroused in the masters: *The Children's Petition: Or, A Modest Remonstrance of That Intolerable Grievance Our Youth Lie Under, in the Accustomed Severities of the School-Discipline of This Nation. Humbly Presented to the Confederation of the Parliament* (London: Richard Chiswell, 1669), pp. 49, 15, 11.

14. Remembering the erotic, howling pleas for mercy from the Victorian pornography, note the following from American comic strips: "Oh! Oh! Father! I'll never do it again! Help! Yow!" ("Buster Brown"); "Oh, Oh, Oh, please don't! No! Please, father, Ow! Ow! Ow! Oh, I'll—sob—be good! Yow! Oh! Ow! How that hurts!" ("Angelic Angelina"); "I didn't mean it—I'll be good! Ouch! Ouch! YEOW! Boo-hoo! BOO-HOO!" ("The Gumps"); and the following remarkable final caption from the July 15, 1928 strip of "Winnie Winkle the Breadwinner" concerning the little boy Perry: "So that's his idea of fun, is it! Wait'll he gets home!! I'll take his clothes offen him an tan him good and proper!!!"

15. *The Standard Edition of the Complete Psychological Works of Sigmund Freud*, trans. under gen. editorship of James Strachey, in collaboration with Anna Freud (London: Hogarth Press and the Institute of Psycho-Analysis, 1953), XVII, pp. 175–204. Further references will be cited in the text.

16. Havelock Ellis, *Studies in the Psychology of Sex* (New York: Random House, 1936), I,ii, pp. 129, 137.

17. Far and away the most subtle and smart of the unsurprisingly rare treatments of this subject is Eve Kosofsky Sedgwick's "A Poem Is Being Written," *Representations* 17 (1987), pp. 110–43.

18. Steven Marcus, *The Other Victorians: A Study of Sexuality and Pornography in Mid-Victorian England* (New York: Basic Books, 1966), pp. 259, 261.

19. See Sedgwick, "Poem," p. 126; and *Child-Loving,* passim.

20. Ellis quotes this from another (unnamed) source, p. 141.

21. Dale Kramer wittily notes the oddity of the tone here and the apparent misdirection of the satire: ". . . that [Jude] was caused pain would scarcely seem to justify the marshalling of the forces of humanity and religious feeling against Troutham": *Thomas Hardy: The Forms of Tragedy* (London: Macmillan, 1975), pp. 151–52.

22. Penny Boumelha offers what seems to me an admirably persuasive and sympathetic reading of Sue's sexual reserve as perhaps her "only rational response to a dilemma," a response that pre-serves her "resistance to reduction to a single and uniform ideological position": *Thomas Hardy and Women: Sexual Ideology and Narrative Form* (Madison: Univ. of Wisconsin Press, 1982), pp. 142–7.

23. See especially his letter to Edmund Gosse (November 20, 1895), where he gabbles on about how Sue, though not an "invert," has but "weak and fastidious" sexual instincts: *Thomas Hardy and His Readers: A Selection of Contemporary Reviews,* ed. Laurence Lerner and John Holmstrom (London: The Bodley Head, 1968), p. 123.

24. *Study of Thomas Hardy and Other Essays,* ed. Bruce Steele (Cambridge: Cambridge Univ. Press, 1985). Lawrence's comments on Sue as the frightening "product" of civilization, a woman with the vital female in her atrophied, are well-known (pp. 108–9). Not so well known is his remarkable turn at the end of his essay toward a poignant sympathy for Sue and a distaste for the men who destroy her: "Why must it be assumed that Sue is an 'ordinary' woman—as if such a thing existed? Why must she feel ashamed if she is special? And why must Jude, owing to the conception he is brought up in, force her to act as if she were his 'ordinary' abstraction, a woman?" (p. 122).

"AFTERWORD"

1. To be more specific, my payment came as a single check constituting the entirety of the remuneration I was told I might expect for preparing this *Afterword.* There would be no second check, nor should I expect one, no matter how massive the sales might be. On the other hand, I wouldn't be asked to return the money if my written opinion did not (as it does not) constitute the sort of puff the publishers seemed (understandably) very anxious to procure.

Index